FOOPS!

30 COMMON FINANCIAL MISTAKES

MANOJ AR

JAICO PUBLISHING HOUSE

Ahmedabad Bangalore Bhopal Chennai
Delhi Hyderabad Kolkata Lucknow Mumbai

Published by Jaico Publishing House
A-2 Jash Chambers, 7-A Sir Phirozshah Mehta Road
Fort, Mumbai - 400 001
jaicopub@jaicobooks.com
www.jaicobooks.com

FOOPS!
ISBN 978-93-91019-71-6

First Jaico Impression: 2022

Page design and layout by R. Ajith Kumar, Delhi

Thank you, Harshita, Arushi and Poonam—the three fairies in my life who are my constant support and motivation to live more meaningfully.

Thank you, Mom and Dad, for giving me life, as well as adding meaning to it.

Thank you, Guruji, for continuing to bless all of us.

CONTENTS

PREFACE

There is a wall clock at the entrance of our house. This is an ordinary clock with nothing fancy about it. It shows time, just like any other clock would. For most of the year, it gets multiple glances from us during the day, which is probably all about it. Through the day, we focus on our work, routine, family, health and other gadgets—probably everything except this clock. A clock's function is to tell us time, and it does so pretty effectively.

Oops... But here comes the day the clock's battery is depleted. Now, all our daily actions are under threat unless the clock is up and running again. Sad but true; we focus on the clock only when the clock battery dies down. For almost the entire year, we never realised or appreciated that it was working seamlessly to tell near-accurate time. We only recognised and appreciated the clock's non-stop functioning after it broke down. This moment of awakening, when *we realise* the presence of something that has always existed, is a vital ingredient of an 'oops moment'.

The clock was always there. The time was always there. But the *awakening* that the clock was effortlessly performing its duties only came when it broke down. It took this moment when time literally stood still to make us realise what we never appreciated earlier.

Awakening Is a Part of an Oops Moment

One of the characteristics of an oops moment is the 'awakening' to something that already existed. However, there is much more to an oops moment.

To understand more about such oops moments, let's consider another example. This time, of the most complex and highly sophisticated machine that each one of us is handling—our body.

For most of us, for the most part of our lives, this machine runs perfectly, and we do not care much about it. We, the owners of our body, subject this extraordinary machine to all kinds of undisciplined habits of eating, sleeping and working, and never realise that our body is continuously engaged in fighting the inhumane behaviour it is being subjected to. As if the widespread diseases were not enough, or as if the pollution, contaminants in food, water and air were not enough, we decided to subject this machine to our own lifestyle tortures.

However, this magical machine keeps adapting non-stop, without a single complaint. But hardly do we realise or appreciate this fact. We are not awakened to the reality that our body is fighting against something disruptive, even right now.

We do not appreciate how good our body was at fighting its enemies until the dreaded day when we fall sick. When the body is unable to fight, we recognise what we ignored all this time—that good health is the greatest asset we possess. We must never lose our health for money, fame, work or, for that matter, anything else in life. Our moment of awakening towards our body only arrives after we fall seriously sick. The body was always fighting against its enemies even when we were healthy. But we were never awakened to that fight. Now, we are. And the day we are awakened, our oops moment arrives.

But, as I mentioned, an oops moment goes much beyond just awakening to an already existing phenomenon.

Don't we keep making the same mistakes again with our health as soon as our body wins its war against its mighty enemies? Don't we get back to our routine habits—the same junk food, undisciplined sleep and everything else that does not help or support our body to get stronger?

If we were truly awakened to our body, we would have given up some bad habits that lead to our ill health. We would have stopped or reduced the junk food intake and started a healthy morning routine with yoga, exercise or morning walks. We would also have included some healthy foods in our diet, switched to more natural foods than processed ones; the list goes on.

For some of us, and it definitely includes me, it may take a much bigger jolt to truly awaken us.

Vinod, one of my very close friends, only got awakened to many realities about his body and the food he used to eat after he was suddenly diagnosed with serious levels of type-1 diabetes (HbA1c of 13.3), very high cholesterol (three times the normal bad cholesterol) and severe thyroid imbalances—all in a single blood test. This diagnosis came at a time when he thought that he was pretty fit. Those aware of diabetes and blood sugar complications would know what HbA1c of 13-plus can do to your body.

Discussing the reasons for such sudden appearance of these modern lifestyle diseases is beyond this book's scope. But the fact remains that this turned out to be a true awakening moment for my friend.

Awakening happened. But as I said, the oops moment goes beyond awakening. Awakening is just the first step of any oops moment.

Massive and Permanent Action Follows Awakening

For an awakening to turn into a true oops moment, the awakening must definitely be followed by massive and permanent action. An oops moment is God's way of teaching, awakening and then enabling us to take massive action. Without action, the awakening is transient. Let me repeat here, for this deserves emphasis:

Post awakening, the action has to be 'massive' and 'permanent'.

If we have decided to gargle twice a week after the last throat infection and continue to do it for many years, that's a permanent action. It is then that we can term our getting sick as our oops moment.

So, here we are with the characteristics of an oops moment: (a) Awakening to something that already existed, though we never appreciated it. (b) A suitable massive and permanent action.

Soon after the diabetes diagnosis, Vinod started to read more about the food he eats and its impact on his body. Following that, he started to bring serious changes in his eating habits. This was massive action—massive because this action involved doing things that went against socially accepted practices and needed serious courage and commitment to create new habits while giving up on the old ones. This involved challenging almost every generally accepted social norm, researching more about it, and coming up with a solution that suited his body the most. Hours and hours of study and weeks of experimentation on his body, for months and years at a stretch—that was massive action.

The body was always there. It was always fighting diseases—known and unknown—every single moment. It was preventing us from getting sick with its own robust immune system. But Vinod was awakened to this fact only when he fell seriously ill and his oops moment arrived. He never appreciated something that was always existent until he was awakened. After his awakening, he took massive and permanent action. He changed many of his habits and slowly started to reverse diabetes. The food and other habit changes enabled his body to self-heal. And within three months, his medicines were reduced to 20% of what he started with. Three months later, Vinod was on with the least possible medication available in the market. If subsequent tests show further improvement, he will be off the medicines for good.

Awakening followed by massive permanent action is key in any oops moment.

The sequence remains as mentioned. You cannot take massive permanent action unless you are awakened.

Oops moments are usually life-changing and life-elevating. They define a new version of you.

There are so many things happening around us, but we see and realise only those to which we are currently awakened. That moment when you get awakened and take massive and irreversible action after your awakening is your oops moment.

Your life is redefined after the oops moment arrives.

There are hundreds of examples around us—strange as things may appear, they are potential oops moments. The day you get awakened to these oops moments, you will start taking massive action to make a real difference in your personal or professional life. To get your thought process rolling, let me share some of the oops moments that I realise, I was surrounded by. Here you go.

Diabetes is not caused by a high intake of sugar. Diabetes is caused by a lack of insulin production or insulin acceptance in your body, which in turn is caused by hormonal imbalances. These imbalances can be fixed just by changing our diet. The day a diabetes patient is awakened to this reality and takes massive action after the awakening, their life will never be the same.

All our physical and emotional diseases result from our past karmas—whether in this birth or past ones. We need to settle our karmas by *serving* ceaselessly. The day we are awakened to this fact, we will never be frustrated by our situations. Instead, we will find opportunities to serve. Life will turn into a beautiful journey of service.

A single sneeze travels at 100 miles per hour and shoots 1,00,000 germs into the air. The day you are awakened to this fact, you would definitely prefer wearing a mask in times of a pandemic. You might also persuade others to do so.

A century ago, apartheid was prevalent. He was living with it for years. Then, one day when he was thrown out of a train compartment, came his awakening. He gets awakened to something that has existed for years and resolves for massive permanent action. He follows through on this resolution, thus transforming his awakening into his oops moment. His name was M. K. Gandhi.

He was rejected from the University of Southern California's School of Cinema Arts—not once, but twice. These successive rejections were his awakening. He took massive irrevocable action and transformed his awakening into his oops moment. Today, he is considered one of the greatest moviemakers who has given us some of the most impressive movies like Jaws, Jurassic Park and Saving Private Ryan. Yes, his name is Steven Spielberg.

And it is not about famous personalities or celebrities alone. Oops moments arrive in everyone's daily life.

I was myself a mediocre student during my childhood, and I was fine with this mediocrity. My grades were slowly deteriorating as my class was progressing. I knew where I was headed until the ninth standard, when the unavoidable happened. I flunked. I knew this was in store. It was no surprise for me. But there was an internal awakening. I was a failure now, and this was not acceptable to me. From that day until today, whether in school, college or a job, I have slogged massively and have always stayed in the top league. It was possible because I was awakened to my oops moment, and I was ready for massive permanent action.

We have all grown with the belief that oxygen is a life-giver and a lifesaver. True. But here is your awakening—oxygen is also your life taker. Yes, this is correct. Oxygen, when it goes inside your body and comes in contact with your body parts, starts to oxidise them. Over many years, this regular oxidation of your body manifests in the form of a degenerating body, weak body parts and, ultimately, death. Of course, you cannot survive without oxygen. It is a double-edged sword. So, you counter the oxygen's oxidation effect on your body by consuming food that is rich in anti-oxidants. It is like putting paint on an iron table to prevent it from oxidation and rust formation. These foods go inside your body and prevent your body parts from oxidising quickly, thus slowing down the degeneration speed and increasing your life span to an extent. That's an awakening. The next obvious step is to understand the foods that give us the most anti-oxidants. There are many. Unlike non-vegetarian food, most fruits and vegetables are rich in anti-oxidants in varying degrees. This is an awakening for many non-vegetarians and also for those vegetarians who are now used to eating processed and packaged foods. This knowledge allowed me to awaken to something which already existed, and take massive action, thus manifesting my oops moment.

One of the most significant oops moments of your life will happen when you are awakened to His existence. You may claim that you are already aware of His existence. Yes, you may be aware that He exists, but there is a big difference between *being aware* and *being awakened.* Awakening is experiencing from your soul. Something goes inside you and shakes you into taking action, and your life is never the same after that.

Oops moments are not restricted to humans alone.

For example, an elephant stays tied to a fragile rope, assuming it cannot break it ever unless it counters its oops moment. When it becomes aware of its own strength, or even the fragility of the rope, it gets awakened and then takes massive irrevocable action. It breaks the rope and enjoys its newfound freedom—this is an elephant's oops moment.

Foops Moments

If you are wondering what these life-changing oops moments have to do with personal finance, then let me share another example—this time from the financial domain.

I always knew that compound interest was more powerful than simple interest. I had heard that compounding[8] was very powerful. I knew the compound interest formula since I was in class ten. My children also know it today. It exists almost since eternity. But my point is not about its existence or knowledge. It is about awakening. Life could have gone the same way unless my oops moment arrived.

The situation so unfolded that I got an opportunity to glance at my elder brother's PPF[38] passbook. There was nothing special about the passbook entries until one entry got my attention. This was a credit entry of ₹70,000 (and mind you, that was 1994—more than 25 years ago). But what was great about this entry of ₹70,000? How did it become my oops moment? What stuck with me about this credit entry was that this money was not deposited by my brother. This was the interest that the bank gave him for keeping his money in a PPF account. This was the interest income for one financial year, that too 25 years back. Moreover, this was all tax-free.

To put the above awakening in perspective, that was the year when I got into a job with Larsen and Toubro. My joining salary was ₹5,410 per month, or approximately ₹65,000 per year, subject to taxes.

The next set of thoughts shook something inside me.

Whatever I earn after having an engineering degree, and slogging for an entire year with one of the best-paying companies in India is less than what my brother would earn by doing nothing—absolutely nothing.

In those times, I was not aware of the concept of investments, passive income, etc. But this seemingly small incident did shake me up. So, while compound interest always existed and was always working, I got awakened on that day. This awakening changed my thought process about money forever. It had a massive, permanent and lasting impact on the remainder of my life. This drove me to explore, research and read more about money. Since that moment, my way of looking at money has changed forever. The fact that it ultimately led to my financial freedom[20] and a beautiful and worthwhile life is a testimony to the impact oops moments can have on your life.

Subsequently, I had many such financial oops moments in my life—awakenings that lead to massive action and life-changing financial results.

All such financial oops moments are, as I call them, the 'Foops' moments of our lives.

We have all grown up with flaws—financial or otherwise. These flaws, though they have always existed in front of us, never lead to our awakening. And there is no action without awakening.

The intent of this book is to awaken you to your possible Foops moments. I will be presenting many Foops moments—some based on my personal experiences and others on my interaction with thousands of freedom seekers across the globe.

Foops is the awakening to a financial law that has always existed. However, you never realised its value. Foops also involves taking massive, irrevocable action after your awakening. No action indicates no awakening. Awakening always leads to action.

If you get awakened to even one or two of these Foops moments, trust me, it can have a life-changing impact on the way you perceive money and the way you will end up financially in life.

The Golden Hand of Experience

Harry Truman once said, "The reward of suffering is experience."

While this is a very optimistic way to look at our suffering and to ultimately get past it, the sad part is that human beings are constrained by time, and it is virtually impossible to experience everything and learn from it—even in a specific domain of our choice.

It may take us decades of action in our area of work to realise that we were doing it wrong all this while. In most cases, we will repeat the same mistake many times before learning from it. But if we are smart enough, we will fix the mistake at the first given opportunity, and not repeat it. But even if we do that, how many mistakes can we find, experience and fix in one life span, probably to start afresh in the next?

If we cannot experience a majority of the mistakes, leave alone fixing them, how can we become true experts in our domains?.

But if there is a problem, there ought to be a solution as well. And the solution is pretty simple. We can save a lot of time by learning from others' mistakes rather than experiencing all of them ourselves.

Sam Levenson, a renowned American author and a television host, once said, "Learn from other people's mistakes. Life is too short to make them all yourself." I cannot agree more.

Warren Buffet, the world-renowned investor, says, "It is good to learn from your mistakes. But it is better to learn from other people's mistakes."

But how do we learn from others' mistakes in our domain? And that too those mistakes which we are yet to experience?

There is no ready-made answer.

If we are fortunate, we may have friends in the same domain. Our regular conversations with our friends might help—assuming that we are ready to share our secrets and admit mistakes we make. But how many friends do we really have today? And, that too, friends who work in the same domain, have the character to accept mistakes and share. This is a rare combination, especially in today's context. We ought to be truly fortunate to have this in our life.

The other alternative is to read books, blogs and articles. It is still tough to learn and believe in everything those books and articles tell us.

What about getting hold of a person who is a coach in our domain, someone who interacts with thousands of people similar to us, and works up close with them, understands the mistakes they keep making and can share those mistakes with us? What if we had access to such a coach who acts as a conduit between us and all the people in our domain who keep making common mistakes?

Yes, this is the solution. We need access to someone connected to all those people who are continuously making mistakes in our domain and is ready to share his experience with us.

When it comes to the personal finance domain, I will be your conduit, your messenger who has access to thousands of financial freedom seekers from across the globe who keep making mistakes as a natural process of their learning and growing.

For the remainder of the book, I will unlock some of the biggest Foops moments that thousands of freedom seekers have experienced in their personal financial journey.

The onus is on you to learn from such experiences of others, identify the Foops moments that relate to you, get awakened and then take massive irreversible action to change the course of your own financial destiny.

Even if you can identify one or two Foops moments from this book and take action on those, you will have saved much of your wealth from destruction. Rather, let me put this in a more positive perspective. If you implement even a few of the Foops moments that I will share with you, then you would not be able to fathom the wealth you would amass in times to come.

FOOPS 1

PAYING THE COST OF LOST OPPORTUNITIES

> **OPPORTUNITIES ARE LIKE SUNRISES. IF YOU WAIT TOO LONG, YOU MISS THEM.**
>
> — WILLIAM ARTHUR WARD

When we are at our workplace, we are losing an opportunity to spend the same time with our family or to meditate or play tennis.

When we are deciding to do nothing, we are very consciously taking a decision to not make use of any of the available opportunities.

When we are angry and disturbed, we are deciding to do away with a choice to be happy and peaceful.

When we decide to continue sleeping in the morning, we are choosing to enjoy the moment and deciding not to invest the same time in the company of nature, surrounded by fresh air and greenery.

When a sales manager decides to pick up an order for his organisation, he is losing the opportunity to serve some other potential customer at that same moment.

When our children decide to go to a particular school or college, they are deciding to give up the opportunity of studying in some other school or college.

When a farmer decides to sow capsicum in his fields, he is losing the opportunity to sow okra, bitter gourd or any other vegetable—and also the profits associated with those.

Every single moment of our lives, we are making decisions. Some of the decisions could be taken after intense and rigorous thinking, while others could just be taken subconsciously. Whatever be the case, the first point that needs to be emphasised is that every single decision that we take, however obvious it may sound to us today, is a trade-off between what we finally choose to do versus what else we could have possibly done.

Or, to put it in other words, we always have a choice. Therefore, we should not feel constrained by a lack of options at any stage.

The second point that I want to table is that with every choice comes the cost of not choosing, which I refer to as the *cost of lost opportunities*.

With each choice we make, or we don't make, we try to do something at the cost of not doing something else. There is an opportunity being lost every moment. Rather, I would say we always choose to grab one opportunity at the cost of another.

Karuna is one of my freedom seekers and an ex-colleague from Tata Consultancy Services (TCS) in New Delhi. When in TCS, we used to have many tea-time discussions. On one of the lighter days at work, during one such discussion, she mentioned that she and her husband watched one of the most horrible movies over the weekend. Curious to know more, I asked her to elaborate on her experience.

Karuna and Sushil were a newly married couple then. They had an interesting love story, which I had the privilege of learning over a previous tea-time session. Last weekend, they booked a couple's ticket for themselves for this latest movie. Not that newly married couples are too bothered about the movie, but in spite of that, Karuna told me that they knew it five minutes into the movie that it was going to be a horrible experience. They were repenting that they did not read the review for the movie before booking the tickets. But then, they had no choice now. Money was already spent, and that too, for tickets in the elite class. The tickets were non-refundable, as is mostly the case; they had to spend the next three hours in hell.

I asked why they did not come out of the movie hall once they knew that the movie was substandard. She expressed her inability citing the ₹1,000 that was already paid for the tickets; they absolutely did not want to waste the money. Since the tickets were non-refundable, they could not justify leaving the movie theatre midway.

Did Karuna and Sushil have a choice? Of course, we just learnt that we all have a choice in every moment of our lives. Did they give up on any other opportunities as they decided to sit through the movie? What opportunities did they lose by deciding to sit through three hours of torture? They could have enjoyed their time in a nearby garden. They also had the choice to enjoy some memorable moments in a fine dining restaurant around the area. They always had the option, and they always had a missed opportunity. They chose to sit through the movie at the cost of many other lost opportunities.

No one should ever have the feeling that they don't have a choice. Everyone is making a choice every moment, even when they are choosing the status quo.

Why did I share the above incident?

I did so to bring home the point that apart from always having a choice and always having to pay the cost of lost opportunities, there is a third lesson that we need to learn.

And that lesson stems from the next obvious question. Is it justified to waste the money they paid for the movie? My take is that *we cannot let a past event influence our future choice.* The reason for this is simple. The past is gone, while the future is yet to come. Neither should influence the other.

The money paid for the movie tickets is gone forever. It is history. By choosing to either sit through a bad movie or spend romantic time in the garden, the ticket money will not come back. It was gone the moment the tickets were booked. What we do with the next three hours (future) has no linkage to the invested money (past). If we try to connect the past with the future, we are most likely to make an irrational decision.

Sitting through a movie, knowing it is subpar, my friend and her spouse made the decision not to enjoy the remainder of their three hours elsewhere and give up many more wonderful opportunities in hand.

This third point of keeping future choices disconnected from past events is vital in many fields of life, including investing your hard-earned money.

To conclude the three key points:

1. We always have a choice. Deciding not to do anything is also a choice we make.
2. With every conscious or subconscious choice, we always pay the cost of some other lost opportunities.
3. We should not connect past events while making rational decisions for the future.

The cost of lost opportunities in investing encapsulates one of the most common errors in personal finance.

Keeping an eye on this cost in every investing decision gives many investors the right tool for a more rational evaluation, including in matters of whether to hold on to an investment or sell it.

This cost of lost opportunities is also termed as the 'opportunity cost', or 'alternative cost' of making a particular choice in microeconomic theory. It says that when an option is chosen from alternatives, the opportunity cost is the cost incurred by not enjoying the benefit associated with the best alternative choice.

My experience dealing with thousands of freedom seekers clearly demonstrates the devastating effects of not understanding this cost. There are many examples from the personal finance space when we just let the situation be, without deciding, and instead assuming that we are in the 'safe zone'.

I will emphasise this point with some of the most common examples that I have observed in the personal finance space. You may connect with some of these examples, get awakened and take massive action to manage the cost of lost opportunities.

1. Holding on to Loss-Making Stocks

One of the most effective mechanisms to take a rational decision on a loss-making stock is to perform value analysis[48] for that stock. To learn about value analysis, you ought to read *The Autobiography of a Stock*.

Even though the value analysis of a stock may clearly indicate to sell it, we tend to hold on to them, especially the loss-making ones, in the hope of recovering at least the invested cost.

In such loss-making cases, we fail to act, just like the couple who failed to act after having invested in a bad movie. We do not appreciate the fact that losses are as much a part of stock investing as profit realisation. We do not come to terms with the fact that it is fine to lose a battle in order to win the war. We forget the basics, and we go with the noise.

When we are not selling our worthless stock and hoping for the stock to recover and come back to its purchase price, we are effectively in a state of indecision, waiting for divine intervention. We keep waiting as if it is our birthright to at least recover our costs. Markets neither understand nor are driven by our purchase costs. This benchmark exists only in one place—our mind. In such a state of indecision, we forget that we are anyway making a subconscious decision, and this (in)decision is as follows

"I am deciding to stay invested in this stock. Therefore, it is my conscious decision not to invest the current realisable value of this stock in a more profitable option."

Obviously, each such (in)decision has a cost attached to it—the cost of lost opportunities.

By holding on to loss making stocks, we display all the three characteristics of this Foops moment.

i. We had a choice. But we decided not to sell the stock even though the value analysis indicated selling it.
ii. With this decision, we are paying the cost of lost opportunities. The ₹10,000 stuck in a loss-making stock with a purchase cost of ₹15,000 can be more effectively utilised by investing in a better-performing asset[2]. The loss of ₹5,000 is likely to be recovered quicker in some other performing asset, rather than keeping this ₹10,000 with a dud stock. And remember that duds sink deeper in trouble much sooner. It is doubtful that we will even have this ₹10,000 after some time. So, today, if we are taking no decision or are deciding to stay with this stock, we are effectively deciding to invest

₹10,000 in a dud stock today vs. investing this ₹10,000 in a better performing asset. Knowingly or unknowingly, we are paying the opportunity cost.

iii. We are connecting past events to the present and are therefore taking irrational decisions for our future. It is just the purchase cost of the past that is leading us to an irrational decision. If you decouple the purchase cost from the scenario, a wise decision can be made much faster because there is no notion of a loss in that case.

This is exactly the same mistake Karuna and Sushil were making—watching a dud movie just because they had invested some money to buy the tickets.

To sum it up, whenever we are in a state of indecision, and if we disconnect the past, evaluate the available opportunities and make a conscious choice, we will be better prepared for our future. In such a case, we would have taken massive action after our awakening—the key to realising the potential of Foops moments.

2. Holding on to Real Estate

This scenario is much more typical among those of us who hold real estate. Of course, real estate decisions are far more challenging to take than stock decisions. The amounts involved are significant, and the running around involved is too much for our comfort.

Especially in India, we buy real estate as an investment and wish to hold on to it eternally. Even if we are ready to liquidate it, we usually wait for the real estate market to hit the *right price* before we sell it. Day in and day out, I deal with investors who feel that the real estate market is currently down and would sell their property as soon as it comes up to their minimum benchmark level.

Our current returns from real estate may be pathetic (even 0% or negative in some cases). Still, we keep holding on to it in the hope of recovery. What we do not realise is that by holding on to it, we are taking a sub-conscious decision to not invest in another investment option which may easily fetch us much higher returns (say 8-10%), higher predictability, improved liquidity[31] and a much better tax efficiency (debt mutual funds[32], for example).

We are paying the cost of lost opportunities. We are losing these 8-10% returns every year by just holding on to the real estate. And in real estate, this 10% can be a very big amount because the cost of the property itself is usually very high. If you do the number crunching, you may very well realise that you start earning about 25% extra on your average monthly salary just by moving your asset base from real estate to a debt-based mutual fund.

I am not sharing random numbers. I am sharing my experiences with you. Let us look at a situation that I once faced in my own financial life.

I had a flat in Delhi valued at around ₹120 lakhs and appreciating by approximately ₹3-4 lakhs every year. Over and above that, it was fetching me a rental income of approximately ₹18,000 per month. All this sounds good, doesn't it?

A flat investment in Delhi was satisfying my ego. An extra ₹18,000 per month was giving me a passive income[36]. But then my Foops moment arrived. The realisation hit me when I did the number crunching. Here is how it goes.

Even if I do not discount all the maintenance charges and municipal taxes I used to pay on that flat, I was earning a maximum of ₹4 lakhs every year in capital appreciation (though that was no assurance in the future) and approximately ₹2 lakhs every year as rental income. This is a total income of ₹6 lakhs per year or ₹50,000 per month.

This sounds fantastic, but only until I apply the base investment of ₹1.2 crores. So, I am earning ₹6 lakhs per year on an investment that is worth ₹1.2 crores. Simple tenth-standard mathematics tells me that this turns out to be not more than 5% ROI. Remember that this still does not account for municipal taxes, house maintenance, unavailability of a tenant at certain times of the year and many other hidden costs. Not only that, my investment is highly illiquid, tax-inefficient and involves dealing with illegal money.

What if I invest the entire proceeds of ₹1.2 crores into a simple debt mutual fund which gives me around 8% returns on average? Firstly, it will be safer and less volatile than real estate since debt mutual funds of this category invest mostly in government-linked and other safe AAA securities. Secondly, an additional 3% return (8% of debt mutual funds compared to 5% of real estate) translates into approximately ₹3.6 lakhs per year or ₹30,000 per month. Now, this is the additional monthly money I get just by shifting assets, not to mention the increased liquidity and peace of mind. For a vast majority of seekers, this is almost 20-25% of their take-home salaries. At the time when I was doing these calculations, this was almost 15% of my take-home salary. A 15% salary increase by doing what? By shifting assets. And whether I get my salary or not, I will surely get this, and I will keep getting this until the last day of my life. This was an awakening. What followed was massive action. Within three months, I had sold off this real estate, a few lakhs here and there. I did not bother much about the sale price. We should not, because we will lose much more in lost opportunities if we delay the sale.

3. Waiting for a Tenant Who Can Pay the 'Right' Rent

Again, not only do I have personal experience with this Foops moment, but I have seen so many falling in this trap; they keep falling until they are awakened. The lure of a higher rent is so pulling that we tend to ignore the basics.

We, as flat owners, do not mind waiting for a few months with an objective to get a tenant who can pay 10-15% better monthly rent.

We tend to ignore the fact that with two to three months without rent, we have already lost 20% of the annual rent—a clear case of the opportunity cost.

So, even if we are fortunate enough to get a tenant at the desired rent after three months, we are already on the losing side.

4. Waiting for a Year to Save Taxes

"My portfolio[37] has not been giving good returns despite the fact that I have been investing as per your recommendations," mentioned one of the freedom seekers to me during a call.

"Ok, let me have a look at it… It seems you have not sold off the assets which I had marked as 'liquidate' six months ago," I replied after looking at his data online.

"Yes, I didn't."

"You cannot expect an optimally performing portfolio when you continue to hold underperforming assets. Please sell the underperforming assets."

After a few days, I checked back with him.

"Have you sold off your underperformers?"

"Not yet…"

"Ok, waiting for something specific?"

"Yes..."

"What?"

"I will sell after four months."

"Why?"

"Because by that time, one year will be competed and I will not have to pay taxes."

"Did you calculate how much tax you would have to pay vs. how much money you would lose by holding on to underperformers for four months?"

"No."

"Then please do that and share your analysis with me. There is an opportunity cost involved here."

And don't be surprised by the analysis that I received. At least I wasn't, because I have encountered stranger stories. She was making losses in her underperformers, and there was no tax to be paid since there were no gains at all.

After going through the above cases, you must have realised that there is one common thread that runs through most of the lost opportunities.

And the common thread is the *waiting period*.

We tend to be in a mode of indecision. We continue to wait and wait indefinitely. We tend to feel that not making a decision is safe. As humans, we do not want to make the wrong decision. But we fail to appreciate that not taking a decision is probably the worst decision we can take.

As Dr. Marc Dussault, a growth strategist, says "It is in your moments of indecision that your dreams are destroyed."

Whenever you feel you are procrastinating a decision, you must remember this Foops moment. You must do your basic number crunching, and I am sure that it will help you choose the wiser option much faster.

At the end of the day, there are no right or wrong decisions. They are what they are—just decisions.

Foops #1: Paying the Cost of Lost Opportunities

Awakening	Action
• We always have a choice. • Not deciding is also an act of choosing. • Every choice is accompanied by lost opportunities. • Each lost opportunity has a cost.	• Do not continue sitting on a bad investment. • You lose money every single day that you do not act. • Get rid of a poor performer quickly and move to a better performer.

FOOPS 2

ASSUMING THAT WE UNDERSTAND MATHEMATICS

EVERYTHING AROUND YOU IS MATHEMATICS. EVERYTHING AROUND YOU IS NUMBERS.

– SHAKUNTALA DEVI

Warren Buffet says that an investor does not need financial degrees but only some elementary mathematical skills.

The fact is that out of the actual functional competence needed to build massive wealth, basic arithmetic skills are one the most important and cherished. Unfortunately, and surprisingly, these skills are extremely rare.

I have personally interacted with hundreds of CEOs, CFOs and top-level CXOs who are either entrepreneurs or working with high-profile Fortune 500 companies. They may have their own specialised skill sets—the ability to work under pressure of deadlines, handling clients, managing plans, domain knowledge and everything else—but the chances are high that they will not be able to pass a tenth-standard exam.

As an example, a lot of us reading this book may have absolutely no clue on how to calculate the ROI (return on investment) of a randomly staggered investment, like in stocks or sometimes mutual funds, over a period of time. The problem is not that we do not know a certain skill. The problem is worse. We do not believe that we do not know.

Even worse is that those who are aware of this lack of basic mathematical skills have hardly any guilt. And since they do not have guilt about missing an essential skill, they do not even attempt to hone the skill.

Number Numbness

In his book *Innumeracy*, the famous American mathematics professor, John Allen Paulos recounts some examples from a test he conducted for potential employees of an organisation he was consulting. Some of the seemingly simpler questions had surprising answers.

One of the questions was that if a quantity grows from 50 to 100, has it increased by 50%, 100% or 200%?

The answers that the candidates gave were all over the place. If you answered anything other than 100%, then I would not blame you for an incorrect attempt, nor should you blame yourself. The underlying concept needs to be well understood, and once we have the right understanding, this answer does not require any great competence.

There was another interesting question in the book.

The candidates were asked the population of the United States, which was about 220 million at that time. The only challenge in this question was that this was not a multiple-choice question. Testees had to actually write down the answer.

About half of them answered it about right. But the interesting part was the analysis of the wrong answers. The wrong answers were neither randomly spread nor were they clustered around the correct answer. Instead, there were cluster of answers around 20 million, and another around 2 billion. Most people had no clue about the scale and only remembered some numbers.

This inability to fathom, compare or appreciate really big numbers or really small numbers is also called 'number numbness'.

For many, it is hard to tell the difference between a million, a billion and a trillion. Politicians seem to make this mistake the most. But a general investor is also not insulated from this phenomenon.

Ok, let us try another seemingly straightforward question. If you are an Indian, then tell us India's total population. You have five seconds to choose your answer—1.3 crores, 1.3 million, 13 million, 13 crores, 130 crores, 1.3 billion? Now verify your answer from Google, and don't be surprised if you got it wrong or took more than five seconds to answer.

You will face this every day, and the lack of this skill will keep haunting you until you learn to tackle the problem head-on and learn tenth standard arithmetic.

Let me share a few more examples with you from the personal finance space. These are some typical examples. You may be encountering many more situations in your financial lives and unknowingly taking incorrect decisions, probably leading to massive implications on your wealth in the long run.

Returns Down by 2%

If the fixed deposit rates are down by 2%, then do not ever think that your returns are also down by 2%. If it was just a 2% reduction in your returns, it would have been quite a manageable situation. Unfortunately, you are definitely worse off.

This 2% reduction in interest rates is an illusion—a mathematical illusion. So, if we assume that your earlier yield was 8%, this 2% reduction in interest rates would lead to your yield being 6% now. The 2% reduction of yield is on a base of 8%. Without referring to a base, percentage reduction or percentage increase calculations are as meaningless as they can get.

It is like saying that someone scored 35 marks. Saying that someone scored 35 marks is a statement that is without a base. Such statements push us to judge whether they indicate a good or bad outcome, depending on our experiences in life. Someone may feel that 2% reduction is not significant enough, and 35 marks are below average.

What if I were to tell you that 35 marks were out of a base score of 40? Now, this is around 88% score, which is definitely not a below-average score.

What if I were to tell you that the 2% reduction in interest rate is actually a staggering 25% reduction in your returns since the earlier returns had a base of 8%? Yes, it is correct. That's 25% reduction in your returns. If you were getting ₹40,000 returns earlier from this asset, you would now be getting only ₹30,000 returns. Foops moment already?

It's simple mathematics. But that's where the problem lies. The simple things usually get ignored, and the consequences of such ignorance can be devastating for your financial life.

Ratiocinitis

A tendency to forget the rules regarding the addition and subtraction of fractions, ratios and percentages is hypothetically termed ratiocinitis. It is an illusion created in people's minds.

Let us say that a store is offering a 30% discount on everything at the time of checkout. Now, a fancy dress that normally sells for ₹100 in the same store has a tag saying 20% off. So, there are two discounts applicable on the dress. Does this mean the total savings is 50%? No, it's not.

The actual savings is just 44%, and not 50%. How? Twenty

percent off ₹100 is ₹80, and 30% off ₹80 is ₹56, which is 44% off of the original ₹100.

Most would get it wrong. But if you have been a mathematical wizard and got it right, then try this one.

Will it make a difference if the store takes the 30% off first and then offers a 20% additional discount at the time of checkout? Most would feel that it should not make a difference. Now, verify your answer by actual calculation. And be prepared for your Foops moment.

Meaningful Comparison

It's a common error to report a seemingly impressive number sans any comparisons.

Every day, vehicles in India produce over a billion tons of pollution. Impressive? Yes! But let me state this statistic another way: every day, the vehicles in India pollute 0.000000001% of our atmosphere. Impressive? Not really. Let me also clarify that this is also a poor way to think about pollution.

But that is the problem with raw numbers. We have to compare them to something else for them to be meaningful. A better statistic could be that vehicles are responsible for more than half of the carbon monoxide pollution.

A Stock Has Fallen by 90%

Let us say that a stock is valued at ₹100 today and falls 10% each day for the next ten days. How much do you think the stock has fallen in total in the last ten days?

If you are finding it tough, let me give you a few choices—10%, 50%, 90%, 100%, 110%, none of the above.

Think about it for some time. Allow your grey cells to do some physical activity. It's healthy for them.

The answer is, 'none of the above'. The actual fall is 65.1% over ten days. How did we calculate that? It is tenth-standard math. The first-day fall is 10% of ₹100, that is, ₹10. So, your stock is worth only ₹90 on the second day. If it falls by another ten percent on the second day, it falls by 10% of ₹90, that is, ₹9 (and not ₹10).

This goes on, and the fall in absolute terms becomes lesser with each passing day. Try solving this in an excel sheet, and you will start to love the illusions of mathematics.

Theoretically, a stock can never fall 100% from today's value. Or, we can also say that a stock that has fallen 100% can never rise again. It has become trash.

Even more interesting is the confusion about how much percentage a stock needs to rise once it has fallen by 90% from its original value. What do you think? Here are your options: 56%, 81%, 90%, 100%, 5000%.

Not many would get it right. But a stock that has fallen 90% needs to rise 5000% to reach its original level. And the reason is pretty much the same. The reference points or the base values when the stock starts to fall and when it starts to rise are completely different.

Averages

Everything in mathematics has a twist and can create illusions. Let us take something as simple as calculating averages.

There are actually three different kinds of averages.

Let us take a sample set of 2, 2, 2, 3, 5, 6, 8. The mode average (the most repeated number) is 2; the median average (the one in the middle) is 3; the mean average (the sum of all samples divided by the number of samples) is 4. Any one of which can legitimately be the average.

In personal finance and its calculations, you will frequently encounter the concept of 'average' . You ought to understand what kind of average we are dealing with, else the outcomes can be far off from the expectations.

Yes, I agree with Warren Buffet that we do not need extraordinary financial skills to deal with investments. We just need elemenatary mathematical skills. But we surely need to master these basic skills.

A wise gentleman once said, "Data is like a mini skirt. It hides much more than what it reveals."

Now that the problems have been put in the right perspective, you have a much better chance to find the right solution. A part of the problem also lies with the media and how it interprets and presents data to investors.

We fail to understand basic numbers because there seems to be no social stigma attached to this inability. People who are embarrassed at making the smallest grammatical mistake happily declare themselves too incompetent to understand these simple calculations. Such people are termed innumerate in Paulos's book by the same name.

Another interesting example during our freedom journey is the tracking of our monthly performance. Each month has a target, and your actual net worth achievement in that month is compared with the target to arrive at your net worth performance. Two different people who are ₹10,000 behind the target may have varying performance depending on the target (or the base number).

Let us say that person A had a target of ₹30,000 net worth for October 2020, and he achieved ₹20,000 (behind by ₹10,000). Another person, B, had a target of ₹70,000 net worth for October

2020, and he achieved ₹60,000 (also behind by ₹10,000). Do you think that the performance of both A and B would be the same? Absolutely not. The absolute amount lag may be the same, but the performance percentage for person B is much higher, which matters more in this case.

These are subtle things that matter a lot in your financial journey towards freedom. We need basic mathematics, not rocket science. This is one place where no one can really help you. You owe it to your financial well-being, and you must take charge of getting this done and dusted.

Foops #2: Assuming That We Understand Mathematics

Awakening

- One need not be a mathematician to invest and build wealth, but understanding of basic mathematics is an absolute must.
- Avoiding concepts of percentages, ratios, averages, comparisons, analysis, etc. does not help an investor.

Action

- If you do not have a mathematics background, revisit tenth-standard mathematics and clear your concepts around ratios, percentages, profits, averages, etc.
- Without clarity on these concepts, numbers may cause illusions, and therefore, incorrect decisions.

RELYING TOO MUCH ON THE NUMBERS

WHEN TAKING KEY DECISIONS, DIG AT THE ROOTS INSTEAD OF JUST HACKING AT THE LEAVES.

– ANTHONY J. D'ANGELO

While understanding the mathematics around numbers as an essential skill for an investor in Foops #2, I also realised that even if we understand numbers, we start relying too much on the absolute numbers themselves.

This over-reliance on numbers is driven by the sheer amount of numbers we are surrounded by and deal with in our daily lives. And we do pay the price of relying more on numbers and less on our intellect. While numbers are important and cannot be ignored, just relying on the numbers has proven to be a recipe for disaster for many investors.

However insignificant you may think this point is, this Foops moment could just be one of the biggest differentiators between being a normal investor and a financially free person. So, let me take a deep dive into the over-reliance on numbers and how we can potentially surmount this over-reliance.

Bollywood actor Aamir Khan says in the movie *3 Idiots*, "Everything is a machine. We are surrounded by machines."

Indeed, we are all surrounded by machines. And as icing on the cake, we are also drenched in numbers. All around us, every moment, we face numbers.

Whether we like it or hate it, our life revolves around numbers, since the day we are born—probably even before that. Your date of birth is enslaved in numbers. Your house number, roll number, mobile number, Aadhaar number, PAN number, car registration number, insurance policy number, employee number, PF account number and the list goes on and on. You need to have an understanding of numbers when you go out shopping—whether for groceries or any other household needs. Even the simplest task like switching to your favourite TV channel needs an understanding of numbers, not to mention that you definitely need a good understanding of numbers when it comes to understanding or calculating your income, taxes, revenue, growth, savings, investments, etc.

Undoubtedly, numbers are everywhere, and they are more important than we think. And if numbers are important, it is also human for many of us to commit mistakes while dealing with numbers. One zero here and there, and our financial life can descend into complete chaos.

So, before we go into the intricacies of investing and start dealing with relatively more complex issues like calculating return on investments, I think it is important for a significant number of freedom seekers to understand relatively simpler yet important aspects of numbers.

Comparing Numbers

There are many interesting aspects about numbers—one of which is the relative comparison between two numbers. A comparison between two numbers allows you to make important decisions or arrive at vital conclusions in life.

The real fun with numbers only starts when you start comparing them and begin arriving at conclusions.

So, let's go.

The red shirt with a 20% discount may still be costlier than the blue shorts with a 10% discount, allowing you to make a purchase decision. Mariappan can save more taxes if he opts for Investment A rather than Investment B. Deepti, not Varun, was declared the class topper since she had the highest marks in the class. The match is won by Team A only when Team A scores more than team B. Kapil's business has grown by 20% this year compared to last year. Amitabh Bachchan is more popular than Sunil Shetty since Mr. Bachchan has many more followers than Mr. Shetty on Twitter.

The number of comparisons is endless.

As you would have realised by now, there are two or more entities involved when we are making these comparisons. Deepti vs. Varun, Investment A vs. Investment B, Team A vs. Team B, Big B vs. Suniel Shetty, etc.

Interestingly, the comparison need not be only between entities. It could also be between an entity and a benchmark. Let me explain.

Although Sunil Shetty has significantly lesser followers than Amitabh Bachchan, we can still call both of them celebrities since each has more than 5,00,000 followers (a pre-set number to define a celebrity). Now, when it comes to being called a celebrity, the comparison is not between Amitabh and Sunil but between Sunil and a benchmark number of 5,00,000. Similarly, Deepti may be the class topper. But when it comes to deciding who all qualify to represent the school for next year's science exhibition, both Deepti and Varun qualify since the criterion is that the top five students qualify for this prestigious show. Again, for the science exhibition, the comparison is no more between Deepti and Varun now. It is between Varun and the benchmark position (top five). Prakhar can be said to be running a high fever since his temperature measurement showed a reading of 100.1°F against the benchmark reading, which is 98.4°F.

So far so good. No rocket science until now. But it was important to set the context. The awakening happens now. Your Foops moment will originate as we go through the remainder of the chapter. So get ready for the fun.

There are two big (and very common) mistakes that most of us, as investors, make when it comes to dealing with numbers. As with any Foops moment, the impact of both these mistakes can have extremely serious consequences on our future wealth. In fact, these mistakes are so common in corporate or personal lives that I will never run short of examples to qualify for this topic.

1. There Is a Lot Behind the Numbers

The first blunder that most of us make is that we just look at the numbers and arrive at a conclusion. We rarely intend to go deeper into the reasons behind the numbers. And, as I often tell my freedom seekers, depth is where the magic is.

Raveesh, my friend and college mate, takes pride in his health and fitness. And it was imperative that I take some lessons out of his health regime for my own benefit. And when I had my coffee-time discussions with him, some of the observations were mind boggling.

For the most part of the last ten years, his bodyweight had been 72-73 kg, which is slightly overweight for a person of his height. And when one is entering the 45-plus age group, it is very important that key parameters like weight be monitored and regulated. And it was not long before he started to lose weight. He moved from being slightly overweight to a leaner version of himself. As his weight entered the 'perfect' range, he obviously felt very good about it. And why not? His weight was now in the range that any fit person would be proud of.

Now, his numbers were perfect. For his height, age and sex, the perfect body weight was 65 kg, and he was right there.

Look at these numbers and make conclusions at your own peril. If you think that they tell you the complete story of his fitness, then the answer is a resounding no. You have made the same mistake again. You probably looked at the numbers and data, compared it with a benchmark of ideal data and came to your conclusions. This is one of the biggest Foops moments for most investors.

A health crisis was about to follow, as I found out on discussing the topic further with him. Unless we find out what is behind these numbers, we could end up in a worse situation like he did. If the weight loss from 73 kg to 65 kg was a result of switching to much healthier eating habits, exercise, yoga, meditation, etc., then these are surely some valid reasons for his perfect weight. But we rarely go to this depth to find out the reasons behind the numbers.

As Raveesh realised later, the reason for his weight loss was not because of his healthy lifestyle but the onset of serious Type-1 diabetes. Now, given the same set of 'healthy' numbers, would you still dare to qualify my friend as fit and healthy?

I am sure not. But what changed? The weight, height, age—everything is still the same. All the numbers are where they were. Only the reason behind the numbers has changed.

The reason behind the numbers is even more important than the numbers themselves.

I worked for IBM India from 2005 to 2015. For the most part of this period, IBM was declaring astonishing results. During 2013-14, the EPS (earnings per share)[15] of IBM was increasing almost every quarter. For anyone outside IBM who is probably trying to evaluate the company from an investment perspective, this was a very good sign. A healthy EPS with a positive trend is always a good sign. But those outside IBM just saw the numbers. That is how we also see a company when we evaluate it for investing. We see the ratios, numbers, make some comparisons with other companies or with some benchmark and try to arrive at conclusions.

What we fail to do is to find the reasons behind the numbers. And we, sitting in IBM, reading some internal reports, were aware that all was not well. Our salary increments had almost stopped, expenditure on travel and training was getting trimmed, even our coffee was not free anymore. And if all that is happening within the company, how can the EPS be healthy?

The answer is hidden behind the numbers. It is possible to still show a healthy EPS, because EPS, or earnings are calculated as revenue minus costs. What the company is doing to keep healthy earnings is to reduce the costs, which included salaries, travel, training, perks, coffee, etc. So, even though the revenue was falling, IBM was able to hit its target EPS by cutting down heavily on costs.

And once we understand this reason, we will be warier about the, so-called healthy EPS and positive trends. Cost-cutting cannot continue forever. They are naturally expected to hit a saturation point at some time. Cost cutting can be a temporary answer to continue to showcase good earnings, but it is not the solution, by any means.

It's very similar to personal finance. You can continue to save the same money despite a reducing salary by aggressively reducing your expenses. But for how long can you continue to reduce expenses? At some stage, income has to stabilise or move up.

After a few years, since nothing major was done to increase the revenue, IBM's EPS soon started to dip. But if an investor had just looked at the numbers, he would have easily missed the trick hiding behind the numbers. And since the reasons behind the numbers are not easily accessible on a public platform, doing the right analysis becomes a challenge.

In April 2017, Jeff Bezos, Amazon's founder, sold $1 billion worth shares of Amazon. What are the implications of these numbers for the shareholders of Amazon?

The owner's share in a company is termed 'promoter shareholding'[39]. The promoter happens to be the one who is closest to the business. If he was confident about the business and its future prospects, he would never sell his own stake. When the promoter shareholding goes down significantly, as it happened in this case, it is usually a matter of concern for the shareholders, since they feel that the promoter is not very confident about the company's future.

So, should the shareholders take these Amazon numbers as an indication to sell, and sell their shares too in such a situation? Many of them actually did. And why not? The numbers were clearly indicating a lack of confidence in Amazon.

Now, let us dig behind the numbers. At that time in April 2017, Jeff Bezos wanted funds, and he was selling his Amazon shares to fund Blue Origin, his aerospace company. Blue Origin aims to launch paying passengers on 11-minute space rides. Jeff sees future potential in this venture of space tourism. Overall, the fundamentals of Amazon never changed. Just because the numbers (promoter holdings decreasing in a specific year) indicated so doesn't mean that you need to get rid of the stock. You need to go behind the numbers, evaluate the reason for the numbers and then take a decision. Amazon stocks have only soared since 2017, by about by about 400% since 2017—from $895 in April 2017 to $3,401 in August 2020.

I shared the above examples so that you can understand the importance of going behind the numbers and try to avoid hastily labelling the data at hand. Let me share another example of how going deeper into the numbers may allow you to select or reject stocks.

Those who invest in stocks, or at least have a fair idea of the key terms, would know that healthy and growing earnings per share (EPS) of a company is usually a good sign. Although this is definitely not the only trigger (as we saw in the case of IBM earlier in the chapter) for an investor's buy decision, it is definitely one of the first and most fundamental indicators.

So, focusing on EPS numbers and seeing them grow over time gives an investor a sense of comfort. But again, EPS is just a number. It just indicates the company's earnings on a per-share basis. There is a lot behind the numbers.

If you dig deeper, the company's earnings can be broadly classified as earnings from operations and earnings from non-operations.

Operating income, also called income from operations, takes a company's gross income, equivalent to total revenue minus the COGS (cost of goods sold) and all operating expenses. A business's operating expenses are costs incurred from normal operating activities and include items such as office supplies and utilities.

So, if I have a factory that produces pens and I earned a revenue of ₹10,000 in a month, the cost of manufacturing the pens was ₹6,000 in that month, and ₹1,000 was spent in giving salaries, perks, operational expenses like travel bills, stationary purchase, etc., then my operating income for the month if ₹3,000. Operating income is important because that is the core business of my company and a healthy operating income is always a welcome news. Operating income becomes a part of my earning (or earnings per share).

A non-operating income, on the other hand, is the income shown in my income statement that is driven by activities that do not fall under the core business operations of my company, that is, income generated from anything other than manufacturing and selling pens. Yes, my company may have some cash which may have been invested, and we may have earned income from it. This type of non-core income stream may take one of many forms like gains or losses due to fluctuation in foreign exchange, asset impairments or write-downs, income from dividends arising out of investment in associates, capital gains and losses from investments, etc. It is also known as peripheral income or incidental income.

If a company's EPS is growing without an increase in operating cash flow or with negative operating cash flow, then this can actually be a red flag for an investor. Negative cash flow from operations may also require deeper analysis of the company financial statements.

So, even when you see a growing EPS, going behind the numbers might reveal an unhealthy operation and therefore a risky future for the company.

Let it sink in. Let it be your FOOPS moment.

Let this concept be applied to all facets of life, be it finance or your relationships. If someone is angry at you, do not do hastily label the person. It is better to go deeper to try and understand the reason behind the anger. For all you know, you might be responsible for that person's anger.

2. The Future Originates From the Past

This is another big Foops moment for many investors. Most investors look at the current numbers to try and predict the future. What they inherently forget is to look at the origin of the future. That is, in the past.

Let me explain.

Vinod and Ronit are two equally qualified professionals who started their jobs almost at the same time. Today, after ten years, Vinod earns a salary of ₹75,000 per month while Ronit earns ₹45,000 per month. They both work for the same industry and have been associated with renowned companies. Whom would you bet your money on if we are talking about their future after three years?

Many of you might bet on Vinod. Some of you may still bet on Ronit just because I am asking you this question. However, very few of you will counter this question with the most pertinent logical point, and it is as follows:

"If you are asking me about the future, you ought to show me the past."

Yes, if you are in a position where you are asked to pre-empt the future, then it is only wise to look at the past and, specifically, the trends in the past before you reach any conclusion.

The farther you want to look into the future, the farther back you need to go in the past.

This was the trend of Vinod's salary over the last three years—₹1,00,000, ₹89,000 and ₹75,000. The downward trend could be because of various reasons. That takes us back to the first point that there is a lot behind the numbers. Of course, you need to analyse the reasons for the consistent reduction in salary for Vinod. It may be an issue with Vinod, like he has not been keeping well, has lost interest in his job, etc. It may also be completely circumstantial. For instance, his department not doing well for the last few years. Therefore, they had to cut salaries across the board. It could even be a combination of both.

On the other hand, Ronit's salary shows an increasing trend—₹36,000, ₹40,000, ₹45,000. Again, do not just go by the numbers. Look for the reasons behind this increase in salary.

Given these additional sets of numbers from the past, would you like to rethink the answer to our original question? Whom would you bet your money on if we are talking about their future after three years?

Take your time. We are talking about the future now, and past trends do become important. The Foops moments must sink in for you to take massive action.

Some of you might want to change your answer. Some others may still be quite unsure and would want more information on the reasons behind the numbers. In either case, it is a win-win because you are now thinking in the right direction.

The selection of the better player cannot be made on the basis of one match or one tournament. You need to delve into the past, look at the trends and reasons behind the numbers, and then come to any reasonable conclusion about the future probability.

Which is a better mutual fund to invest in—the one with 10% ROI or the one with 12% ROI? First, get behind the numbers. Was the 2% difference in ROI achieved by taking significant additional risks? If you are convinced that it was not the case, then look at the past trends. Has the latter fund been giving a similar performance for the last 1, 3, 5, 7 or 10 years—across all market cycles? If yes, then go for it.

Which is a better stock to invest in—the one with 30% promoter share or a 60% promoter share? A higher promoter share is generally a good sign for a stock. Same rules—check the reasons behind the numbers, and check the past trends. The one with a 30% promoter share may be the one where promoter share is continuously going up and the other way around for the latter stock.

Who is likely to recover faster—a person with a fever of 100°F or the one with a fever of 101°F? We cannot arrive at a conclusion unless we know the reasons behind the fever and see the past trends.

The examples are limitless, and they apply to all fields—be it personal finance or any other area of life. You got to get behind the numbers and then look at the past trends if they are available.

After the book *The Autobiography of a Stock* became a national bestseller, many readers asked me a very obvious question. If stock selection is as simple and process-oriented as the book depicts, then why can't you develop an automated tool to select the stocks—a tool which picks up the entire company data (current as well as historical) from some central database, applies all the formulas, calculates all the ratios, finds the intrinsic value, compares it with the current market price and just makes an automated decision on our behalf. In such a case, there would be no human error. Moreover, we will also be able to eliminate any emotional bias towards a particular stock or a set of stocks.

First, I thought through this entire point of view, assuming that this may be a great idea. Subsequently, when I researched on the internet, I realised that I am not the first one being presented with this idea.

Artificial Intelligence-based mutual funds have already existed in the market for many years. In India, we also call them 'quant funds'. Quant Funds are managed by an alogrithm, thus eliminating emotional bias. They also have access to virtually infinite data of the past, thus ensuring best possible future predictions. They have infinite processing power, thus ensuring that all scenarios are covered and there are no misses or human errors.

If quant funds have such distinct advantages, they should have been performing much better than mutual funds managed by humans. But the reality, as I found out, was quite different.

For example, in August 2018, a quantitative team at Aberdeen Standard Investments started a $10 million artificial intelligence global equity fund, betting that an algorithm can be more effective at figuring out the complex world of factor investing than a human portfolio manager. A year later, the AI-based fund had underperformed the broader stock market's powerful rally, and its assets had grown by only half that of the market.

When I further researched the reasons for such a failure, I was not surprised at all. While the robot has all the data, it may never have all the reasons behind the numbers. And as we know by now, the numbers are never as important.

So, while numbers are key, the reasons behind those numbers are as vital as the numbers themselves, if not more.

Foops #3: Relying Too Much on the Numbers	
Awakening	Action
• Analysing numbers is a good starting point, but there is a lot more behind the numbers. • When we are trying to predict future numbers, we need to go deep into the past numbers.	• When evaluating any investment, dont just look at the numbers for taking a decision. Look at the reasons behind the numbers as well. • When projecting the future of an investment, drill back into the past trends to get a fair picture before taking a decision.

FOOPS 4

RISKING YOUR EQUITY BY INVESTING VIA SIPs

RISK COMES FROM NOT KNOWING WHAT YOU ARE DOING

– WARREN BUFFET

Those who have invested in equity-based mutual funds need no introduction to the concept of systematic investment plans (SIPs)[45]. They are born with SIP in their DNA. But not all who are reading this book may have exposure to equity mutual funds or other volatile investments like gold or stocks. Even if you are a long-term investor in equity, you will find it rewarding to read along as we revisit the real problem and the proposed solution from scratch.

Additionally, equity investing veterans might also get awakened to their Foops moment when I will tell them that SIPs are meaningless, in fact detrimental, for mutual funds—in many cases.

Before we talk about the redundancy of SIPs, we must understand the basic working principle of SIPs and how it is one of the best techniques to invest in a volatile investment vehicle like mutual funds.

Even before that, I must take time to classify investments broadly into two categories: debt-based investments[10] and non-debt-based investments.

Debt-Based Investments

Debt-based investments are all those investments where the coupon rate[9] (or the rate of return, or the return on investment) is decided before getting into the investment. Fixed deposits[19], recurring deposits, public provident fund, employee provident fund, post office schemes, senior citizens saving schemes, RBI bonds, peer-to-peer lending are all debt-based investments. You know the returns before you enter the investment. So, the curve of your investment value vs. time is almost perfectly linear.

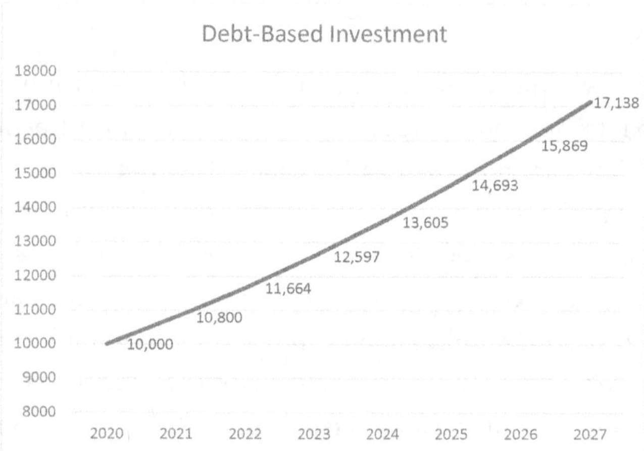

Figure 1

So, in the above chart, we see the typical life of our investment growing in a debt-based instrument. If we had invested ₹10,000 in the year 2020 for seven years in a fixed deposit at a coupon rate of 8% per annum compounded interest, the investment would continue to grow every year and would end up exactly at ₹17,128 in 2027—neither a rupee more nor less. The final amount at a future date is known to us even before we actually invest our money.

For the moment and for the sake of simplicity, we are ignoring the tax applicability of returns.

Also, it is important to note that the returns are not perfectly linear (the line is not perfectly straight; its slightly curved); that is the impact of compounding[8] on your money. We will deal with compounding in Foops #6.

For now, for practical purposes, we will assume that the returns are close to linear.

Non-Debt-Based Investments

Non-debt-based investments are those investments where the maturity value is not clearly known at the time of investment. Also, since the maturity value is not clear in most cases, the investment period is also not fixed. This vagueness adds the risk[40] element to such investments.

All investments like equity-based investments (stocks, equity-based, mutual funds), real estate investments, commodity[7] investments like gold, silver, etc., are 'non-debt-based' investments.

Such investments do not follow a linear path and are usually volatile. Some investments like stocks may be more volatile than others like gold. Moreover, the curve of their volatility[49] is quite unpredictable since it depends on various micro- and macro-economic factors, which are usually beyond the investor's control.

Have a look at how gold prices have fluctuated between 2011 and 2019 (see Figure 2).

You can see that the graph is not linear. Also, the future is unpredictable, unlike in debt-based investments. No one knew where the average price of gold would end up by the end of this year. It was hovering at ₹54,000 in mid 2020 and close to ₹47,000 in mid 2021—true to its nature of unpredictability.

Let us look at another non-debt-based investment—the equity market. The chart in Figure 3 traces the trajectory of the equity market for 12 months in 2020.

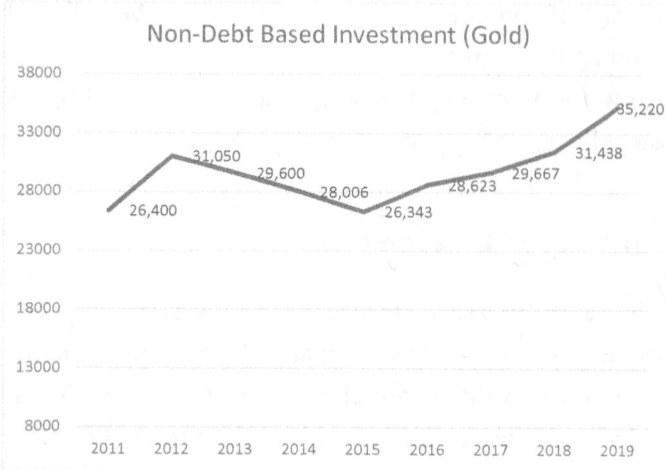

Figure 2

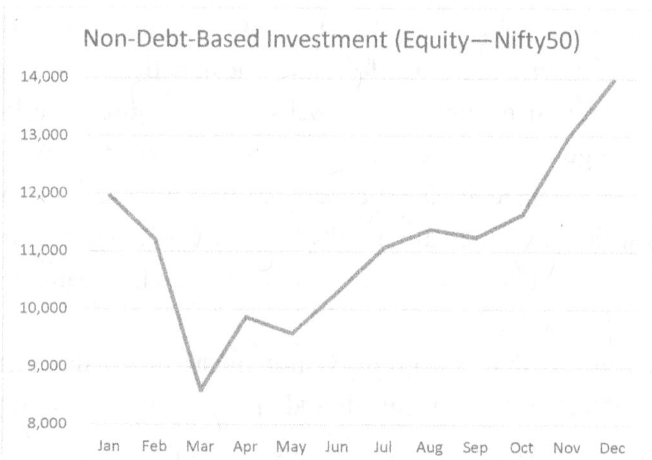

Figure 3

Again, the graph is non-linear, volatile and also unpredictable. It can swing in either direction in the short term (anything less than five to seven years is considered short term for a long-term investor). As you would have noticed, the equity market curve is far more volatile than the gold curve.

A similar curve drawn on real estate prices would show a different kind of volatility.

Common Ground in Non-Debt-Based Investments

Volatility is the common ground for all non-debt-based investments, whether equity, real estate, commodities, etc. For all such volatile asset classes[3], it is not easy to predict the future considering their nature.

And when it is not easy to know the direction in which our investments will swing, then there is definitely an element of risk involved in such investments.

Well, all investments have some level of risk. For example, you may have a 'safe' debt-based investment in an instrument like a bank fixed deposit. But the bank where you have a fixed deposit may itself go bankrupt, and there have been many such cases of late. But by nature, a fixed deposit is not tagged as a risky investment since its outcome is quite predictable. We will deal with the risk in investments later in this book. But when we talk of risk here, we are talking about the nature of investment itself rather than force majeure situations like a bank going bankrupt, which can happen with any investment.

Now, having known that non-debt-based investments are riskier, why would anyone enter into such investments?

Of course, the rewards follow the risk. While a typical FD may give post-tax returns of anywhere from 4% to 6%, gold as an asset class has fetched close to 8% returns. On the other hand, the equity market has been fetching around 10-11% returns over a long period. Greater the risk, the greater the reward.

Now, when we deal with risks, and it is not possible for us to eliminate it (as in the case of non-debt-based investments), we develop techniques and strategies to mitigate the risk, SIP being one of them

Risk Mitigation for Volatile Investments

A systematic investment plan (SIP) is among the most powerful techniques to mitigate the risk[42] of volatility.

In this technique, we keep investing a defined amount at defined intervals, say, monthly. As the markets fluctuate month on month, you would buy cheaper in some months and costlier in other months. Overall, with time, you will average your cost of purchase.

This is far better than buying everything at a high price but definitely worse than buying everything at a low. But since it is not possible to predict the highs and lows, the SIP technique turns out to be much safer. It involves average risk and, of course, average rewards, but even average rewards from the equity market can surpass the best returns of a fixed deposit.

The SIP technique demands discipline and commitment to keep investing the same amount every month, for years together before you can see the rewards; that is where it may not work for everyone. But with financial maturity of an investor, it should.

Awakening to the Reality of SIPs

SIP is a great technique. But even great is not great enough. SIP is simple and wonderful. But it makes no sense, and is in fact, detrimental in many cases.

Now, this may be a Foops moment for many hardcore, disciplined SIP followers. But as with any other Foops moment, it is better to awaken to reality and take massive and urgent action to correct your past mistakes.

Let me dish out a few instances where SIPs could actually be harmful for you.

Equity to Equity Movement

When we invest in equity, one of the ground rules is that we do not go with a lump sum investment. The reason is simple. The markets are volatile and unpredictable, and we may enter the market at its peak with a hefty sum, only to see our hard-earned money eroding as the market falls post our investments. We reduce the risk and go only via SIPs (systematic investment plans) or STPs (systematic transfer plans)—both of which try to average our entry costs in a volatile market. This is well understood, practised and appreciated.

But this is where our Foops moment lies.

The above practice was proposed and works well *only when* moving our funds from *a non-volatile asset class* (like a savings account, FD, debt fund, etc.) to *a volatile asset class* (like mutual funds, gold, etc.).

In investing, could there be situations other than this movement from a non-volatile asset class (specifically non-equity) to a volatile asset class (specifically equity)? That is, for example, do we have practical situations wherein we move funds from equity to equity? Our initial reaction may be negative, but if we dig deeper, an awakening awaits us.

In many situations, we wish to move our funds within the same equity market. Not only do these situations exist, but they are also pretty common. Every day, we face such situations with our freedom seekers, whose assets are reviewed for performance every six months.

When we review the assets for their performance, it is quite possible that one or more equity assets have been consistent underperformers, and we may want to move the funds lying in underperforming assets to the assets which are better performers. For example, if one mutual fund is not performing, we may want to move our funds to another better performing mutual fund in the same category. Thus, performance tuning is definitely one situation where we would move funds from equity to equity.

Performance may not be the only reason to move funds from one equity asset to another equity asset. We also see that an individual's risk profile changes over time. With the changing risk profile, we may also have to move funds from certain high-risk equity assets (like small-cap equity mutual funds) to relatively low-risk equity assets (like large-cap equity mutual funds) or vice versa—again, a movement involving two equity-based assets.

There could be other reasons for this movement too. Over-dependence on a particular fund house, holding too many stocks within the same industry, and many more reasons could trigger the movement from one equity-based asset to another equity-based asset.

Whenever such a movement is needed, the most prudent technique is, in fact, a lump sum movement. Such a lump sum movement involves no movement risk at all, irrespective of the current market situation. Compare this with a SIP-based movement, and you are at a significantly higher risk.

Let me explain.

Lump Sum Movement within Equity Has Zero Market Risk

Moving funds within equity involves selling one asset to buy another. The first step is, quite obviously, to sell. This is where the first mental roadblock arises for many seekers. When it comes to selling, most of us have been tuned to the notion that we must not sell when the market is low.

And this is logical, but only if you are selling funds from equity and moving to any debt-based investment or because you are selling to consume the funds, say, for your child's education. In such cases, yes—selling when the market is low does not seem to be prudent.

But this notion does not hold true in case we are moving funds within equity. If we are selling our underperforming asset cheap (when the markets are low), remember that we are also going to buy the target asset cheap. We are in the same equity market when both selling and buying. The sale of asset A and purchase of asset B can be completed in two to three days or even earlier. So, even if the market was low, it helped us sell low and buy low—a zero-risk scenario.

A similar scenario pans out when the markets are at a high. In such scenarios, seekers are quite prompt in selling but have a bottleneck for buying. They hesitate when buying high. With the same logic as above, if they look at the overall scenario, it carries zero risks since they are selling high and buying high.

Thus, irrespective of the market conditions, a lump sum movement of funds within the equity market happens to be a zero-risk scenario. Or, as I say, equity-to-equity movement is market neutral.

SIP Movement within Equity Has High Market Risk

If, when moving funds from equity to equity, we happen to liquidate asset A quickly but wish to move to asset B via SIPs, we must remember that we are adding a time factor until all funds are moved from asset A to asset B.

This time factor is where risk kicks in. This time gap could be of months or years, depending on the distribution of the SIP. And if those extra years happened to be the time when the market rose sharply, then two things would have happened to our funds:

a. They missed the market growth post liquidation of asset A since they would have been lying somewhere in a debt fund or our savings account.
b. We are going to buy asset B at a higher net asset value (NAV)[33] in a strong market, effectively yielding us lesser units.

Now, you may argue, "What if the markets fell after we exited asset A?" In that case, don't we stand to benefit? Yes, we do. But that is the whole point. Since there is no way to predict whether the markets will fall or rise, we are taking a risk if we are waiting via SIPs to move funds from asset A to asset B. This is precisely the risk we avoid when we move a lump sum amount.

In a nutshell, the movement between equity has to be very quick, as quick as possible—preferably within a day or two. The more the time gap, the more is the risk.

There have been times when the markets have been extremely volatile, so much so that there is a surge or a dip every other day, as was happening in Covid-19 days. In such extreme cases, even two to three days of delay in moving funds from asset A to asset B within equity can carry risk. In such extreme cases, I have even suggested that many of my freedom seekers use the same-day movement strategy.

Same-Day Movement Strategy

Liquidating and receiving funds from an equity-based asset(mutual fund or a stock) could take two to three working days after placing an order. Then reinvesting those funds in another equity-based asset could take another couple of days before they appear in your portfolio. The entire movement, however prompt you are, could take four to five working days. When the markets are extremely volatile, every day matters.

In such extreme market situations, especially if the amounts involved are significant, I have sometimes recommended many seekers to adopt a same-day movement strategy, where we move the funds within a day.

Some of you may be wondering how that happens because the liquidation and reinvestment delays are mostly from the broker or the fund house's side. How can we eliminate that? As I have always emphasised, personal finance is nothing more than tenth-standard mathematics and some common sense.

Assume you have to move a fund of ₹5 lakhs from asset A to asset B within the equity market. Below is the method you can adopt for the same day movement strategy:

a. Instead of straight away going for liquidation of asset A, this strategy involves arranging for ₹5 lakhs from any of your existing debt-based assets like FDs, savings accounts, etc. We would need these funds for two to three days. We can even take a loan from any of our friends or relatives for two to three days if we do not have liquid money in our portfolio. Many times, it is even fine to use our emergency fund since this requirement is only for a couple of days.
b. Pick a day when we are going to make this movement; ensure that your savings account has liquid funds.
c. On that day, you are going to place two orders:
    i. One of them will be a sell order to liquidate funds from asset A.

   ii. The other order will be a buy order for asset B. The buy order will be executed based on the temporary funds you have arranged.

d. Since both the orders are placed on the same day, there is zero time gap between the movement of funds from asset A to asset B. This is a same-day movement, which has absolutely zero risk of market volatility.
e. When your sell order materialises after two to three days, and you get back your funds in your savings account, you can return the funds to your friend or replace the emergency fund if you used that.

Instances of Equity-to-Equity Movement

Now, you might be wondering whether these situations of equity-to-equity movement are rare.

When we learn to manage our wealth, and especially when we have reached our ideal portfolio balance, then this equity-to-equity movement would perhaps form a majority of our transactions. Yes, the majority—may be as much as 90% of the transactions. Let this be your Foops moment. Let this sink in. Let this awaken you, and let this force you to take this seriously and act. Don't follow the SIP method blindly.

Here are some known instances when you may have to use these techniques:

1. **Performance Reviews**

   This is the case we just discussed. When we review the assets for their performance—which we should definitely do once in six months—it is quite feasible that one or more equity assets have been consistent underperformers. We may want to move to better-performing assets. For example, if mutual fund 1 is not performing, we may move our funds to a mutual fund 2, which outperforms it in the same category. This is a clear case of an equity-to-equity movement. And this movement is quite common.

2. **Changing Risk Profile**

   Performance may not be the only reason to move funds from one equity asset to another equity asset. The risk profile of an individual also changes over time, and with the changing risk profile, we may have to move funds from, say, certain small-cap (high risk) assets to large-cap (relatively low risk) assets, or vice versa—again, a movement involving two equity-based assets.

3. **Overdependence on a Fund House**

   This can happen when we keep buying different equity mutual funds over time. It is also common among seekers who do not review and tune their portfolios every six months. Overdependence on any fund house can surely add risk to our portfolio, which we definitely want to eliminate. We saw various examples of risks associated with fund houses in 2020. Franklin was one of the major ones. When we decide to move to equivalent funds from a different fund house, we are making an equity-to-equity movement again.

4. **Overdependence on One Industry**

   Holding too many stocks within the same industry is another common risk in many portfolios. This could happen because of the investor's affinity towards one industry, future prospects of that industry, or the investor knows a lot more about a particular industry, having worked in it for a good part of their career. Whatever be the reason, the risk always exists. To mitigate this risk, you will need to move some funds across industries.

5. **Need to Churn Money**

   Churning money is a technique many seekers use to avoid the long-term capital gains (LTCG) tax[26] up to ₹1 lakh per year. This technique is also used to save taxes under Section 80C without making any investments. We will be talking in detail about this technique in Foops #9. But its relevance right now is that it involves liquidating investments to save tax and then reinvesting the same immediately, probably in the same funds. This is also a clear case of equity-to-equity movement.

The above list is obviously not exhaustive. There could be other times when we move our funds from one equity asset to another. And we must remember that this is a Foops moment.

Everyone around us will recommend we go via the 'safer' SIP route. But a little bit of common sense will help us realise that lump sum movement, in some cases, carries far lesser risk than SIPs. SIP is a great technique, but a blind follower of SIP may end up on the losing side.

Foops #4: Risking Your Equity By Investing via SIPs	
Awakening	**Action**
• SIP is an investing technique for investing in equity-based investments[16]. • SIP mitigates risk in debt to equity movement. • On the other hand, SIP increases risk when moving funds from equity to equity. • Lump sum fund movement from equity to equity is market neutral.	• If you have to move funds from equity to equity, move them lump sum rather than systemtically. • Follow the single-day movement technique, if feasible. • Get rid of a poor performer quickly and move to a better performer in one shot—lump sum.

FOOPS 5

GETTING DELUSIONAL ABOUT MUTUAL FUND DIVIDENDS

GETTING RID OF A DELUSION MAKES US WISER THAN GETTING HOLD OF A TRUTH.

– LUDWIG BORNE

Lagaan, a 2001 Hindi film, stars Aamir Khan in the lead role. The film is set in the early 1890s, during the late British period of India's colonial British Raj. The story revolves around a small village in central India; the inhabitants have been burdened by high taxes and several years of drought. Soon, they find themselves in an extraordinary situation as an arrogant British army officer challenges them to a game of cricket as a wager to avoid paying the taxes they owe.

The dividend taxation system in India is not better placed than a *lagaan* in British times.

Actually, in purely technical financial terms, the concept of dividends is flawed in itself, especially for mutual funds. They serve no purpose at all. They are artificial and misleading marketing tools. It would be wiser not to call them dividends in the first place.

Not only are dividends useless and do not add any value, but they also do the reverse for you. Mutual fund dividends, in reality, drain your money—courtesy of the wonderful taxation rules in our country. Is this your Foops moment? Did you always believe that dividends are good? Did your parents, well-meaning friends or your financial advisor always tell you to invest for dividends?

Taxes on dividends is more like paying a *lagaan* on our own money without any reason. This essentially implies that our equity mutual fund dividends lead us to pay more needless tax than what we should be paying.

This was actually a powerful Foops moment for many investors and freedom seekers. I am sure many readers would be unconvinced about dividends' futility. And I am going to take time to delve a little deeper into this topic for precisely this reason.

The dictionary definition of dividend is "a sum of money paid regularly (typically annually) by a company to its shareholders out of its profits (or reserves)."

Investopedia says, "A dividend is a distribution of a portion of a company's earnings."

The Wikipedia article starts with, "A dividend is a payment made by a corporation to its shareholders, usually as a distribution of profits."

These (and other) definitions all point to the same thing. When companies make a profit, they bring some of it back into the business and distribute the rest to shareholders as *dividends*. Obviously, the management of the company has a choice in the matter. It's up to them to decide how much (if any) dividend to distribute. There are plenty of companies that distribute very little or none of the profits as dividends for various reasons.

As far as being shareholders in the company is concerned, so far so good. But absolutely none of this applies to mutual funds. In a mutual fund, all the profits made by the fund, whether through capital appreciation or dividends of the stocks and securities in which the fund invests, is reflected in the NAV of the mutual fund.

There is no rocket science in understanding that the delta of the NAV is all for the investors to keep as this is a mutual fund investor's capital gains, except for the fund house's management expenses. This delta can be calculated with this formula:

The NAV as of today – (minus) the NAV at the time of investment

Now, if the NAV of the mutual fund has increased over time, investors can choose to withdraw their money partially. They could either sell some mutual fund units (this keeps the same NAV but with a reduced number of units) or get paid in dividends (this keeps the same number of units but with a reduced NAV).

Whether the money comes to the investor as a dividend or withdrawal makes no difference, making dividends useless.

> "The idea of dividend reinvestment in mutual funds is nonsensical."
>
> –Dhirendra Kumar, Value Research

To top it and make dividends such a poor choice is the deadly and unnecessary effect of taxation in dividend payments.

With a simple example, I will try and uncover not one, not two, but three Foops moments related to dividends. Let us tackle them one by one.

The Dividend Is Not a 'Bonus' or 'Free' Money

Many investors are sitting on the idea that dividends are free money that comes to us as a bonus, over and above the regular capital appreciation that happens to the NAV in the mutual funds over time. Let us face this Foops moment first.

Let us assume that we own 1,000 units of mutual fund X. The current NAV of each unit is exactly ₹100. That makes the total current value of our investment in this mutual fund to be exactly ₹1,00,000.

Let us say that the fund now gives us a 5% dividend, that is, ₹5 per unit. Since we were holding 1,000 units, we would get ₹5,000 as a dividend. But this is a Foops moment for many investors. Many of us are under the impression that this ₹5,000 is an added bonus. That is how we always visualised a dividend, probably based on our experience in the stock market.

However, we need to be awakened to the fact that this dividend is not free money at all for mutual funds. Even before the dividend amount reaches your bank account, the NAV value of each fund unit would now be reduced from ₹100 to ₹95. And the investment that we would be holding post the dividend payout will be reduced to ₹95,000 from the earlier ₹1,00,000.

Assuming that many of us may miss the key point of this Foops moment, let me reiterate it for everyone's benefit.

When we get paid dividends by fund houses, the NAV gets reduced by an equivalent amount.

And this is why we see the same fund house having two different funds in the same category—one which pays a dividend and the other one which does not pay a dividend. They do this just so that the NAV of these funds can be tracked differently.

Let me show you a real example. The chart in Figure 4 shows you key details of Axis Bluechip Fund Growth as of September 10th, 2020.

In it, the key values that you must note in the context of our topic are highlighted appropriately.

Observe the one-day growth of the fund (1.07%), one-year return of the fund (7.00%), fund start date (January 5th, 2010), and the latest NAV of the fund (₹31.03) as of September 10th, 2020.

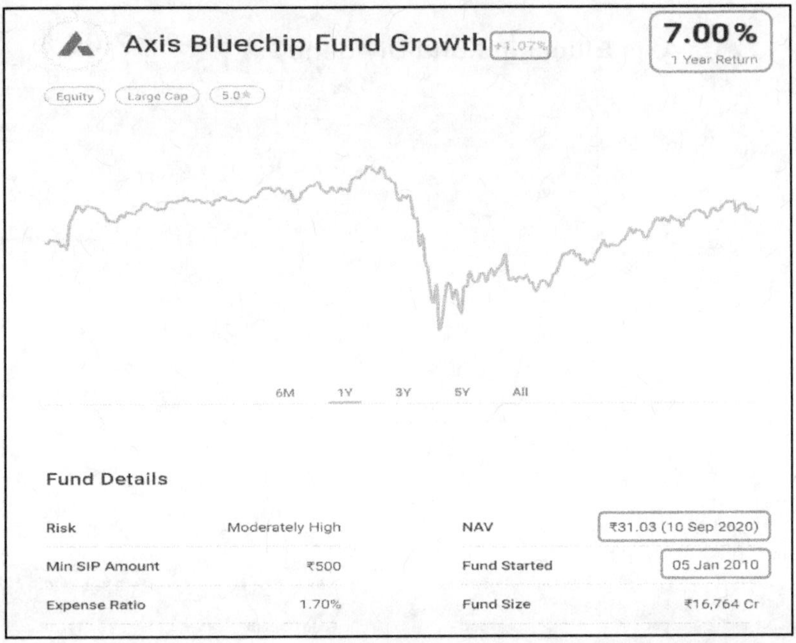

Figure 4

Now, let us look at the dividend-paying equivalent of the same fund reproduced in Figure 5 (next page).

If you are not yet Fooped, then let me reiterate the highlighted content of these charts for you in plain and simple language:

1. There is no difference between the two funds. Both these funds started on the same day (January 5th, 2010) and have the same returns until date (September 10th, 2020). Of course, the difference is that the first one does not pay us any dividend, while the second one does.
2. Does the dividend-paying feature of the second fund make the second one a better choice? Not at all. And the reason is straightforward. As explained earlier, every time the second

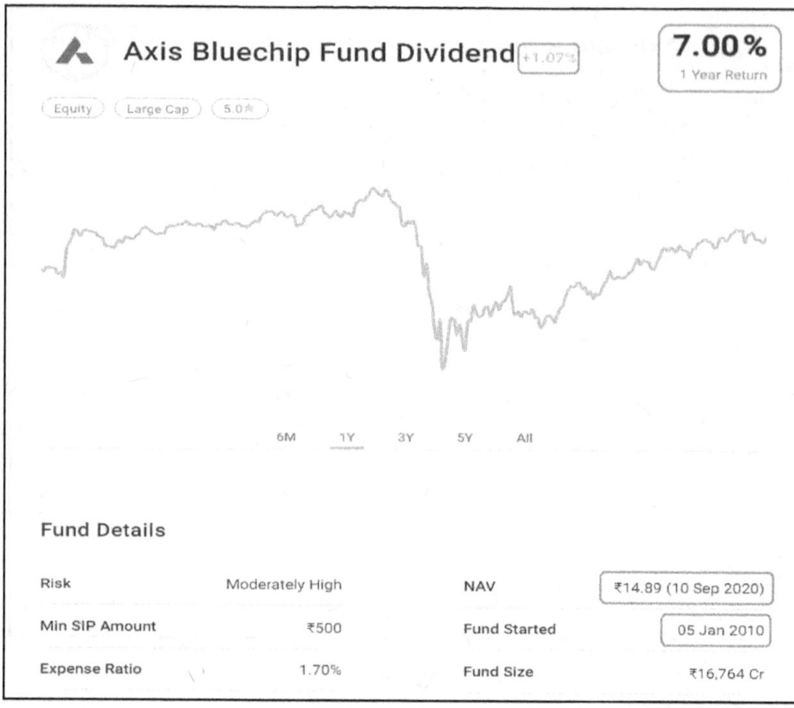

Figure 5

fund paid the dividend, its NAV was reduced by the same amount. As you can see, the second fund (the one that pays a dividend) is currently running at a NAV of ₹14.89, while the first one (which never paid us dividend and kept the money within the fund) is running at a NAV of ₹31.03.

3. So, while we might be feeling elated after receiving regular dividends, the fact remains that this fund is now worth that much less. If we were holding 1,000 units of the dividend-paying fund, then it is worth only ₹14,890. The first one is worth ₹31,030—the difference being paid to you in the form of regular dividends.

Some of you may have this query in mind: if this is how dividends work, then what is the difference between taking dividends and regularly withdrawing money from the fund?

That is a logical question, and the answer is that there is absolutely no difference. To reiterate what I said at the beginning of this chapter, the concept of dividends in mutual funds is flawed. The so-called dividends serve no purpose at all. They are artificial and misleading tools, simply used for marketing certain products.

Dividends Are Worse than Systematic Withdrawal

Let the Foops moment sink in that dividends are no more than a marketing gimmick. They are used by fund houses to sell their products by encashing the perception around the term 'dividend'.

But, here comes our next Foops moment.

Receiving dividends are actually not the same as withdrawals from mutual funds—they are far worse.

We just saw that dividends are the same as withdrawals, then how can I claim they are worse? My claim until now was on the gross returns from mutual funds, that is, pre-taxation. We saw how the NAV was adjusted so that, in effect, we have the same amount of money. But that is all before taxation.

What happens when the dividend actually lands in our savings account? It is not tough to figure out. As soon as the dividend is *realised* (credited into our account), it becomes liable to taxation.

Let us continue with our earlier example wherein we were supposed to receive a dividend of ₹5,000. And let us take the case of dividends received from an equity mutual fund and a debt mutual fund separately because of how the taxman treats both these types of mutual funds.

Dividends from Debt Mutual Funds

If it is a dividend-based debt fund, we will receive only ₹3,558 instead of ₹5,000. Why? Because the debt fund house withholds a mammoth 28.84% of the dividend and pays that as tax to the government.

Hold on. Read it again. Almost 30% of our dividend is lost en route from the fund house to our bank account. And remember that this loss is instant since tax on dividends is deducted at the source.

It would have been much better to simply withdraw the amount or set up a systematic withdrawal plan.

If we had withdrawn the funds in less than three years, short-term capital gains (STCG) would have been applicable to us. Our payable tax would be as per our existing tax slab, which could be anywhere between 5% to 30%. The chances are that we will lose less money to the taxman here than with the dividends option, in which case, we are sure to lose close to 30%.

And suppose you did a bit of planning and started withdrawing your money after three years of investing. In that case, you are subjected to a long-term capital gains (LTCG) tax, which is a flat 20% post indexation. This tax would be quite close to 0%, assuming an average 6% inflation[23] every year.

So, you could be taxed anywhere between 0% to 30% depending on various conditions if you would make a systematic withdrawal from the mutual fund. But you would be charged nearly 29% tax if you opt for dividends for your debt funds.

Dividends from Equity Mutual Funds

There was no such tax on the dividends from equity funds just a year back. But now, even in an equity fund, there's a 10% tax on the dividends. Accounting for the surcharges, you will get ₹4,353 as the dividend while your NAV goes down in equivalent to ₹5,000.

If, instead, you opted to withdraw after a one-year holding period, you would be subjected to long-term capital gains tax in equity. This could be 0% if the withdrawals are less than ₹1 lakh per year or a max of 10% for anything above that.

So, in almost all cases, dividends fail to meet up to their own promise. And they come out worse than a simple withdrawal from the fund. In case we need regular monthly income, then we can easily set up a systematic withdrawal plan (SWP)[46] from our fund.

It, therefore, makes no sense to opt for a dividend plan. Fund houses are giving us our own money and the government turns out to be the biggest beneficiary by taxing us a heavy *lagaan* on it.

You Pay At Least Six Times More Tax in Dividend Option

Foops moments do not cease to exist when it comes to dividends. Here is the third one.

What if I told you that there is a bigger Foops moment hidden in the taxation of dividends?

In dividends, the entire dividend amount is taxable. While in a withdrawal, the entire withdrawal amount is not taxable—only the gains are.

If you are wondering about the significance of this, let me elaborate with an example.

Continuing with the same example from earlier in this chapter, if we receive a dividend of ₹5,000, we would be taxed 10% (for equity funds) and 28.83% (for debt funds). Fair enough. But the more important question is that on which amount this tax is levied. It is on the entire dividend amount of ₹5,000. So, let us say, in our example, in the case of debt funds, our tax will stand at 28.83% of ₹5,000, which is approximately ₹1,442.

Instead of that, we could have opted for a withdrawal of ₹5,000 from our fund. Even in the worst case, where we are taxed 30% as short-term capital gains for debt-based mutual funds, this tax is not on the withdrawn amount but on the gains. Assuming that the debt fund gained 8% every year, we had a total gain of approximately 16% in two years. When I withdraw this amount after two years, I would be taxed 30% on 16% gains of ₹5,000, which comes out to be 30% on ₹800, which comes out to be ₹240.

Compare the tax outgo in the worst case of the withdrawal option (₹240) with the dividend option (₹1,442). You would realise that we would be paying six times more tax if we opt for the dividend option. On the other hand, in the best case, you would be paying nil taxes with the withdrawal option, since you may be in the 0% tax bracket, or you may not have had any gains in that year, or the inflation may have been high, resulting in the indexed cost beating the gains—resulting in no effective gains and no taxes.

In fact, some older investments are getting an even worse deal. Once upon a time, a method of investing called 'dividend reinvestment' was popular because it led to lower taxation. Now, it actually destroys your money because of the tax on dividends.

The tax on capital gains comes into play only when you sell your investment. However, the tax gets deducted by the mutual funds at the source every time they pay a dividend paid or reinvest it. In effect, your money keeps diminishing in the reinvestment option. Your eventual returns will be severely impacted because the dividend tax constantly reduces the amount available for further growth.

The answer is simple. Instead of opting for the so-called dividend plans, we should opt for the growth plans and just withdraw a certain amount regularly, as per our need, by setting up a SWP. The tax incidence is going to be many times lower.

Foops #5: Getting Delusional about Mutual Fund Dividends

Awakening

- Mutual Funds dividends are simply a marketing gimmick.
- Dividend option for mutual funds end up making us poorer vis-à-vis simple withdrawal from the fund.
- We may end up actually paying six times, or even more taxes on dividend mutual funds.

Action

- Liquidate all your mutual funds running with dividend option.
- Move the money to an equivalent growth option.
- If you want regular inflow of money, use systematic withdrawal plans (SWPs) rather than the tax inefficient dividend option.

FOOPS 6

UNDERESTIMATING THE POWER OF COMPOUNDING

> **THE MOST POWERFUL FORCE IN THE UNIVERSE IS COMPOUNDING.**
>
> – ALBERT EINSTEIN

This is a small story set 200 years ago.

Rama was a poet living in a remote village in India. While he was highly skilled in poetry, he could never find worthy customers in his village. As such, his family was suffering because of financial issues. The situation became so bad that he had to do something drastically different for his and his family's survival.

Rama decided to meet the king and display his art. After a few days of travel, he reached the palace and met the king. He showcased his poetry to the king and the attendees in the palace. The king was highly appreciative of Rama and asked him what he would like as a reward.

This is where Rama surprised the king once again. He requested the king for an empty chessboard. The king obliged. Rama then declared that all he wants is one grain of rice in the first box, two grains of rice in the second box, four grains of rice in the third box and so on until the entire chessboard is filled up.

The king was rather shocked by this wish. Not only was it strange, but it also seemed trivial to be asking the king for a few grains of rice as a reward. Anyway, the king did not mind fulfilling Rama's wish. So, he ordered his staff to honour the poet's request.

As the staff started to count the number of grains needed to fulfil the wish, the gravity of the situation dawned on them. By the time chessboard's first row was completed, there were 256 grains of rice—not much by any standard. But what do you expect would have happened when the second row was completed? No, it was not 512 grains of rice. The last box of the second row demanded 65,536 grains of rice—which was approximately one sack of rice. And by the end of the third row, it was not two sacks; it was 256 sacks of rice, or 1.67 crore grains.

The king realised this enormous demand and ordered rice from outside his capital. By the time the fourth row was completed, the need was for 65,536 sacks of rice or 4.29 trillion grains of rice. This was just half the chessboard.

And guess the numbers by the time we reach the end of the chessboard. Of course, you know it is not going to be just double. Here, let me share the exact number: it was 4.29 trillion sacks of rice. The kingdom itself had not produced these many sacks of rice in the last ten years put together. And 4.29 trillion sacks were just for the last box of the chessboard. If we add up the rice needed for the previous 63 boxes, the total number is mind-boggling, to say the least. And it all started with one grain. And there were just 64 boxes to be filled.

The wise king made just one mistake. He underestimated the magical power of compounding—grossly.

Here is another question, which I often discuss with audiences during my seminars. Among the thousands of attendees I have interacted with, I am yet to see even one person come close to the answer for this question. So, I am throwing an open challenge to you to see if you can come close to the answer without using a calculator. I am aware that you will go big on your guesses, but let us see how far your mind can go.

Here you go…

Take a regular sheet of paper, which is generally around 0.1 mm thick. Fold it across the centre to double its thickness. What would be the thickness after one fold?

0.2 mm. Good.

Now, let us do one more fold and double the thickness again. How much is the thickness after two folds?

0.4 mm. So far so good.

Here goes the question: what is the approximate thickness of this sheet of paper if you fold it 50 times? Please do not use a calculator. Try and make a guess to get an idea of how badly you underestimate the magic of compounding.

The closest answers I have gotten say 500 meters thick. Imagine folding a paper 50 times and arriving at something which is half a kilometre thick. This seems wild to imagine. How can the paper have a thickness of 0.5 km? Never heard, never imagined.

But here is the right answer: 11.2 crore km thick. Yes, this is the paper's thickness with just 50 folds of 0.1 mm thick paper. To put the 11.2 crore km thickness in perspective, the distance from the earth to the moon is around 3.84 lakh km—nowhere close to the thickness of our paper after 50 folds. Our paper's thickness would be close to the distance from the earth to the sun, around 15 crore km.

Did our imagination go wrong? Ok, let me give you another chance to get it close.

Let me give you, the informed reader, a simple choice. I give you two options. The first option is to take ₹1 lakh a day, every day, for the entire month. The second option is to take ₹1 on the first day, ₹2 on the second day, and so on, until the month's end. Which option would you choose? I know many of you are now inclined to seriously look at the second option. Our mind is probably starting to understand the seriousness involved with compounding and its immense power. Well, the answer is that the first option would fetch you ₹30 lakhs, while the second option would fetch you more than ₹100 crores. It is not just that the second option is better—there is simply no match. The power of compounding is immense.

"Compound interest is the eighth wonder of the world. He who understands it, earns it; he who doesn't, pays it," says Albert Einstein.

And the fact is that most of us end up on the latter side; that is, we do not understand it.

Don't believe me? Then you may want to believe Morgan Housel, the internationally acclaimed author of the bestselling book *The Psychology of Money*. This is what he writes in his blog:

"No matter how many times you study compounding, it is so big that you can barely wrap your head around it. In 2004 Bill Gates criticized the new Gmail, wondering why anyone would need a gig of storage. You never get accustomed to how quickly things can grow."

Of all the examples we discussed in this chapter, did any example change your life? Probably not. What it likely did was to surprise you because the results intuitively didn't seem right. Linear thinking is so much more intuitive than exponential thinking.

Michael Batnick once explained it.

"If I ask you to calculate 8+8+8+8+8+8+8+8+8 in your head, you can do it in a few seconds (it's 72). If I ask you to calculate 8x8x8x8x8x8x8x8x8, your head will explode (it's 134, 217, 728)."

Physicist Albert Bartlett put it like this:

"The greatest shortcoming of the human race is our inability to understand the exponential function."

As Morgan Housel further elaborates,

"Good investing isn't necessarily about earning the highest returns because the highest returns tend to be one-off hits that kill your confidence when they end. It's about earning pretty good returns that you can stick with for a long period of time. That's when compounding runs wild."

So, what happens when the money compounds? Does our imagination go wrong? Why can't we visualise the results of compounding to any fair degree of accuracy? Why can't humans project the impact of this simple principle?

Research carried out in the US by George Washington University in 2016 found that only a third of Americans understand how compounding works.

Equivalent research by the Pensions and Lifetime Savings Association in 2018 revealed that 80% of Britons are not saving enough for retirement, primarily because they underestimate the power of compounding.

Lusardi and Tufano, in 2009, examined 'debt literacy' regarding interest compounding and found that only one-third of respondents knew how long it would take for debt to double if one were to borrow at a 20% interest rate. This lack of knowledge confirms conclusions from Moore's 2003 survey of Washington state residents, where she found that people frequently failed to understand interest compounding.

The fact is that, by default, the human mind is not designed to conceptualise and visualise the magic of compounding. We have been taught and shown linear growth all around us. We see ourselves and other species growing old linearly—one day at a time, day by day. We realise when we deal with our jobs that the more time we put in, the money that we can earn increases—linearly. The harder a student works, the greater their probability of getting better marks—a somewhat linear relationship.

Our minds have been trained to visualise linear growth.

Having said that, we do see a lot of non-linear growth as well.

If we monitor the stock market every day, it is absolutely non-linear and highly volatile. A drug may be ineffective until a certain dosage before becoming effective or become progressively more potent over a specific range, but then turn harmful—both examples of non-linear growth. If we exercise twice for 20 minutes, we are not likely to lose twice the weight. Exercise for one minute twenty separate times, and we will have drastically different results. The world is full of non-linear growth examples.

However, there is a special case of non-linear growth, which we hardly study or relate to in real life. This happens to be compounded growth. This is because we have not seen enough examples of it. Even if many examples exist around us, we haven't really studied them in-depth and appreciated the outcomes. Or we have just not been patient enough to wait for the magic of compounding to showcase itself. Our mind, therefore, has not been tuned or developed for appreciating compounded growth.

What is the way out?

Well, there seems to be no shortcut. The mind needs to be trained repeatedly, with ample examples, to grasp this important concept's seriousness so that it starts to visualise compounded growth. The mind will only start taking it seriously enough, only when it starts to visualise it. Then, we will start taking actions in our daily life that support the power of compounding.

Now, let me take you to a simple, real-life financial example—which you all should be able to relate to.

Do you remember Figure 1, the chart of a debt-based investment like a fixed deposit over time, where the curve is almost perfectly linear? Let me reproduce it here for your convenience.

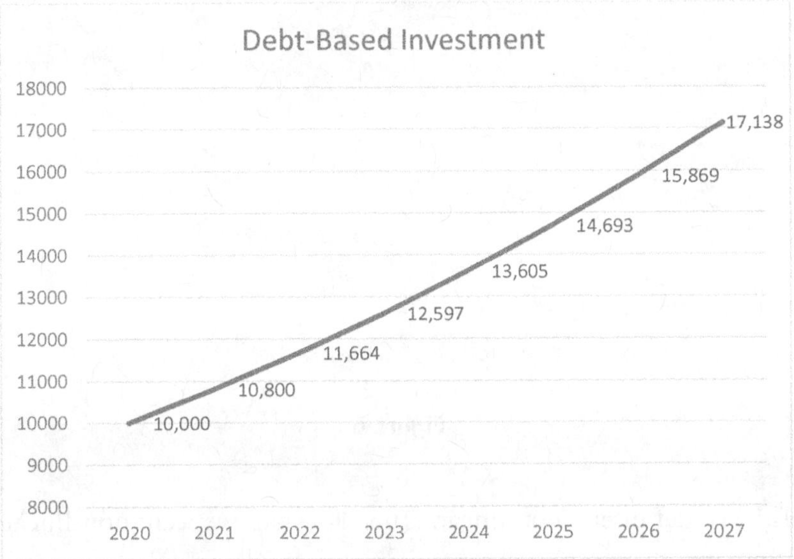

Figure 5

So, this curve shows how ₹10,000 in your debt-based investment grows at an annualised rate of 8% for the next seven years. The curve is not perfectly linear. Instead, it seems to be curving upwards.

What if we were to continue investing for another seven to eight years? Let us look at the curve for the same investment, the same ₹10,000 invested at the same 8% returns now extrapolated to 35 years, rather than seven years. The more you extrapolate, the more you will realise the presence of non-linear compounded growth.

Here is how it looks:

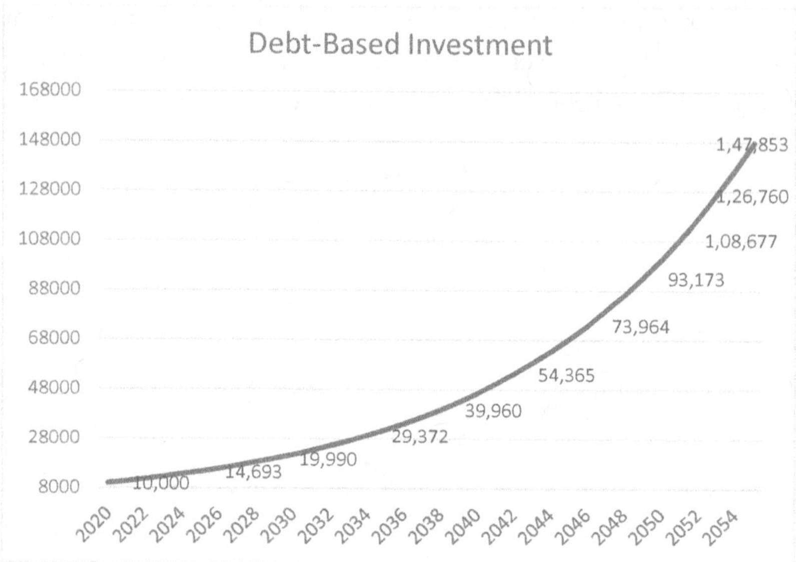

Figure 6

This is definitely not linear. This is what we call non-linear compounded growth.

Here is an even more interesting part of such growth. If you look at the first seven years in this graph (2020-2027) and hide the remainder of the graph by keeping your hand over it, you will see an almost flat line with a small 15- to 20-degree angle from the horizontal. That's what we saw in Figure 5.

Now, go to the last seven years of the graph in Figure 6 (2048-2055), and hide the previous years by keeping your hand over it. You see another straight line but with a significantly steeper climb, almost like a 65-70-degree angle with the horizontal.

It is the same rate of interest for the same amount. Nothing has changed, except that time has elapsed, and compounding has been able to play its magic.

The more time you give it, the more magical it becomes. So, if a paper took 50 folds to reach a thickness of 11 crore km, it will take just one more fold to achieve another 11 crore km. You achieve in just one fold, what was achieved in 50 folds.

Warren Buffet's wealth was not created just by making good investments. In fact, there were, and are, better and smarter investors than Buffet. But there is hardly anyone who has been invested for close to 75 years. Compounding has played a significant role in Buffet's wealth, and that's something which is extremely difficult to beat.

And how can we give more time to our investments? The most logical way is to start investing at an early age.

Age is such a vital factor in compounding and wealth creation that it can never be overemphasised. Still, I see so many investors waiting for the right opportunity to start their financial freedom journey. Some wait for the current family situation to settle, to get into a better role before starting, to understand everything in-depth before going ahead, or whatever else.

We do not realise that with every passing day, we are diminishing the impact of compounding. And while everything else can be theoretically recovered, time lost can never be.

And that is the strongest reason why I conduct programs for school students where we talk about money, passive income, interest, compounding, inflation, etc. If nothing else, I wish to make a dent in our next generation's psychology towards money.

Compounding still remains one of the most underrated yet powerful mechanisms to generate massive wealth. If we can identify this Foops moment early in life, it can have a far-reaching impact on our future and on the coming generations.

Foops #6: Underestimating the Power of Compounding	
Awakening	Action
• The human mind cannot fully comprehend compounding and its amazing power. • Thats probably because we havent seen enough examples of compounding in our daily life.	• Start investing early in life, as early as practically possible. Time, once lost, is not recoverable. • Let money compound. Don't keep unnecessarily moving it from one asset to another.

FOOPS 7

FOLLOWING THE STUPID APPROACH OF 'KEEP INVESTING'

> THE AVERAGE INVESTOR'S RETURN IS SIGNIFICANTLY LOWER THAN MARKET INDICES DUE PRIMARILY TO MARKET TIMING.
>
> – DANIEL KAHNEMAN

Here is one of the oldest Wall Street jokes that many of you may have heard before. But it is worth replicating in the current context.

This is how it goes.

A newcomer into the market asks a grizzled veteran,
"How do I make money in the stock market?"
The old master replies,
"Why this question? That is the simplest thing to do. Buy low and sell high."
So, the young man asks, "Yes, but how do I actually do that?".
The reply comes, "That's a very difficult question indeed. It takes a lifetime to learn this art."

Well, this may not be the greatest joke around, but it fits very well in the context of the Foops moment that I'm about to reveal. And this is not only true for stock investing; it holds equally true for any volatile asset class—be it stocks, mutual funds, real estate, gold, etc. But for the sake of our understanding, let us limit the discussion to equity markets only (equity markets comprise both stock investing as well as equity-based mutual fund investing).

It seems almost self-evident that the most common interpretation of 'buy low, sell high' is to buy when the markets have fallen to their nadir and sell when the markets have risen to their zenith. And this is not only common sense but can also be proven with enough evidence from history that shows those who bought during corrections and sold during euphoria were the biggest gainers.

But then, what is so difficult in this to actually practise? And if this can be practised in real life easily, then everyone investing in equity should be filthy rich.

As per www.researchandranking.com, 90% of investors in the stock market lose money. Not only that, but a similar percentage of day traders lose money. This is also reflected in the fact that 80% of day traders quit the market within the first two years. But, have you ever wondered why so many people are losing money when the winning formula is as simple as buying low and selling high?

The reason is pretty straightforward. You can adopt this strategy only if you know the lows and highs of the market in advance.

Let me reiterate the fact that could awaken you to your next Foops moment. The fact is that the market high and low cannot be known ahead of time. They cannot be known even presently. They can, in fact, be known only in hindsight.

That the market has peaked can only be known after it has crashed, at which time it is too late to take any action anyways. And if the highs and lows of the market cannot be known ahead of time, how in the world are we going to buy low or sell high.

Media statements like, "The markets have 'corrected'. Is it the right time to buy now?" only add to the confusion.

The biggest challenge with buying in 'correction' is finding when the market has been 'corrected'.

How does one know that the market is now 'correct' and would not become 'even more correct'? And then what happens if the market becomes, say, 'extremely correct'. How long should one wait before the market becomes 'incorrect' yet again? In hindsight, these are the easiest questions to answer, but when looking ahead, this can get as tough as you can imagine.

It might sound confusing to many. But remember that confusions are usually good. They indicate that we are on the brink of expanding our minds, a potential awakening to our next Foops moment.

Let me help you override any confusion by taking you through a small exercise.

I will show you a few real-life market situations from the past and expect you to predict the market over the next few weeks. If you do this exercise without accessing the internet, you will find it not only interesting, but you will also get a very important message for the rest of your life.

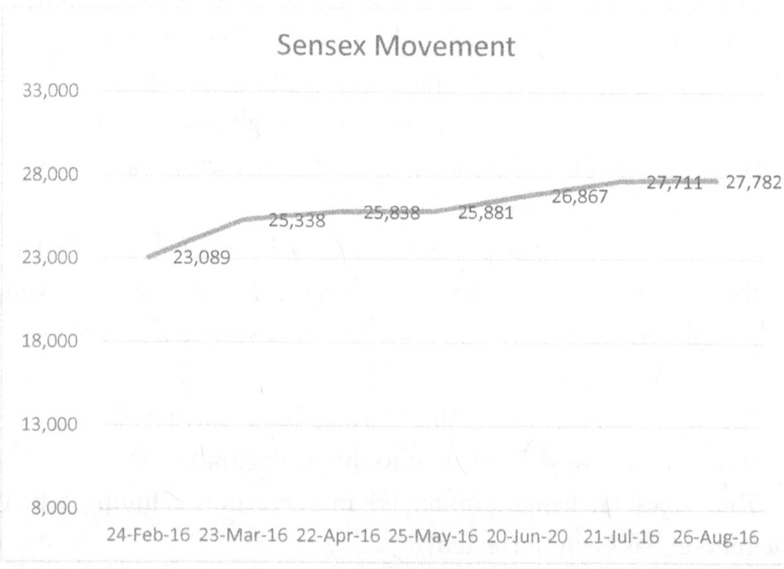

Figure 7

The above figure shows the sensex[44] movement during a random six-month period from February to August 2016. Now, assuming you understand the core principle of stock investing (which is to buy low and sell high), what would you likely do in September 2016? Buy or sell?

Considering the past six-month period, it seems that the market is already at a high, having risen almost 20% in six months (from 23,089 to 27,782), which extrapolates to around 40% annualised returns. So, what do we do now? Buy? Sell? Or do nothing?

A majority of us would actually do nothing because we are fearful of buying more at a high and too greedy to sell it at the same time. But remember that taking no decision is also a decision that we take—as we understood in Foops #1.

Momentarily ignoring those who do not take any decision because of fear or greed, the next lot of people, who are brave enough to take some decision, would go for a seemingly logical action—which is to sell and, as they say, *book some profits.*

Fair enough. But then, the common challenge in a volatile market is the unpredictability of its near-term future. How do we know that the markets will not go even higher, having gone high for the last six months? That's a perfectly valid question, and no one in the world will ever have an answer to this question.

Before we look at the reason for this market unpredictability, let us see the markets exactly a month later, in the third week of September 2016 (see Figure 8).

As you see, the markets actually rose in September 2016, thus touching another high. Fair enough. You cannot blame the market for being illogical. That's how it is designed to be—unpredictable and volatile. Actually, as we would see later, market volatility is precisely what can give you stellar returns from this asset class.

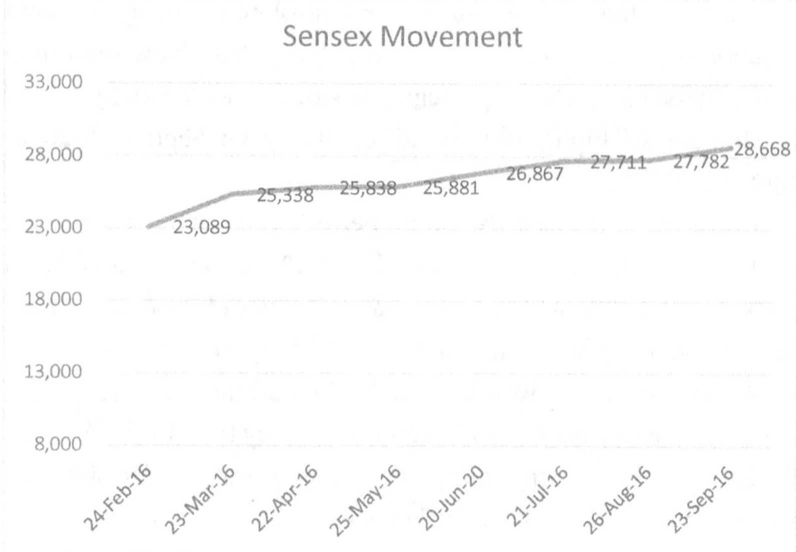

Figure 8

But the key question is, what next? Should we sell now? Or do you think that if the trend is likely to continue, we should actually be buying more? Of course, no one in the world knows this. So, we can just make a guess, at best.

Figure 9 shows the data as of October 2016.

What next?

Should we buy now, since the market has come to a relatively lower point? We don't know. It is all guesswork.

Let us look at the next three months and see in Figure 10 if your guesses were anywhere close and whether you were able to make the correct buy or sell decisions.

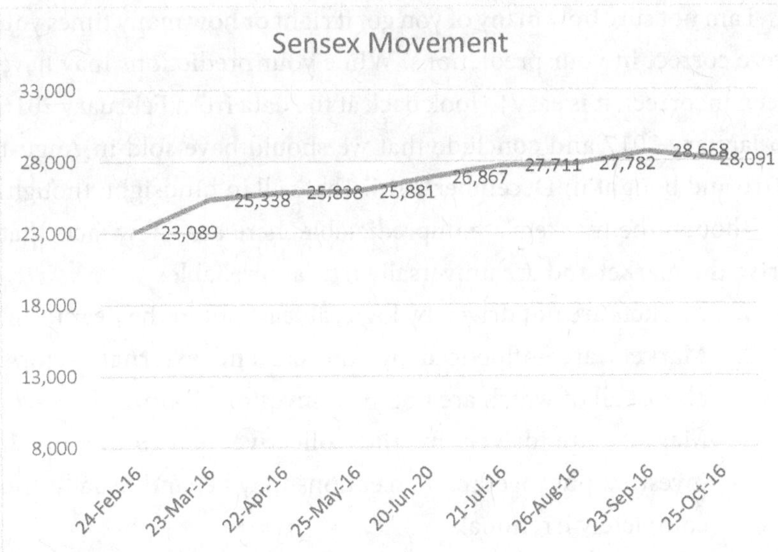

Figure 9

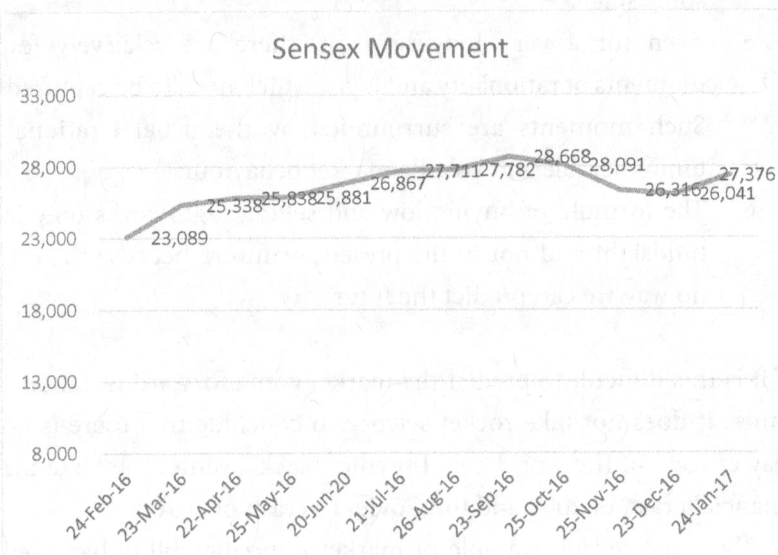

Figure 10

I am not sure how many of you got it right or how many times you were correct in your predictions. While your predictions may have been incorrect, it is easy to look back at the data from February 2016 to January 2017 and conclude that we should have sold in August 2016 and bought in December 2016. That's all in hindsight, though.

Though the markets are unpredictable, here are a few facts that drive the market and are universally true and reliable:

1. Markets are not driven by logic, at least not in the near term.
2. Markets are influenced by internal and external factors, almost all of which are not in an investor's control.
3. Markets are driven by the collective perception of all investors put together. Perceptions may be, and usually are, completely irrational.
4. Unless you have a very long perspective (seven-plus years), you have all the chances of being fooled by the market at some stage.
5. Even for a very long horizon, there are relatively few moments of rationality and logic, which need to be captured. Such moments are surrounded by the usual irrational, unpredictable and volatile market behaviour.
6. The formula of buying low and selling high works only in hindsight and not in the present or future because there is no way we can predict the future.

If it is this difficult to predict the market going forward in rational times, it does not take rocket science to conclude that there is no way anyone in the world could predict black swan events[4] like the financial crash of 2008 and the Covid-19 crash of 2020.

The most recent example of market unpredictability has been the meteoric rise of the market after the first three months of the

Covid-19 lockdown—completely unpredictable and illogical but very true to the nature of the market.

At the end of the day, we conclude that the *market is the king*. There is no way to judge the market's future direction even with reasonable accuracy, at least in the near term. So, what do we do? Though the strategy 'buy low, sell high' is simple and logical, it is impossible to implement by looking at the market. We must accept this fact. We must succumb to a higher power.

Look Inside Rather than Outside

Acceptance about anything in life is usually confused with giving up. But the fact remains that only acceptance allows you to think in a new direction, possibly trying to solve the problem. If we do not diagnose a disease, we will never take remedial action. If we do not accept that we are full of anger, we will never work on it. Acceptance is vital for solutions.

Having accepted that we are full of anger, we must stop looking at solutions outside us and work towards getting calmer over time. We have to look inside, rather than outside, for the solution. Easier said than done, but this concept of looking inside goes a long way in finding solutions to handle the mighty markets.

Once we accept and respect the fact that the market is the king and we cannot predict its future, our minds are opened up to new possibilities.

But we have to think out of the box to implement this possibility.

The challenge is that we were looking at the outside data points (at the market and its movement) to decide when to buy and sell. This strategy, as we have seen, just does not work in any situation. The chances are high that you will fail.

In this case, the only strategy that works is to look inside (at our own financial portfolio and our own investing strategy[24]) and use a simple and effective 'Portfolio Balancing Tool'.

Let me explain how this tool works and how it helps us effectively implement the 'buy low, sell high' strategy extremely effectively.

This tool does not work on the usual 'keep investing' principle but on the 'keep balancing' principle.

'Keep Investing' Principle

The 'keep investing' principle, which many advocate, gets implemented in our portfolio in two ways:

1. **Blind Investing Method**

   The first method to follow the keep investing principle is the blind investing method (via SIPs). Here, we must keep investing a fixed amount in equity-based assets at regular intervals, irrespective of what is happening in the market or to our portfolio. We are *blind* to any situation—whether outside or inside—and we just keep investing.

   Of course, we are well aware of the SIP method of investing—the truest form of blind investing.

   This is like saying to ourselves that I do not care even if I am full of anger. I will continue to live my personality. I do not bother about what others think about me or whether this anger impacts me adversely or not. I am what I am. This is definitely one way many people live their lives, simply because it keeps us in our comfort zone. It's easy. There is no hard work to be done. Whether it is the right thing or not is your call to make.

Expectedly, most investors follow this method because it is highly propagated by most financial advisors. And, guess what—it's damn easy. This method may have several positives, but the merits of this method outweigh the demerits only for naïve investors—just to get them in the habit of saving and investing.

The same SIP method becomes a burden and a drag once we become disciplined because there is a better way out ('keep balancing', which we will discuss soon).

2. **Conscious Investing Method**

In this method under the 'keep investing' principle, we do not invest the same amount every time. In fact, we try to look at the market lows to invest more. At the same time, we are looking at the market highs to invest less.

But this method, though theoretically better than blind investing, is fundamentally weak since the market highs and lows make sense, as we saw earlier, only in retrospect. Additionally, it demands more time involvement from an investor, which may not be feasible in every case.

And then, human emotions come into play. How long will we keep investing if the markets continue to rise? And how much? And if the markets dip, how long will we keep investing if it continues to fall? When do we stop?

This is like saying to ourselves that, "My anger is not my problem. It is the other party that is instigating this anger. Therefore, they must be blamed for my situation. I am just reacting to the situation." Another easy way out.

Irrespective of whether we use the blind investing method or the conscious investing method, there is one fundamental flaw with the 'keep investing' principle. It is either completely blind (as in blind investing method) or outward-market-looking (as in conscious investing method). Neither approach is good enough since we are either closing our eyes to reality or trying to predict the market's future, both of which are recipes for failure.

The 'keep investing principle' thus does not sound successful.

There has to be a better way, and there is.

'Keep Balancing' Principle

The 'keep balancing' principle is not blind but inward-looking, which happens to be the most practical and logical approach to wealth creation.

It looks inward—towards our investing strategy and portfolio balance and strives to maintain the right balance of equity assets in our portfolio.

This is like saying, "If I am angry, I need to change internally despite all the instigation. I need to have better control over how I look at the situation." This is hard work, but definitely worth it.

Let me explain how this principle works step by step.

Step-1: Decide the Optimal Portfolio Balance

A balanced portfolio gives you the most optimum returns across all market conditions. A good financial consultant will consider your risk-taking capacity, risk-taking tolerance, liquidity needs, ROI needs, age and many other financial and non-financial factors to arrive at the right portfolio balance for your needs.

As you will see in the subsequent chapters, a perfect portfolio balance is not all about the best returns. It is about optimum returns while taking care of other constraints that you will have in your life. For example, it may be a stupid idea to continue investing in equity if you need the money for your child's education in two years. Likewise, it might be foolish to invest in small-cap equity stocks if your risk tolerance[43] levels are below 50%.

So, we need to decide the right mix of equity, real estate, commodity and debt investments for ourselves. Remember that this is a fairly customised mix for you in the given situation. The mix may change over time, but once formulated, it should stay the same for the next few years.

We do this exercise for every single freedom seeker in the ELITE program[11]. For Rohitesh, one of our freedom seekers from Mumbai, the investing strategy suggested an equity portion of 45% for his portfolio. The remaining 55% comprised a combination of commodities and debt-based investments. Real estate was marked as 0% for him.

Step-2: Hit the Right Balance

Once we have decided on the correct portfolio balance, we have to make efforts to reach that right balance. Rohitesh had around 22% equity allocation when he learnt that the right equity balance for him was 45%. This gap between 22% and 45% needed to be bridged to arrive at the right balance.

To bridge this gap, we decided to work on a two-pronged strategy.

Firstly, he was advised to move some money from his debt-based investments to equity-based investments. Keeping in mind the lock-in period with many of his debt-based investments like EPF[14], PPF, etc. and his liquidity needs for money in the near future, this movement was limited and definitely insufficient to reach the optimal balance of 45%. But still, something is better than nothing. However, it is essential to understand that this movement cannot be done in a lump sum manner due to the risks involved when moving from debt to equity. Therefore, we decided to split the movement across the next 24 months via SIPs.

He was likely to hit around 33% equity post this movement. But that still keeps him short of the optimal target of 45% by approximately 12%.

The next step was to alter how his monthly surplus was being invested. Apart from the mandatory investments in debt like EPF, we asked him to stop any further debt-based investments for the next two years. It was clear that all other surplus funds should be moved to equity to bridge that additional 12% gap.

These strategies worked in parallel over the next two years. Finally, after two years, Rohitesh was right there, very close to the ideal 45% balance—in fact, a little higher, at 47%.

It is important to note that we should not get too caught up with numbers here. While 45% is an ideal balance for Rohitesh, plus or minus 5% is fine too. Therefore, to ease the nerves for our seekers in the ELITE Program, we have the concept of red, amber and green bands for equity balance rather than a fixed number.

Step-3: Keep Balancing

We have understood what's the right balance for us.

We have hit the right balance over time.

Now comes the most exciting part, that is, to maintain the balance.

You got a new car. Excellent! Everything is so good about this new beast, including the wheel balancing. It is just so perfect and smooth.

Over time, of course, as you drive your car, the wheel balance is quite likely to get disturbed. And you cannot afford to let it be that way. Not only will it lead to faster wear and tear of your car wheels, but your driving experience will never be as enjoyable. So we ensure that we get the wheel balancing checked and tuned with every car service.

It is precisely the same with our investments and our portfolio. Even if we have brought the portfolio at the perfect balance, the portfolio keeps getting out of balance as our investments grow. We need to continuously tune it for the most optimum returns.

Therefore, once you have reached the target balance, you have only one job to do as an investor— keeping the portfolio balanced as per your investing strategy. If you can understand and learn this art of balancing your portfolio, you will be automatically executing the 'buy low, sell high' strategy with amazing results—even without any attempt to predict the market highs and lows.

Why Would a Portfolio Become Unbalanced?

Some of our seekers often have this question, and some of you may want to know this too. Car wheels becoming unbalanced is understandable since the car has to run on roads; why would any portfolio go out of balance after it has been balanced once? A perfectly valid question, but many factors influence the portfolio balance on an ongoing basis.

I will list down three of the most important factors for your understanding:

a. **Monthly Investments**

Though the portfolio is balanced in a particular proportion as per your investing strategy, a regular monthly investment is also flowing into your portfolio. This regular monthly investment is made from the net investable surplus (NIS) that you generate month on month. These investments must also be routed to the respective asset classes in the same proportion as the desired balance.

To continue our earlier example, we created an NIS allocation plan for Rohitesh. He was advised how his monthly net investible surplus would get split among various equity and non-equity assets, the total equity asset proposal being 45%. If you go a bit deeper, this 45% allocation to equity gets split into various stocks, equity mutual funds, etc. in a specific proportion—again depending on Rohitesh's investing strategy.

If the monthly investments are not properly allocated, or we are unable to invest in specific months (because of various life situations), then it is quite likely that the portfolio will go out of balance over a period of time.

b. Different Returns from Different Asset Classes

This is one of the most significant reasons why your portfolio will keep getting unbalanced. Once you have set the portfolio in balance at, say, 45% equity and 55% debt, what happens if the equity portion keeps growing at 13% per annum and the debt portion grows at 7% per annum?

Assuming there is no other input or output to the portfolio, after three years, your equity and debt will almost be in a 50%-50% balance rather than the planned 45%-55% balance. Just in three years, the difference between the two grows by 10% because of the difference in returns from different asset classes.

It's also true in the case of negative returns from equity, which is quite feasible in some years.

c. Equity Volatility

It is not just that the equity returns are different from debt returns, but the equity market is also volatile. In this nature of the market lies the biggest opportunity to buy low and sell high.

Let us see how it happens.

i. **Case 1: Markets Rise**

Assuming our portfolio was perfectly balanced at 45% equity and 55% non-equity assets, let us understand what can happen if the equity market rises by 25% over the next six months. Yes, this is quite possible considering the true nature of the market. At the same time, the debt portion is growing at a fixed rate of 7% per annum, or 3.5% half-yearly.

If this happens, the new portfolio balance would be almost 50-50 in six months flat. If you are in the habit of reviewing your portfolio every six months, you would see this as a warning sign that your portfolio's balance has shifted. The natural response to this imbalance would be to do something to correct it. And what can you do to get a portfolio with 50% equity back to the right balance of 45% equity? Of course, it does not take rocket science to conclude that you need to sell some equity and move those funds to the debt portion of your portfolio.

So, what did we just do? The markets were high, and we sold equity. That is the 'sell high' part of your 'buy low, sell high' strategy.

But how do we buy low? For that, the markets have to fall, which they will, sooner or later.

ii. **Case 2: Markets Fall**

Now, you balanced the portfolio back to where it was by selling high. And now, your portfolio is back in 45%-55% balance.

After a few years, let us say that the markets fall by almost 25% in six months. So, your equity portion will fall by 25%, while your debt portion will continue to rise at 3.5% in six months.

When this happens, the new balance of our portfolio with the falling market would be approximately 37% equity and 63% debt. Again, if we have been reviewing our portfolio regularly, we will act to rebalance the portfolio back to 45%-55%. To do that, all we must do is buy more equity by moving funds from the debt side to the equity side. This is how we naturally 'buy low' in the market.

The above two cases of markets rising or falling as per its nature prove the fact that if we regularly track our portfolio and follow the 'keep balancing' principle, we automatically implement the 'buy low, sell high' strategy. Moreover, we do this by looking at our portfolio rather than the market. Thus, we allow the market to play as it wishes to, and we buy or sell based on our portfolio balance movement.

Of course, to implement the above strategies, you will need the help of certain tools. For example, you will need to know your current portfolio balance and, more importantly, the right portfolio balance for you, etc. Most of these tools are available for free on our official website (http://www.manoj-arora.com).

d. **Withdrawals for Life Special Events**

This is another situation where we have seen significant chaos being created in portfolio balance. Life special events are major events that need high-ticket expenses like international vacations, child education, child marriage etc.

In any such event, most investors withdraw funds from one or more assets without considering how these withdrawals impact the portfolio balance.

Let's say our portfolio was optimally balanced at 45%-55%. We withdrew the entire amount for a special event from the debt portion (say FDs, PPF, EPF etc.). This amount turned out to be, let us say, 10% of our portfolio. In this case, we can clearly gauge the imbalance that gets created with this withdrawal.

Therefore, the withdrawals in a balanced portfolio should almost always be made in the same ratio as the balance. This means that if I were to withdraw ₹10 lakhs from my portfolio (for a special event in my life), which is correctly balanced at 45%-55%, I would ideally withdraw ₹4.5 lakhs from the equity portion and ₹5.5 lakhs from the debt portion so that the portfolio remains balanced after the withdrawal.

Now, since all the above factors—regular monthly investments, the difference in returns, volatility and withdrawals—are working in tandem, it might be difficult to project the future balance of your portfolio. Therefore, it becomes imperative to keep reviewing your portfolio balance and taking action whenever we see the portfolio is running out of balance.

So, the age-old practice to keep investing in the market is not what fetches you great returns. It was a Foops moment for me. I made the same mistake for many years—just investing and investing. 'Keep Investing' never returns you the most optimal returns.

We must become aware and awaken to the fact that we need to look inside, to our portfolio balance, and then take action accordingly rather than investing aimlessly or acting based on market dynamics—both of which can be disastrous for our portfolio.

Foops # 7: Following the Stupid Approach of 'Keep Investing'

Awakening	Action
• Market highs and lows cannot be known in advance. • Thus, our investing decisions should never be governed by market performance but by our portfolio needs. • We ought to learn the art of balancing rather than investing aimlessly. • A portfolio that is balanced as per our investing strategy is designed to give us most optimal returns at all times.	• Never try to enter the market thinking that it is at its low. The same way, never exit the market thinking that it is at a high. • Too many people have burnt their fingers trying to time the market. • Decide your investing strategy • Hit the target equity equity percentage. • Keep balancing the portfolio around the target equity percentage.

FOOPS 8

GETTING SWAYED BY THE HYPE OF NFOs AND IPOs

> **YOU CANNOT BE DISTRACTED BY THE NOISE OF MISINFORMATION.**
>
> – JAMES DALY

Imagine that you are the Indian cricket team's selector. You have a crucial decision to make—to select an opening batsman for the team. And you have to pick one of two options in front of you. On the one hand, you have an experienced batsman with a proven track record. On the other hand, you have a new batsman who has never played at the international level before. However, the new batsman has received a lot of attention from the media and is hyped to be the next big thing. So, who do you pick? Most of you would go with the experienced batsman, which would be the right decision in my opinion too.

In rare cases, the selector may go in for the new batsman over the experienced one. This could be because of various reasons related to the technicalities of the sport like the pitch suiting his batting style, left-right combination, the new batsman's X factor or the fact that the captain has recommended him. Yes, there could be reasons and genuine ones too. But these are rare. You would not replace Sachin Tendulkar with a Mr. X just because of the latter's potential.

I gave you this example so you can relate Mr. X to an NFO[34] or an IPO. I always tell my readers and all freedom seekers to dig deeper when tracking—whether assets and their returns, expenses and savings, portfolio balance, risk profile or anything they wish to improve, for that matter.

"Anything that gets measured, improves."

– Peter Drucker

I fully agree with Peter Drucker. The key word here is 'anything'. It does not say 'a few things' or 'many things'—it says 'anything'. So, it could be your weight, your exam score or your wealth. If you measure it, it has to improve.

The reason is simple. Our mind is always striving for improvements. But it needs to see some data points which can show some progress over time.

And the better you measure it, the more magic you will see happening with it. Depth is always magical. So, before you awaken yourself up to your Foops moment related to NFOs or IPOs, we need to go deeper and understand what these investment types are, how they operate and how they are different from a regular mutual fund or stock investment.

NFOs

As Investopedia says, "NFOs (or New Fund Offers) are the first subscription offering for any new fund offered by an investment company or a fund house." A new fund offer occurs when a fund is launched, allowing the firm to raise capital for purchasing securities.

In simple terms, if any fund house, like Axis Mutual Funds, has to launch a new fund, say, BlueChip Fund, it would come up with an NFO for this fund. Of course, the NFO would clearly state the objectives of the fund, where all it would be investing the money, the risk categorisation, the fund manager details, etc. The objective of an NFO is to raise money for itself so that it can go and buy securities as per the objectives of the fund.

This definition of an NFO and our experience with mutual fund NFOs tell us many things about an NFO.

1. **Unproven Track Record**

   We are being too liberal if we say that NFOs have an unproven track record. The fact is that there is absolutely no track record. None. Zero. Zilch.

   An NFO is like the cricketer Mr. X who has never played before but has now applied for his selection in the national cricket team. In fact, Mr. X may have even played some domestic cricket, but it's even worse when it comes to an NFO. They are trying out for the very first time—with your money. They have never operated in any kind of market earlier. They are a newborn baby. There is no historical data to tell us whether it is likely to perform well or pathetically. When we buy an NFO, we are choosing to go with Mr. X as against an equivalent mutual fund in the market that may have existed and proven itself for many years, or even decades.

2. **Higher Expenses**

   During the NFO phase, you will never have a clear idea about the maximum charges levied by the scheme. This is because the actual total expense ratio is disclosed only later.

   Moreover, newer funds initially charge a higher expense ratio as their corpus (also called as assets under management or AUM) is very small in the beginning, and they need to manage their fixed costs. As its asset base expands, the costs may remain more or less the same, but with a higher base of assets, the expense ratio starts coming down. So, essentially, you are paying a premium to buy mutual fund units during an NFO.

3. **The Beginning is Not at all Cheap**

   Some investors believe that they will be able to buy units at a lower launch price of ₹10 if they enter at the time of NFO. Well, yes, they can buy at ₹10, but whether it becomes ₹5 or ₹50 after six months will depend on the change in the value of underlying securities during this time period.

   It is a Foops moment in itself for many seekers when they are made aware of the fact that a mutual fund unit has no value by itself. Its value is determined by the securities it holds. The change in the NAV of a mutual fund is determined by the change in the value of the securities during this time. Therefore, you are not buying either expensive or cheap if you enter at the initial stage of an NFO.

Considering all the above reasons, it may not make sense to buy NFOs. Was this one of your Foops moments? Even if it was not, read on. There are many more awakenings on the way.

Nevertheless, there could be genuine reasons for an investor to choose an NFO over tried and test mutual funds. For example, we might have a very good experience with the fund manager who is going to manage the new fund, or we have a lot of faith in the asset management company (AMC) which is coming up with the NFO, or the NFO's unique offering may just bridge a gap in our own portfolio.

But these are rare situations and should remain rare. Even if we go with the NFO, we must remember that the risks are high. NFOs become more like a lottery to get lured into. But I have observed so many investors grabbing NFOs as if there would never be a second opportunity to invest in them, or they are going to lose out on a big opportunity if they do not invest now. This behaviour stems from the way NFOs are marketed and hyped.

Another reason why we sometimes get attracted towards an NFO is our experience or observations from various stock IPOs[25] (initial public offerings). We may have seen that there have been many IPOs that have opened at astonishingly high prices. And some of us may have regretted missing the opportunity to invest in the IPO when the stock was available for cheap.

However, investors usually make the mistake of looking at an NFO in the same vein as a stock's IPOs. They tend to overlook the fundamental differences between the two. Let me try and explain the way both work.

NFOs Are Not Like IPOs

The price of a stock is driven by the demand-supply equation because the number of shares is limited, that is, there is a definite and countable number of shares of a company available in the market at any given point of time. On the other hand, the supply of a mutual fund unit is unlimited.

All it means is that you can buy only as many shares of a company as are available for sale. If no one is ready to sell a stake, you cannot buy, irrespective of the price. Now, if you are very confident about a stock and want to buy it desperately, you may lure someone to sell, and for that, you may have to quote a higher price. If the seller agrees to your quoted price, he will sell, and the transaction is completed. Thus, the higher price was a factor of lack of supply and higher demand. The same goes for lower prices. If there are no buyers or fewer buyers than sellers, sellers may have to reduce the price to successfully sell, which drives down the share's price. So, selling and buying shares is quite a fair mechanism.

Now, coming to mutual funds, once the NAV is declared (based on the value of the securities the fund holds), you can just buy as many units as you wish to. There is no seller constraint here. The seller is the fund house, and they may allow you to buy any number of units. If you are a buyer, just buy at a given price (NAV). Interestingly, the demand for units of a particular fund does not increase the value of the funds or the NAV. The reason is simple. There is no limit to the number of units, and the units have no intrinsic value. Separate units are created by the fund house when required for investment, and these units cease to exist at the time of redemption. So, there is virtually an unlimited supply of units. Therefore, the demand for the fund's units has no effect on the fund's NAV.

Look at it this way. Even if there is a huge demand for units of a particular fund, its NAV may still drop the very next day, depending on how the underlying securities perform.

IPOs, on the other hand, may get listed at a premium because their demand exceeds their supply.

NFOs are, therefore, merely marketing tools to kickstart a new fund's campaign. Fund houses use NFOs to create excitement and push their funds. Investors should just learn about the new fund on offer and invest later when the fund is open for sale and repurchase on an ongoing basis. Many new equity schemes have been launched through NFOs in the last decade. These schemes are launched because they are an easy route to capture management fees and increase the fund house's asset base.

For example, in 2019 alone, 125 NFOs were launched. This is huge. This means that a new fund was being launched in the market every three days. And they are being marketed and campaigned through all kinds of media. You actually do not need even one of them, simply because there already are more than 2,500 funds in the market. We better learn to choose from the proven 2,500 funds rather than the new 125 funds.

Also, as an investor, we should be aware that there are many hidden reasons for a fund house to come up with NFOs. More recently, between October-December 2020, 25 NFOs were launched, almost all of them under the ESG (environmental, social and governance) theme—the new buzz in the market. Why are so many fund houses after ESG NFOs? Are these NFOs launched because there is a massive opportunity in this domain? That is what a lot of investors like us might perceive. But that's just what it is—a perception, albeit a false one.

These NFOs have been launched for a very different reason. SEBI has restricted the fund houses from launching more than one scheme from the same category, and ESG is a new category. If the fund houses have to market themselves with something fresh and complete their portfolio, they have no choice but to launch new funds in this category.

Sure, some new funds may turn out to be great and outperform their categories, just like a new batsman may score more runs than an experienced one. But then, investing isn't just a cricket game for you. It has a higher risk factor, and as far as the investor is concerned, there is much more at stake—their hard-earned money. Therefore, it pays to be a little bit more cautious.

Now that we are clear that NFOs are marketing tools and nothing else, what about IPOs? They sound reasonable to invest in, don't they?

Undoubtedly, IPOs are fairer than NFOs. But just by a whisker. And the reasons are not difficult to understand. But before we get into the Foops moment for IPOs, let us understand what an IPO is.

IPOs

As per Investopedia, "An initial public offering (IPO) refers to the process of offering shares of a private corporation to the public in a new stock issuance. Public share issuance allows a company to raise capital from public investors."

What NFOs are to mutual funds, IPOs are to stocks. However, there are subtle differences that you ought to be aware of. While NFOs represent the birth of a new fund, IPOs are not the birth of a company but the announcement of its entry in the public domain. This is the first time the company is moving to the public, even though it may have existed for decades as a private company.

The Lure of Instant Gratification

IPOs attract a similar craze as NFOs. In fact, IPOs have existed much longer than NFOs. So, in the real sense, NFOs are cashing in on the sensation around IPOs. IPOs, undoubtedly, generate a lot of excitement in the market. It is not difficult to understand the reasons for the same.

Most of the time, people who make serious money in stock markets are the ones who invest for the long term—at least seven years, and usually, decades. Such long-term investments need a lot of patience and appreciation of delayed gratification. IPOs, on the other hand, provide instant gratification. Most people want to buy shares during the IPO to get in at a specific price band today and expect that the listing price, usually announced within 2-3 weeks, will be many times higher. This pull of instant gratification makes it exciting and highly risk-prone.

But are IPOs any different from NFOs? Well, just a shade, but not much. This actually turns out to be a big Foops moment for several investors who tend to go with the hype surrounding IPOs.

One of the differences between an IPO and an NFO is that the marketing, promotion and branding of IPOs can significantly influence the opening and subsequent short-term price of the share. And the reason is that, unlike mutual fund NAVs, share prices are influenced by the demand-supply relationship. Unlike mutual fund units, which are unlimited in number, shares are limited to a number defined at the time of the IPO.

To explore this further, let's look at the IPO details of Mazagon Dock Shipbuilders IPO, which was launched in 2020. Its total shares, which were up for grabs, are precisely defined.

Mazagon Dock Shipbuilders IPO

Open Date:	Sep 29 2020
Close Date:	Oct 01 2020
Total Shares:	3,05,99,017
Face Value:	₹10 Per Equity Share
Issue Type:	Book Building
Issue Size:	413-444 Cr.
Lot Size:	103 Shares
Issue Price:	₹ 135-145 Per Equity Share
Listing At:	NSE,BSE
Listing Date:	October 12 2020

With the total available shares capped at ₹3.05 crores, any demand over these numbers would lead to an 'oversubscription' of the IPO. Oversubscription creates curiosity and further demand, which leads to a vicious cycle. There have been cases where IPOs were oversubscribed by many hundred times.

For example, Happiest Minds Technologies, which came out with an initial public offering (IPO) in 2020-21, was a big success in the capital market, leading to oversubscription by 151 times. Such oversubscription means demand far exceeds the supply, and the supply is already capped. This demand-supply gap naturally results in shooting up its share price at the time of launch.

This euphoria, however, can both be a boon or a bane for an investor. When such big money can be made so quickly, there usually are legal and illegal players around. And the one that suffers the most in such cases is common retail investors like you and me.

IPOs definitely make more sense than NFOs. But many factors still make them an unworthy investment for retail investors like us.

1. Opaque Track Record

Unlike NFOs, the company which is coming up with an IPO does have a prior track record as a private company. And the track record could be in decades and even centuries. Flipkart, a retail giant in India, was established around 15 years ago and is still a private company when writing this book. Mother Dairy was founded in 1974 and is one of the top private limited companies in India. Parle, a brand recognised in every home, was established in 1929 and is still a private company. Founded in 1865, Cargill is a massive agricultural conglomerate and the largest private company by revenue in the United States.

So, is it safe enough to buy IPO shares of a company that has existed for centuries? No, there is an issue here. The issue is in the transparency as a private limited company. As the name suggests, the data of such companies, including the financial data, is privately held and therefore opaque. So, while they may be known brands that have existed for centuries, we have no clue what is happening behind the scenes. It is like a new movie with an excellent, top-of-the-line star cast, but just having such a star cast may not be sufficient evidence of a great movie.

So, with an opaque track record, we are taking a huge risk when we buy the company's shares. As the data has been held privately so far, there is hardly any way we can do value analysis to conclude whether the offered price band is worth the value or not. It's like getting into a lottery keeping our fingers crossed.

2. IPOs Are Expensive

Many investors assume that an IPO is an opportunity to get in at lower prices because this is the first time the company is going public. However, remember that the company is not starting up at the time of IPO. They have already existed and done serious business for many years. It is just that they are going public now.

By the time you buy a company's shares in its IPO, other parties have almost always invested earlier at lower prices—often much lower prices. Before you even knew about the company, there were probably three or four rounds of private investments, and the per-share cost of ownership usually goes up with each round.

In fact, one of the big reasons for a company to launch an IPO is to allow previous investors—founders, venture capital firms, large individual investors—to cash out at least a portion of their investment.

That is why most IPOs are, contrary to popular belief,

often expensively priced when compared to what their true value would be. They are not priced to offer you a piece of the business at low or reasonable prices but to find greater fools who can get in when the privileged few are getting out. If you are not aware of the greater fool theory[21], you must take the time to search about it on the internet.

Don't ever believe investment bankers when they say that IPOs are cheap and attractive. Their incentive lies in first fixing the IPO price (whatever the promoter wants) and then working backwards to justify the same.

3. Sales Pitch Is Too Noisy

This is how I would term the difference between an IPO and a share in the secondary market:

Shares are bought. IPOs are sold.

It's important to understand that the investment bankers and underwriters of IPOs are salesmen. The whole IPO process is intentionally hyped up to get as much attention as possible. Since IPOs only happen once for each company, they are often presented as a once-in-a-lifetime opportunity for the promoters and large shareholders to cash out.

Promoters and investment bankers thus weave noisy stories around this whole process. That is why you often hear terms like listing gains, bright future, long-term story that entice you to believe them as soon as you hear them.

Amid all this noise in the media and our close circle of investor friends, we forget to see beyond this sales pitch and scrutinise the IPO to see if it is truly so bright and beautiful.

We should not buy a stock just because it's being sold via an IPO. If at all we need to, we must check for the value of the investment by performing our independent value analysis.

Those who need help performing value analysis may refer to the book *The Autobiography of a Stock*.

Now, the biggest challenge with doing all this analysis in the case of an IPO is that all the historical records of the company so far were private. Therefore, we are not usually very sure of their authenticity. Herein lies the entire problem with IPOs. The risk is always higher.

Warren Buffett writes in his 1993 letter,

"An intelligent investor in common stocks will do better in the secondary market than he will do buying new issues… [IPO] market is ruled by controlling stockholders and corporations, who can usually select the timing of offerings or, if the market looks unfavourable, can avoid an offering altogether. Understandably, these sellers are not going to offer any bargains, either by way of public offering or in a negotiated transaction."

One of the most popular articles on moneycontrol.com clearly states the reason, and it is pretty simple.

"In the secondary market, prices are determined based on buying and selling that a particular counter is witnessing. However, since the price of a stock that is about to be listed only reflects the level at which investors would buy, such issues tend to become over-priced initially and which shows up in the long-term performance. In simple terms, the optimists set the price of an IPO."

4. Grey Markets are involved

Back in 1992-93, when I was doing my engineering at Aligarh Muslim University, we had to go and buy first-day-first-show movie tickets. The number of tickets was capped, and the demand was high, especially for the first-day movie tickets. And when money can be made quickly because of the massive demand-supply gap, the grey market takes birth. Some local agents, who were in cahoots with the cinema management, would buy tickets in bulk at the listed ticket price and then sell them at a premium.

We had two choices in this case. We could stand in the serpentine queue for the ticket, wait for our turn, and pray to God that some tickets are left for us by the time our turn comes. But since the agents already purchased tickets in bulk, the number of tickets left for public is far too less. We often ended up on the losing side of this unique battle. The other way was to forget the queue, contact the agent, pay some premium and easily get our ticket. I clearly remember a Salman Khan movie ticket that I purchased at a premium of ₹50 on a ticket price of ₹40. Paying ₹90 for a ₹40 ticket was big money in college times.

A very similar scenario arises with IPOs, where there is a significant demand-supply gap between the number of available shares and their self created and hyped up demand. As a result, the grey market shoots up.

This grey market in IPOs is driven by high-net-worth individuals (HNIs). They usually put in bids for large chunks of shares in IPOs, just like a local ticket agent buying movie tickets in bulk. This pushes up overall subscription levels for the issue and, in turn, lures investors to buy shares in the grey market at a premium.

The grey market premium for Computer Age Management Services's (CAMS) ₹2,242 crore initial public offer (IPO) was running at ₹500 a share. This meant that anyone who wished to buy the shares of this company during the IPO had two choices—he could apply legally and following the right process, or he could buy them at a premium of ₹500 per share from the grey market. However, the chances of his official application for shares would likely be turned down because most of the shares are gobbled up by HNIs.

So, if you have been awakened to the Foops moment that NFOs are useless, please also be aware that IPOs are also unworthy of any sane investment. This could be another Foops moment. It can have a massive impact on your future wealth, depending on how much you have already been into NFOs or IPOs which carry more risk than they are worthy of.

Foops # 8: Getting Swayed by the Hype of NFOs and IPOs

Awakening	Action
• Investing in any mutual fund at the time of NFO makes absolutely no sense. • Investing in stocks at the time of IPO is almost as meaningless. • IPOs are generally beneficial for insiders. • The risk that we take when we invest in IPOs or NFOs is just not worth it.	• Insulate yourself from the hype created by marketing teams of the fund house or investment bankers to buy NFOs or IPOs. • They are NOT cheap, as hyped. • Study the existing mutual funds, or analyse the existing stocks for a more rational investment. There is no shortcut to wealth.

BELIEVING THAT INVESTMENT IS A PREREQUISITE TO SAVE TAXES

UNTIL THE WRONG BELIEF LEAVES, WE WILL CONTINUE TO BE ROBBED.

– DADA BHAGWAN

Can a dish taste sweet without sugar? Can we build strong relationships with our family members without investing time with them? Can we win a lottery without investing in a ticket? Can a child top an exam without investing in hard work? And last but not least, can we save taxes without investing any money?

Well, the answer to all the questions, except for the last one, is a clear no.

When it comes to investing and personal finance, the math runs a little different.

Usually, we must invest our money to save taxes, be it in PPF, ELSS funds[12], EPF, VPF, tax-free bonds[5], health insurance, life insurance[30], charity, home loan, etc. Depending on the instrument and the amount invested, we are eligible to claim tax rebates.

But here is your next potential Foops moment.

We can actually save taxes without making even a single rupee of investment.

Don't believe me? Never mind, you will soon be awakened to this reality.

I have seen many people struggle to meet their investment target to save taxes every year. Usually, the insanity is at its peak during the last month of the financial year, typically in February-March every year. The chaos is so intense that people often buy useless insurance products and get locked in with a lifetime commitment just to save some taxes.

Worse are those investors who borrow money to invest haphazardly to achieve the same end. Unfortunately, there is no dearth of such investors who believe that the sole purpose of investment is to save your income tax or capital gains tax.

I have seen seekers who blindly invest in infrastructure bonds to save capital gains tax, ignoring the lock-in period, pathetic returns, and the worst—an analysis of whether they actually save or lose money by investing in infrastructure bonds. Yes, this is true. You may actually lose money while trying to save taxes. This is because the other option of paying capital gains taxes and then investing the balance in a slightly better option could eventually leave them far wealthier after five years—a clear case of the cost of lost opportunities.

But this analysis is for some other day. For now, I wish to elaborate on the Foops moment that we can save taxes without actually investing any money. This could very well be the Foops moment of a lifetime.

We will use a technique that I call 'investment churning' to save taxes without investing any money. But first, let us understand more about it.

What Is Churning?

Let's play a small game to try and understand what churning actually is.

Imagine a cylindrical pipe—open at both ends—which can hold up to five balls, one behind the other. From one open end of this pipe, you are allowed to push in only one ball in one year. If you do not put in a ball in any particular year, the rule says that you will be penalised for defaulting.

Being a disciplined person, you commit and start putting in one ball every year.

In year one, the pipe will have one ball. Then, the pipe will have two balls at the end of the second year, and so on, until you reach year five when the pipe fills up to its capacity of five balls.

Now, what do you do in year six? You can either skip putting in the ball and pay the penalty or do what I would call ball churning and avoid paying the penalty while effectively not putting in any ball and still following all the rules.

To avoid paying the penalty for not inserting a ball into the pipe, you push the sixth ball into the pipe from one end. What will happen? Since the pipe is open at both ends, the first ball that you inserted in year one will come out of the pipe from the other end. That ball is for you to keep.

So, in a nutshell, you added one ball to the pipe and got one ball back from the pipe. In effect, you did not add anything. However, you avoided the penalty because the penalty was for not adding the ball in a particular year; and you did add the ball, didn't you? This process is called ball churning or simply churning.

You can apply the same concept to your investments and churn your investments to save taxes while effectively not making any investment at all.

Let us delve deeper into it.

Investment Churning

How does the idea of investment churning sound to you? This means that you have a technique to churn some investments, that is, not invest anything but still gain from it. How does it feel? It is exciting indeed.

Let me show you how you can manage this—both with debt- and equity-based investments.

Investment Churning in Tax-Saving Debt Investments

Now, let us apply the concept of ball churning to our debt investments and tax savings.

Let us say we have a PPF Account. Consider this account similar to the pipe in the above example.

As per the current rules, we can invest at most ₹1.5 lakh per annum in our PPF account. Every time we invest ₹1.5 lakhs, we avoid getting penalised with income tax on the invested amount in that financial year and save taxes on this ₹1.5 lakhs.

So, in year one, we invest ₹1.5 lakhs and avoid taxes. Next year, we invest another ₹1.5 lakh, avoiding the tax penalty of year two. We keep investing ₹1.5 lakhs every year to avoid getting penalised with income tax.

Now, what happens after five years? After five years, we can start investment churning.

We can invest another ₹1.5 lakhs from one end. But now, we can also withdraw our earlier invested money in the PPF account. We may argue that it is disallowed to withdraw from the PPF Account for 15 years. Well, this statement is only partially true. We can start drawing partial amounts from the sixth year. So, even if we cannot withdraw and churn the full ₹1.5 lakhs, we can churn a significant amount at least.

So, in a nutshell, in year six, we would be theoretically investing nothing, or at least less than the mandated ₹1.5 lakhs. However, we would still take the full benefit in tax savings on the entire ₹1.5 lakhs you invested from one end.

We will not be penalised even though we did not invest a net amount of at least ₹1.5 lakhs. This is because we were able to churn the money. This, precisely, is investment churning. It can be a pretty effective technique if we are short of liquid cash for investments in a particular financial year.

PPF is not the only debt-based asset class that can make use of investment churning.

There are other debt-based tax saving options, too. For example, a five-year tax-saving FD. This tax-saving FD is a simple vehicle to invest money in and save taxes. In this, we make a fixed deposit for five years, and we save taxes on the entire invested amount (up to the max limits as per Section 80C, which is currently ₹1.5 lakhs). You keep investing every year for five years from one end, thus creating a full pipe of fixed deposits. Your first FD will mature in the sixth year, and you will get back your principal and interest. Just reinvest this amount to create a new FD in the sixth year, thus saving 100% taxes.

How much did you actually invest in the sixth year? Yes, this is the Foops moment that should inspire you to take action. You saved the entire tax amount by making absolutely nil investments.

Therefore, investment churning is a very effective strategy in debt-based tax saving instruments to save money without making net investments in proportion to the tax saved.

Investment Churning in Equity Investments

The above examples of investment churning in PPF or a tax-saving fixed deposit, which are debt-based investments, have only one major benefit. And the benefit is that we can take care of our liquidity crunch by churning money while still saving taxes.

The same technique can be applied to equity-based tax saving instruments as well.

For example, we can also apply investment churning to an ELSS-based (equity-linked saving scheme) mutual fund.

Any investment in ELSS mutual funds are applicable for tax savings as per Section 80C limits but the investments are locked in for three years.

So, if we have to save taxes every year via ELSS mutual funds, we have to keep investing a reasonable amount every year. But again, as in PPF and tax-saving FDs, we can save taxes by investing in ELSS funds, even without effectively investing anything after the lock-in period of three years. In the fourth year, we can withdraw our investments and reinvest the same amount immediately on withdrawal, thus saving all taxes without a single fresh investment.

On top of that, we do not need to bother about market conditions when churning since we are withdrawing and reinvesting under the same market conditions.

Therefore, investment churning is also market neutral.

As if this Foops moment was not enough, there is another distinct advantage of churning equity-based investments. (mutual fund or stock investments). Not only we can save taxes by churning our investment under Section 80C at the time of entry, but we can also save ourselves long-term capital gains tax (LTCG) at the time of exit if we are smart enough.

Let me elaborate on this with an example.

Let us say that we invest ₹1.5 lakhs in an ELSS fund every year, and we save taxes as per Section 80C. After the lock-in period of three years (that is, from the fourth year), we can start churning our investments and continue to save taxes without effectively investing new money in our ELSS funds.

Let's not stop here and go a step ahead.

All equity funds must pay a long-term capital gains tax (presently 10%) whenever they are realised.

If we start to churn money after the three-year lock-in of ELSS Funds, we also take advantage of the long-term capital gains tax waiver, up to ₹1 lakh per year. How? Let me explain.

Since we would be selling units after the third year as a part of the churning activity, we will incur long term capital gains (or losses, as the case may be). However, because of the churn, our mutual fund units are sold off, and the capital gains are realised. Therefore, the capital gains are actually never accumulated beyond a certain amount.

For most investors, the three-year accumulated gains may remain below ₹1 lakh per financial year if they regularly churn their investments. And that is how they can, even wholly, avoid paying any long-term capital gains tax.

Was that a good enough Foops moment for you?

Let me now share a combined example of how we can bring all of this together to work seamlessly.

A Combined Example

Consider a case where we invest ₹1.5 lakhs every year in an ELSS fund to save taxes and get good returns on our long-term investments.

The following table lists the annual investments made each year (₹1.5 lakhs every year) which allows for tax-saving on investments. The next column in the table mentions the cumulative balance of our assets at the start of the year. And the last column denotes the approximate value of our investment at the end of each year (assuming that we earn 10% returns every year on the cumulative balance at the start of the year).

Year	Annual Investment at Start of the Year	Cumulative Balance at Start of the Year	Cumulative Value at End of the Year (With 10% Returns)
Year 1	1,50,000	1,50,000	1,65,000
Year 2	1,50,000	3,15,000	3,46,500
Year 3	1,50,000	4,96,500	5,46,150
Year 4	0	5,46,150	6,00,765

Liquidate Year 1 units worth 1,50,000 (after the three-year lock in is over) and move the funds as an investment for Year 4

Figure 10

Now, at the end of Year 3 (beginning of Year 4), we have ₹5,46,150, our lock-in for the investments done in year one is over, and we can now take out what we invested at the beginning of year one.

If we are smart, we would churn our investments and take out, say, ₹1.5 lakhs from our ELSS fund and reinvest it at the start of year four. The impact of this investment churning would be as follows:

1. We have churned the investment, and without making any net investment in year four, we will save the full tax as per Section 80C.
2. Also, since our long-term capital gains would be only around ₹0.5 lakhs (@ 10% per annum for three years on ₹1.5 lakhs invested in Year 1), and this amount is much lower than the limit of ₹1 lakh per financial year, the entire capital gain would be tax free.

Thus, we saved taxes at the time of entry into the investment. And we also saved taxes when exiting the investment by saving on any LTCG taxes.

Investment churning is, therefore, a big Foops moment. In equity-based investments, our capital gains calculations may become a little complex. Still, it is worth the amount to be paid to your CA. Unfortunately, I have not seen many investors using this method for equity based investments. In debt-based investments, it is obviously simpler to use.

The best part of churning equity investments is that it is insulated from market volatility since we are exiting and entering the equity market at the same valuation.

When used smartly, it can help us save on income tax in times of liquidity crunch. Additionally, it helps us save LTCG tax by keeping our gains below the taxable cap every year.

Foops # 9: Believing That Investment Is a Prerequisite to Save Taxes	
Awakening	Action
• Investment churning allows you to re-invest the same money and still save full taxes. • This technique can be used both on debt- and equity-based investments. • It can help us save taxes under Section 80C as well as taxes on long-term capital gains (LTCG).	• Start churning your money lying in PPF, tax-saving FDs or ELSS funds to save taxes without investing and locking in any new money. • When churned annually, we can keep our capital gains below a threshold and save significant amount of long-term capital gains taxes.

FOOPS 10

OVERLOOKING THE VITAL ROLE OF EXPENSE MANAGEMENT

IT'S THROUGH OUR EXPENSES THAT WE BECOME RICHER OR POORER, REGARDLESS OF HOW MUCH MONEY WE MAKE.

– ROBERT KIYOSAKI

"A penny saved is a penny earned."

Do you agree with this statement? Maybe, you do. But I entirely disagree with this statement. It does not hold expense management in the esteem that it so truly deserves. Though conceptually, this statement is in the right direction, it undermines the importance of savings to a considerable extent.

While writing an article for a popular Mumbai-based magazine, *Complete Wellbeing*, I rephrased this statement to the following:

"A penny saved is five pennies earned."

Now, this is just not an emotional statement. This is a statement based on facts. It not only underlines the importance of savings but also puts it in the correct perspective. And the perspective is that this statement goes beyond the fact that you have to earn that much less if you save more. Actually, you have to earn far lesser.

And this statistic of five pennies is based on data from hundreds and thousands of freedom seekers I have worked with very closely via our ELITE program.

In the ELITE Program, we track every individual's income and expenses (therefore the savings) on a one-to-one basis. And this is what I realised.

On average, people save approximately 20% of their income.

So, if someone earns ₹50,000 a month, they are very likely to save ₹10,000. Of course, this is feasible only under the assumption that they are disciplined. Remember that this is average data. It may vary with each individual and depends strongly on one's family situation and the strength of one's dreams.

Now, let me check a bit of your mathematical competency.

If an individual typically saves 20% of the income, how much more would they need to earn to save an extra ₹1?

Go for it.

C'mon. Take your time. You can do it. Personal finance is all about fundamental mathematics—nothing more, nothing less.

I am sure many of you would have been able to solve this riddle. For those who are tight on mathematics, just like I once used to be, I will show you a simple way to do this calculation.

The easiest way to solve all percentage-related questions is to take an example with ₹100 as the base. So, if ₹100 was the person's income, he was saving 20%, that is, ₹20. Now, if his savings are increased by ₹1, the total savings will become ₹21.

This ₹21 savings would have been possible only if the person was earning ₹105 (20% of ₹105 is ₹21). So, in effect, a ₹1 impact on savings can be achieved by earning an additional ₹5 (₹105 instead of ₹ 100).

Therefore, I can comfortably conclude that if the person saves an extra ₹1 from his income, then this is equivalent to earning an additional ₹5.

Therefore, my statement, "*A penny saved is five pennies earned.*"

Give this some time to sink in. It is simple mathematics. It always existed around us. There is nothing new in this. But the concept must sink in because it can alter how we look at earning money and spending it once it is earned. The whole equation changes. Our focus will shift from earning more to spending wisely. A bigger lever is available in spending wisely than in earning more.

This could potentially be the *Foops moment* that could trigger a new era in your personal finance.

Now, you might just start to appreciate how your parents or grandparents never had a financial crisis in their life, despite their limited income. They were usually tight on their budget because of low incomes, but the families rarely descended into financial crisis. The key always was very optimally managed expenses. We see more income today, but at the same time, we see more financially ruined families. Need I say more?

I know you might argue that while expense management is good, it deteriorates the quality of our life. That is another myth that must be shattered. In fact, it is the other way around. Prepare to absorb this Foops moment as I guide you further.

I will share five other reasons to conclusively prove that managing expenses is a far more vital skill to lead a quality life than earning higher income.

Reason #1: Expenses Are the Only Thing in Our Control

Building wealth has little to do with our income or investment returns but a lot to do with our savings rate. I say this because we see a lot of uncertainty and risk in the first two levers.

Whether we can sustain a high income in today's times of gig economy or not and how long can we sustain that income and job profile without reskilling ourselves are questions without a straight answer.

Investments are a great tool to build massive wealth, but for how long can we be assured of top-quality returns? Are the factors that govern our return on investments in our control? Forget great returns. We have seen enough examples just in the last couple of years where our invested amounts are themselves at risk—be it bank failures, fund house bankruptcy, Covid-19-influenced economy crash or anything else which we may not understand and appreciate today.

So, incomes and returns are not really in our control. Controlling how much we spend and, therefore, how much we save is the only factor that we control to a large extent.

We can build wealth without a high income, but we can never build wealth without a high savings rate. Someone earning ₹1 lakh and saving ₹10,000 is definitely worse off in wealth creation than someone earning ₹50,000 and saving ₹20,000. It all boils down to self-control, discipline, and commitment—arguably the toughest part of personal finance.

Reason #2: More Satisfaction, Less Pressure

The impact of expense control on our life does not reduce the quality of our lives. In fact, it does just the reverse.

We tend to focus on increasing our income for most of our lives—be it with our jobs or business ventures. We give our best to get the next promotion, the next salary raises, the next cool business idea, the next client.

This is all driven by an erroneous belief that increasing income leads to a luxurious and well-lived life. This may sound theoretically correct since increased income can potentially lead to more liquid money and more ways to live a luxurious life.

But nothing is practically farther from reality.

The fact is that with increased income comes the pressure to sustain and justify the higher income. And this pressure is immense. If we fail to sustain the high income for any reason, it needs tremendous mental strength and acceptance to reduce our expenses in the same proportion. Unfortunately, in most cases, people are unable to tone down their expenses if and when income declines. And the result is negative savings—ultimately eating into your earlier savings and then your quality of life.

As Ken Honda says in his bestselling book *Happy Money*,

"Typically, when more money is coming in, then going out, we feel very good about life. This is absolutely the time in life when we should be enjoying life. All the hard work and perseverance of the past is flowing back to us as a reward. Some people start to feel that this will go on forever, and raise their standard of living—and then, they struggle to survive."

But the point is not only about sustaining such high income. Even if we can sustain the income, the pressure to do so takes away crucial time from our lives—the time we need to build strong relationships within our family and friends, chase our true passions and do something to elevate the world around us. Time, incidentally, happens to be our biggest asset; it is limited and running out every moment. And we keep losing time as our income increases, adding more stress to our lives, thus deteriorating the quality of our lives further.

If we now understand that controlling expenses can have five times more impact on our wealth than increasing income, you would adopt saner ways to save more. Not only savings has five times the impact, but it also does not put you under the kind of pressure that increased income would. In fact, it actually gives you a very satisfying feeling since this could be one of the rare things in your life which you have control over.

Reason #3: Income Is Transient, Expenses Are Permanent

If you were given a choice to choose one relationship you would want to nurture—your school friend or your sibling, which one would you choose? In most cases, it would be the latter. Why?

One of the strongest arguments is that family relationships (brothers, sisters, parents, children, etc.) will last much longer—probably until the end of our lives. And since family relationships will last longer, it is our family that will come to your rescue in times of real need. Of course, there have been exceptions where friends have served stronger than families. But in general, we tend to focus on those relationships that are likely to last longer so we can help each other in times of need.

Now, let us compare income and expenses as far as their longevity is concerned.

How long do we think our income is going to last?

If it is a job, then probably until the age of 58 or 60. If it is a business venture, then probably until the age of 70 or 75 at the most. Whether it is 60 or 75, we are assuming that everything else in life goes perfectly as per the plan. There have been enough cases where incomes have been lost much earlier.

What about expenses? How long do we think our expenses would last?

How long do we need groceries or medicines? How long are we going to pay for our utility bills? The answer is actually a no-brainer. Expenses will last until the last day of our life, the dying moments as well. Even after our death, our family will have to spend money on our last rites.

Income is, therefore, transient in nature. By income, I, of course, mean active income[1]. While income is transient, expenses are perpetual. And if expenses are going to be with us forever, where should we focus our energy? We need to build a stronger relationship with which one? What needs better management?

This question needs no special skill to answer. If you focus on managing expenses more, that skill will help you until the last day of your life.

Reason #4: Expense Management Skills Are Easier to Pass On to the Next Generation

Unlike the skills we possess for generating income, the most valuable aspect of expense management is that our family automatically gets involved in it.

They may initially feel constrained with what we are trying to do but would appreciate its value sooner rather than later. Also, it will help us build solid relationships with our family members, especially our children.

We can also easily pass on these habits to the next generation. They can learn how to control expenses just by looking at our style of managing them.

On the other hand, on the income side, the next generation may not have much to learn from us since it is quite likely that they would forge their own career paths and ways to earn income. Their passion, interest areas, industry needs are most likely going to be completely different from ours. Just look at the income-earning skills of your parents and try to visualise how different your own income-earning skills are. There is almost no commonality. But you cannot say the same about expense-management skills. I am sure there are skills that you inherited from your parents on the expense management side, and you exhibit the same even today.

Usually, on the expense management side, it has been, and will likely be, almost all the same skills from one generation to the next.

Reason #5: Expense Management and Inflation Make a Good Team

Another important aspect in personal finance that we must never forget is *inflation*. Now, income and expenses are opposing forces when it comes to working with inflation.

We would always want inflation to be our friend rather than our enemy. However, inflation becomes our enemy when we focus on increasing our income. Foops moment already? Let me explain, with a simple example, how increased income makes inflation our enemy.

Let us assume that after all the hard work, stressed days and time away from our families, our job or business venture awards us with an increased income of 10%. Well, this is good, but only until we account for the running inflation. If our running family inflation[18] is 6%, then we are effectively dealing with a 4% increase (10% – 6%) in income. You see how inflation works against increased income. It brought down the 10% increase to a mere 4%.

Well, we may feel that even a 4% net increase is not bad. But do not forget the price we had to pay for this increase—our relationships, health and lost opportunities to chase our passion.

On the other side, expense reduction works as a team with inflation, rather than against it. This means that if we focus on managing our expenses, inflation comes to our rescue.

Let me explain to you how that works. Let us say that instead of focusing too much on our income, we worked smart and started to look at areas within our house where we can reduce our expenses without compromising on the quality of our lives. One of the key areas I have observed is the wastage of raw and cooked vegetables.

There were times in our house when we used to throw away stale vegetables—both cooked and raw. But then, goal-setting can help us do wonderful things. Slowly, we turned smarter and more conscious about the quantity of vegetables we order and put on our plates. After some initial teething issues, we managed to reduce grocery wastage in our house by around 2 kg in a month. Let us say that these 2 kg vegetables cost us ₹100 per month. So, in effect, we managed to reduce our expenses by ₹100 this month, or ₹1,200 per year.

Now, we have got ourselves in the habit of avoiding wastage. The same 2 kg vegetables would not cost ₹100 next year. It would cost ₹106 instead, courtesy of the same 6% inflation. So, next year, I would be saving ₹106 every month rather than ₹100. Just extrapolating these savings, it becomes ₹112 per month a year later, ₹321 after 20 years and ₹1028 after 40 years.

Did you observe that inflation has now become our friend? With the same habit, we are saving more every month.

Isn't this exciting?

We have to decide whether we want inflation to work with us as a team or against us.

Expense management is so underrated that I never shy away from sharing multiple examples. Let me share one more.

Sandhya Sharma from Pune is a very committed freedom seeker. She is disciplined in her daily tracking and quite passionate about achieving financial freedom at the earliest. She earns well and spends well. She had joined the ELITE program two years ago. Since then, we have been tracking her financial freedom goal together with utmost sincerity. Her investing strategy calls for a slightly constrained exposure to equity, and accordingly, all her investments have been structured. She loves tracking as she approaches her goal of being financially free seven years from today.

All is going well for her except for one thing. She wants to get financially free in three to four years, rather than waiting for seven years. She is ready to take more risks with her investments. But as her mentor, I keep pushing her back. Her risk tolerance levels are low, which means that while she is excited to take risks, it is likely that she might display irrational behavior once the risk materialises. She also needs liquidity because of the upcoming education expenses for her children over the next two years.

In one of our regular interlocks, she was persistent about getting financially free faster. She kept nudging me on what best can be done to achieve the goal quickly. She was pushing me to allow her to take more risks. But I stayed adamant.

It is very clear to all subscribers in the program that they have the liberty to make their own decisions. I act as their mentor to help them sail through as quickly as reasonably feasible. I do not control their investments. But I definitely recommend the path which is right for them, based on my experience and understanding. So, Sandhya had all the right to go and take risks, but she was looking for my nod, which never came.

Patience and acceptance of *delayed gratification* are the biggest virtues for an investor.

When she persisted, I had to tell her that there is one way we can try getting it done: by making some sacrifices in her life and reducing her expenses by 5%.

"And then what?" she asked.

"That's it," I remarked.

Obviously, she wasn't convinced that simply reducing expenses by a seemingly insignificant amount of 5% and doing nothing else to our investments will even impact her financial freedom year. At the end of the day, as we understood in one of our earlier Foops moments, compounding's power is and will always be underappreciated. She was not accounting for the power of inflation adjustment of this 5% extra savings over the next 55 years of her life. So, I had to put the numbers in front of her.

"What's 5% of your expenses today, Sandhya?"

"Hmm... approximately ₹2,000. But I do not think that ₹2,000 every month can help me be financially free in lesser time."

"Let's forget about what we think. Let's calculate. You have approximately 50 years more to live your life. So, ₹2,000 expense reduction per month today will be about ₹59,000 per month expense reduction in your 50th year, assuming an average inflation rate of 7% every year."

"Oh wow, ₹59,000 per month is cool. I never thought about it that way. But still, I am not sure that how ₹59,000 per month will help me when I need about ₹4 crores to become financially free."

"I knew you would ask this. So, here is how. If you sum up the amount you saved from today until the next 50 years, it will come to about ₹1.04 crores."

"₹1.04 crores? Are you sure?"

I can only smile when someone asks me if I am sure about these calculations. Our brains are not designed to understand and appreciate compounding. The moment she heard ₹1.04 crores, she forgot about her risk-taking investments. She went back to the expense analytics charts available on our website. She looked at specific expense heads where she spent more year on year and targeted them for more control. Not only was she able to pull her freedom year closer by two years, the important thing is that she had to take no extra risk. She could improve the quality of her life by just leading a more disciplined life and managing her expenses well.

Who Will Save More?

A person with great humility is more likely to save more than a person with a bigger ego. There is an ongoing race out there—among your neighbours, on social media, at your workplace—to outdo each other regarding the quality of life that is up for display. Only those who decide to quit this race tend to save more. They do not bother about what others think. They bother about how good they feel when wealth can give them the choices in life.

Saving is enhanced by spending less. We spend less if we desire less, and we desire less only when we do not care a damn about what our neighbour, co-worker or social media friends think about us.

By the way, lesser desire also leads to happiness—which is a wonderful byproduct of saving more.

Some Expense Management Ideas to Get You Moving

Now that you have understood the importance of managing expenses, it is my obligation to get you moving. So, get set as we explore some of the most practical techniques to manage expenses shared by our ELITE program freedom seekers from across the world.

1. **Zero-Day Counting Technique**
   This technique involves counting the number of days in a month when you do zero expenses. Each such day is called a *zero-day*. In this technique, we are expected to keep track of our daily expenses and if in a day there is no expense, then tag that day as a zero-day. Count the number of zero days in a month. If it's more than five, we must make sure that we reward ourselves.

2. **Spend Cash Technique**

   This technique involves doing your regular monthly expenses in cash mode as far as possible. Though cards and other digital ways are being promoted for multiple valid reasons, cash spending helps control expenses. There is an emotional connection when our brain sees cash moving out of our wallets, through our hands and on to someone else. We feel that we just gave away what we earned with our hard work. Our brain starts to tune itself to limit this outflow, resulting in lower expenses over time.

3. **Monthly Budgeting Technique**

   This technique involves giving yourself a budget every month. However old-fashioned it may sound, monthly budgeting helps control unwanted expenses. First, give yourself a budget and then stick to it. This technique aligns well with a time-tested wealth management principle that says, "Pay yourself first."

4. **Daily Tracking Technique**

   This technique involves tracking your expenses every single day. Just before you go to bed, log your expenses for that day. It does not take more than two to three minutes a day but can have a massive impact on controlling your expenses. This technique aligns well with a time-tested management principle that says, "Whatever gets measured, improves."

5. **Delaying Technique**

   This technique involves delaying your expense by a day or more. If it is not a mandatory expense for this month, we ought to ask ourselves if we genuinely need to make the expense. If we are not 100% sure, then delay the expense by a day or even more. This technique aligns well with a time-tested management principle that says, "Luxury is a tide of mind."

6. **Family WhatsApp Group Technique**
   This technique involves creating a WhatsApp group with all your family members, specifically for expense jotting. Whenever any family member spends money, they are supposed to jot it down in this group. This way, you do not miss recollecting where the money was spent and how much. Also, looking at all the expenses creates a subconscious wall to limit the amount of expenses.

Foops # 10: Overlooking the Vital Role of Expense Management

Awakening	Action
• Expense management has a more far-reaching impact than income creation as far as wealth accumulation is concerned. • Tighter control on expenses eventually leads to a much better quality of life.	• Start tracking your expenses. • Track them every day, involve your family and have a budget. • Repeat such habits, every day, month on month, and see the magic unfold over time.

ASSUMING THAT 'FAMILY INFLATION' IS THE SAME AS 'INFLATION'

INFLATION TAKES FROM THE IGNORANT AND GIVES TO THE WELL INFORMED.

– VENITA VANCASPEL

Despite all the talk and noise around inflation, I have observed, and it is apparent, that most investors fail to understand the impact of inflation in their planning. Consequently, and not surprisingly, their freedom journeys fizzle out. Worse and riskier still is that many journeys end up with an insufficient corpus, courtesy inflation.

Therefore, if you are serious about building massive wealth and pursuing financial freedom, you must not only understand inflation (which most claim they understand—just like compounding), but you must also calculate and find out two specific types of inflation: *family inflation* and *lifestyle inflation*[28].

You may not hear a lot about these two types of inflation, and the reason is straightforward. Just like in compounding, our constrained brain fails to comprehend its magical powers; we fail to understand the severity with which inflation can degenerate our corpus. Owing to this lack of seriousness towards inflation, we hardly bother about digging deeper and trying to understand family inflation and lifestyle inflation.

But let us start with inflation. And do not make the mistake of skipping the following section, even if you have the feeling that you know all of it. Because that is precisely where the challenge lies.

Our Foops moments are usually hidden in the subjects we think we know.

What is Inflation?

Investopedia technically defines inflation as "The rise in the general level of prices where a unit of currency effectively buys less than it did in prior periods."

In a slightly lighter vein, Sam Ewing defines the inflation monster as follows: "Inflation is when you pay fifteen dollars for the ten-dollar haircut you used to get for five dollars when you had hair."

The Inflation Formula

The inflation formula is simple.

If something was being sold at ₹100 per unit last year and is being sold at ₹108 per unit this year, then inflation is simply calculated as the difference (₹8) divided by the original selling price (₹100). This comes out to be 8%. There is no rocket science in this formula, and there is no robotics involved in implementing this formula to calculate our future wealth needs.

The Challenge with Inflation

If inflation is all so simple to calculate and implement, then what is so challenging about inflation is the concept on which it is based. It is based on something that we have already read about in this book: compounding.

Just as we understood that a human mind cannot fully comprehend compounding and the massive impact it can have in building our wealth, it is almost impossible for a human mind to grasp the destructive impact of inflation on our wealth. However hard we may try, it is tough, really tough.

I usually refer to the relationship between inflation and compounding with this quote:

"Inflation is a destructive reciprocal of compounding."

While compounding plays a mostly positive role in elevating a seeker's life, inflation is just the reciprocal of compounding. Again, considered too simple and therefore too easy to be taken seriously, it has the potential to devastate the financial life of the impacted seeker without the seeker even being aware of it.

And it is not difficult to explain the impact with an example.

Let us assume that you buy 1 kg of mangoes at ₹100 per kg today.

Case 1: 5% Inflation

With 5% inflation, you will have to shell out ₹105 for the same mangoes after a year. After two years, you will be paying ₹110.25 per kg for them.

Can you guess how much you would be paying after 40 years?

Whenever I ask this question in front of an audience in seminars or presentations, the general answers I get are around the figures of ₹250 per kg, and extreme responses are around ₹500 per kg.

But the actual answer is around ₹700 per kg.

Well, mangoes at ₹700 per kg are a little tough to imagine, but the guesses, in general, were not too far off from the correct answer. And that is where the problem actually begins. Since the audience is not too far off, they usually start believing that they have now grasped the idea of inflation to a considerable extent. And this attitude can virtually kill you. Let us see how.

Case 2: 10% Inflation

Now, let us assume that the inflation was 10% instead of 5%

With 10% inflation, after a year, you pay ₹110, and after two years, you pay ₹121 per kg for the same mangoes.

Can you guess how much you would pay after 40 years?

Whenever I asked this in front of an audience in seminars, the extreme answers were ₹1,000 per kg and average answers were around ₹800 per kg—which is not surprising. The human mind is trying to double the previous answers as the rate of inflation has doubled.

But the actual answer is that it will cost you around ₹4,500 per kg for the same set of mangoes. Yes, it's nowhere even close to ₹1,000. It is off by as much as 350%. Something went missing this time. Yes, you would be spending close to ₹5,000 to buy a single kilogram of mangoes in just four decades.

Is This a Serious Miss?

No, this is not a serious miss. This is actually a life-threatening miss. And trust me, I am not exaggerating here.

Let's say someone misses their financial planning by 350% (with an extreme answer of ₹1,000 instead of the actual ₹4,500) or by 550% (with an average answer of ₹700 instead of the actual ₹4,500). Then, you know that post-financial freedom or retirement, their life is nothing but financial chaos.

Someone targeting ₹3 crores at retirement might realise in the sunset years of their life that they actually needed around ₹12 crores. Massive chaos, isn't it?

The person would actually need three to five times the corpus they actually accumulated or retired with. Imagine corpus deficit of three to five times—and this miss was not because inflation was not factored in the plan. Inflation was factored in, but the destructive impact of inflation was not understood.

Worse still is realising this massive gap when inflation starts to play out in the later years of life. In most cases, that is the stage of life when there is no way you can compensate for this loss by earning some extra money.

And such financial chaos, at that age, can surely be life-threatening.

What Is the Irony?

The irony is that not many of us are ready to sit down, focus and appreciate these nuances of wealth management.

People usually want to talk about big new ideas, innovative investment options, smart entry and exit points in the market, etc. Many freedom seekers ask me about the future of India's economy, how serious the current financial crisis is and when it is going to recover.

Well, I try not to comment on such issues for various reasons. First, there already are too many financial advisers giving *gyan* on these topics. Moreover, our economy is too complex and globally integrated to be so predictable in the short run. Also, the economic volatility is actually of no concern to a long-term investor—except that it is an assurance for great returns if we sustain our investing strategy.

But the most important reason I try to avoid answering such questions is that there are far more fundamental matters that need to be understood, realised, experienced and appreciated—like inflation or compounding—before we predict other things like the Indian economy's future.

The rudimentary target for any investment should be to compound at a rate more than the inflation rate. Remember that if your corpus is not growing (compounding) faster than inflation, you are actually losing money every year—and much before you realise it, you will run short of funds.

One of the most fundamental solutions that may be cropping up in your mind is that if you can somehow take 10% as your inflation value and calculate the corpus requirement for financial freedom, you should be covered. Well, the answer is a big NO.

I say this because even if we take a buffer in our inflation numbers, the problem is that we have never ever tried calculating—forget tracking—family inflation and lifestyle inflation.

This Foops moment will focus primarily on the importance and calculation of family inflation. Lifestyle inflation is another hidden demon, which deserves a separate discussion.

Before we calculate these relatively lesser-known inflation terms, we ought to understand how inflation figures are arrived at.

We might think we already know how to calculate the inflation in mango prices if we see the product's price for the last year and this year. Yes, we can do that for sure. But the challenge lies in including these inflation figures into our financial freedom plan. The inflation for each fruit might be different. The inflation for each vegetable might be different. Inflation of every single expense head will be different across different years. And knowing that we are dealing with something as serious as inflation, we cannot get complacent at all.

Well, such tracking is indeed a herculean task and therefore, we try and strike a balance. So, on the practical side, we track our expenses at the level of expense heads (such as grocery) and then use the government-published figures for that expense head to dovetail its inflation into our plan.

Things will become clearer as we get deeper into this unavoidable monster called inflation. Let us first see how the government measures inflation for various expense heads.

Measuring Inflation

Every country has their own way of calculating inflation numbers, and so does India.

There is not one but multiple types of inflation values that are calculated and tracked as *inflation indexes*. An index figure reflects the change in a set of associated variables over a period and in a particular direction.

India's most commonly used inflation indices are the consumer price index (CPI) and the wholesale price index (WPI).

Some countries, including the US, use another fairly popular index called producer price index (PPI).

WPI

The WPI (wholesale price index) is a popular measure of inflation, which measures and tracks the changes in the price of goods in the stages at the wholesale level (just above the retail level). While WPI items vary from one country to another, they mostly include items at the producer or wholesale level. For example, it includes cotton prices for raw cotton, cotton yarn, cotton grey goods and cotton clothing.

CPI

The CPI (consumer price index) is a measure that examines the weighted average of prices of a basket of goods and services which are of primary consumer needs. They include transportation, food and medical care.

CPI is calculated by taking price changes for each item in the predetermined basket of goods and averaging them based on their relative weight in the whole basket. The prices in consideration are the retail prices of each item, as available for purchase by the individual citizens. Changes in the CPI are used to assess price changes associated with the cost of living, making it one of the most frequently used statistics for identifying periods of inflation or deflation. CPI is what matters the most to us.

WPI vs. CPI

WPI measures only the cost of products and does not include the cost of services. Since WPI accounts for changes in the general price level of goods at the wholesale level, it fails to communicate the actual burden borne by the end consumer. So, as individual retail consumers, we are much more concerned with CPI and its impact on our financial planning.

Overall Inflation

Once we know the correct figures for the CPI index (published by the government at regular intervals), calculating the overall inflation rate is as simple as using the following formula:

$$\text{Inflation rate} = \frac{\text{CPI (this year)} - \text{CPI (last year)}}{\text{CPI (last year)}} \times 100$$

The CPI Index Heads in India

The CPI Index is measured and published across various heads. Some of the common ones are listed below.

- Milk and milk products
- Oils and fats
- Fruits and vegetables
- Pulses

- Clothing and footwear
- Transport
- Recreation
- Education
- Personal care

Two sub-categories of the CPI index in India are CPI-R (CPI rural) and CPI-U (CPI urban). Depending on where you live, you might have to refer to the specific sub-category to calculate the correct inflation in your area.

Every country publishes their inflation figures in a structure that is more or less similar. It is quite interesting to look at the Indian government-published excel files on inflation of various categories. As of writing this book, the government published CPI index figures were available at https://data.gov.in/catalog/all-india-consumer-price-index-ruralurban

Global inflation rates are also published by World Bank. To view the World Bank-published Inflation figures for India and every other country in the world, you may refer to this link: https://data.worldbank.org/indicator/FP.CPI.TOTL.ZG. This gives you a holistic view of the world economy as well.

To keep things simple, I would take an example of how the running inflation is calculated for a particular head for a specific year. Once you download and open the Indian government-published CPI index file as per the link mentioned above, it is very simple to understand and calculate the running inflation using the formula that we discussed earlier.

Here is one example for you.

If you download the CPI inflation index figures published by the government of India and look at the 2018-19 data, you would realise that:

CPI (Urban) in January 2018 for milk and products was 139.6.

CPI (Urban) in January 2019 for milk and products was 141.7.

Once you have this basic data, the calculation of inflation is as simple as this:

Inflation percentage = (141.7-139.6) / 141.1 x 100

This comes to 1.48%

Thus, the milk and dairy products went through inflation of 1.48% in 2018-19. You see, it is not at all tough to calculate. We all can do this simple calculation. But did this 1.48% figure ring any alarm bells in your mind? Did it catch your attention? Was it way off your expectations?

When I first looked at this figure, I thought that there was some mistake in my calculations. How could dairy inflation be as low as 1.48% when the country's inflation, as we hear it, is in the range of 7-8%? But then, I did not find any mistake in my calculations.

Confusion and surprises often lead to innovative thinking.

I started to ponder whether the inflation for family A is the same as that for family B if both the families had strikingly different consumption levels of dairy products? If some heads have such low inflation, won't some other heads have very high inflation, resulting in an average of 7%? What if a family has a significant monthly expense of one head which has double-digit inflation? Can such a family still use the generally published inflation figures of the country to calculate their corpus need for financial freedom?

All this inner turmoil ultimately led me to the power of what I call family inflation.

Family Inflation

Let us explore this concept with an example.

Ratnakar's is a beautiful, lovely family. Both Ratnakar and Sumedha come into our review calls together and are passionately building up their wealth with the intent to set themselves financially free in the long run. They have a daughter, Anaha, who is currently in playschool.

They are on this journey towards financial freedom. When we were planning for their financial freedom, the first hunch is always to go ahead and take the generally published inflation figure of 5-6% in India. But then, our process mandates us to calculate the family inflation. This is so important because we all understand the consequences of misjudging inflation.

To calculate family inflation, it is vital to understand the head-wise expenses for the family. Below is the approximate distribution of their average monthly expenses:

Expense Head	% Spend
Grocery Items	25%
Utility Bills	10%
Children Education	10%
Eating Out, Entertainment, etc.	13%
Travel	23%
Car, Fuel, Maintenance, etc.	15%
Misc.	4%
Total	100%

Figure 11

To arrive at the kind of average monthly data as listed in the table above, we need a certain level of disciplined tracking for at least

12 months. Unfortunately, not many are able to do that. People are usually too busy creating wealth. They hardly have time or energy left over for a task as seemingly trivial as managing their wealth or enabling their accumulated wealth to generate more wealth. Of course, they miss out on the power of small things.

Anyways, Ratnakar's family was not like anyone else's. They were quite disciplined and could seamlessly adopt the habit of tracking their cash flow. In the ELITE program, we tend to focus on habit creation around regular income and expense tracking, regular assets and liability[27] tracking, performance tracking, etc. It often tends to bore some of the freedom seekers. But if boredom is the price to pay for financial freedom, so be it.

Coming back to our calculations.

To calculate the true family inflation for Ratnakar's, we went ahead and downloaded the latest government-published CPI data. On downloading the data and opening the Excel file, we added three filters in the below sequence to make the data more informative for us and our calculations:

Filter 1: We filtered out the data to show the records for only the urban sector.

Filter 2: We filtered the year to show the data for only the last two years, 2019 and 2020. We have a choice here. We wanted to look at the inflation since last year. But if someone is keen on looking at average inflation over the last many years, one can filter and choose the years accordingly.

Filter 3: We filtered the most recent month for which the data was available—June.

After applying the above three filters, that is, sector, year and month, we now had only two records being displayed in the excel file—June 2019 and June 2020.

Below are some of the key observations from the filtered data.

Grocery Items

There was no separate head for grocery in the downloaded file displaying the CPI figures for each of these heads for both the filtered months: June 2019 and June 2020. However, there were individual heads for grocery items like cereals, eggs, meat, milk, fruits, vegetables, pulses, sugar, spices, etc. Since Ratnakar's family were non-vegetarians, we decided to include eggs and meat in our calculations.

So, we took an average of the available CPI data for both months for all the heads mentioned above. The result was this:

June 2019: Grocery (all heads included): Average CPI: 142.85

June 2020: Grocery (all heads included): Average CPI: 155.83

With this data and usage of the inflation calculation formula above, we arrived at the grocery inflation for the last year as:

Inflation Percentage = (155.83 – 142.85) / 142.85 × 100

This came to 9.08%

So, here is the first jolt. The real inflation on groceries is 9.08% for this family, not 5-6% that we are used to taking as a quick fix. If you still wish to know the impact of this 3-4% variance in inflation, you should read this chapter from the beginning.

Along the same lines, we calculated the inflation based on the available CPI data for all the remaining heads for Ratnakar's family, and this is what we arrived at:

Expense Head	% Monthly Spend	CPI Inflation (2019-20)
Grocery Items	25%	9.08%
Utility Bills	10%	5.06%
Children Education	10%	2.42%
Eating Out, Entertainment, etc.	13%	6.48%
Travel	23%	8.12%
Car, Fuel, Maintenance, etc.	15%	13.83%
Misc.	4%	6.28%
Total	100%	

Figure 12

Having arrived at the head-wise CPI inflation figures, calculating the family inflation was not that difficult.

We first need to calculate the weighted inflation for each head by multiplying the percentage of monthly spend [A] by CPI inflation for the respective head [B].

For example, the weighted inflation for grocery items would be the percentage of monthly spend on grocery items (25%, which defines the weight of grocery items in the monthly expenses) multiplied by the CPI inflation for grocery items, that is, 9.08%. The result is 2.27%, as listed in the weighted inflation column in Figure 13.

After repeating the process for each row, we sum up the weighted inflation in column [C]. The result is the family inflation percentage. This figure comes out to 8.05% for Ratnakar's family, as shown in Figure 13.

So, instead of taking 6% as the inflation figure for Ratnakar's family, we had to take 8% and include that in our financial calculations. Such family inflation calculations not only tell us the real inflation that a family is facing but also teach us many more subtle things.

Expense Head	% Monthly Spend [A]	CPI Inflation (2019-20) [B]	Weighted Inflation [C] = [A] x [B]
Grocery Items	25%	9.08%	2.27%
Utility Bills	10%	5.06%	0.51%
Children Education	10%	2.42%	0.24%
Eating Out, Entertainment, etc.	13%	6.48%	0.84%
Travel	23%	8.12%	1.87%
Car, Fuel, Maintenance, etc.	15%	13.83%	2.07%
Misc.	4%	6.28%	0.25%
Total	100%		8.05%

Figure 13

Takeaways from Family Inflation Calculations

1. Every family is different. Every family's distribution of expenses varies across different expense heads. So, family inflation is bound to be different for each family.
2. Even if the total expenses for two families are exactly the same, just the distribution of expense heads can lead to significant variations in inflation that each family must cater to in their financial planning.
3. Distribution of expenses for a family will change over time. For example, as the children grow up, the expenses on children's education will grow, and probably that on travel will reduce. Thus, family inflation will never remain the same and should be recalibrated at least every two to three years.
4. If a family goes ahead with the general inflation figures without calculating the actual family inflation, the results can be catastrophic. This is one of the biggest reasons why financial plans fall apart. As we can see in the case of Ratnakar's family, a 2% difference in inflation ultimately resulted in a corpus need that was significantly more.

Build Your Own Inflation Repository

The family inflation calculations above are based on the published CPI figures for urban India.

While this is an excellent starting point to counter inflation, can inflation vary significantly across two different urban cities, say Mumbai and Kolkata? The answer is a resounding yes. What do we do then? The government does not publish any city-wise CPI inflation data.

Even within the same city, inflation can vary for two families with different shopping styles. For example, one family orders their groceries online while the other gets them from a supermarket or other vegetable vendors. The answer is again a very resounding affirmative. If that is the case, how does the above calculation work?

The fact is that it is very difficult to predict the family inflation for our family with pinpoint accuracy even with the published data and all the calculations. So there is only one way out, and that is to build our own family data on expenses.

Once we start tracking our family's head-wise expenses, then within a few years, we will have a big enough data repository to measure the actual inflation for our family over the last few years. This kind of inflation data will be the most accurate data possible. And if we are still undermining the importance of this accuracy, we may continue to do so at our own peril.

We have created the Cash Flow Analytics tool on our website (http://www.manoj-arora.com) for this exact reason. We use this analytics tool to measure the family inflation with a family's actual data and see which specific heads are undergoing more inflation than the others. This gives a lever to the family to have tighter control on specific heads and control the overall family inflation.

Such measures help us rein in the inflation monster, and therefore, the corpus need for our future is significantly lower. We just learnt in the previous Foops moment (#10) that anyone who has mastered restraint over their expenses has always led a more meaningful and financially savvy life.

If you were never awakened to the disastrous impact and the financial misery that an under-judged inflation figure can cause, then let this be your Foops moment. Take charge. Take action. Right now!

Foops # 11: Assuming That 'Family Inflation' Is the Same as 'Inflation'	
Awakening	Action
• Every family is different, and even with the same overall monthly expenses, the inflation figures for two families can vary vastly. • Misjudging inflation figures is the most common cause of financial misery in the later years of life.	• Start tracking your family's head-wise expenses accurately and consistently. • Compare the inflation of each head and estimate your family inflation, which can be vastly different from the publicly published inflation figures. • Incorporate your family inflation in your financial freedom planning.

FOOPS 12

LOCKING INVESTMENTS IN A VOLATILE ASSET CLASS

BUY NOT ON OPTIMISM, BUT ON ARITHMETIC.

– BENJAMIN GRAHAM

The year 2020 will be remembered for many things, but primarily for locking us all inside our homes while the deadly pandemic was spreading its tentacles across the globe. As of writing this chapter, India reported 49,000-plus new cases every day, with the number of cases continuously moving northwards. The US, the world's #1 economy, was the worst-impacted country—both in terms of the number of cases as well as deaths.

As the Covid-19 pandemic spread through the globe, there was an obvious sense of panic all around, not all of which was unfounded. Economies all across the world were at their nadir in many decades due to widespread lockdown and travel as well as business constraints.

If you think that travel, aviation, dining, entertainment, etc., were the only industries to be impacted, then I cannot blame you for having absolutely no clue about the impact's severity.

As of the second week of July 2020, the United States' biggest dairy co-operative, Dairy Farmers of America, estimated that 3.7 million gallons (14 million litres) of milk were being dumped out every day because of disrupted supply routes. Unfortunately, this was not an isolated incident.

Plantation owners could not get their products to the market due to social distancing restrictions, disrupting the usual international flow of labour across the globe.

US oil prices had turned negative for the first time in history. A negative price means that the seller will give you the oil and also pay you for taking it. Yes, this happened because the storage costs for the surplus oil were so high that the sellers found it cheaper to sell it at a negative price. There are hundreds of stories like these from across the globe.

In this panic situation, governments were trying to infuse more liquidity into the market to encourage the revival of businesses. In addition, the federal banks had lowered interest rates, thus making it easier for commercial banks to borrow money and lend at cheaper rates to businesses in need.

Whether this stimulus was enough for the revival of businesses or not is not the point. The business recovery was muted, at best. But if we keep businesses aside for the moment, there was an equal struggle in every family. Estimates of job loss showed that 80% of jobs were affected in the Indian urban economy. Many bread earners lost their jobs permanently. Many had to go through severe salary cuts. And those who escaped both had to be taking more stress than ever—just to sustain their jobs.

And it was not only restricted to jobs. Governments were trying to pump easy, liquid money into the economy. As investors, most were severely impacted. Easy liquidity led to a severe dip in the interest rates on fixed-term instruments like term deposits and bonds. These unexpected lower returns from debt-based instruments had posed a big question on the other possible investment options.

As any experienced investor would tell you, when the world is in turmoil, one asset class stands strong, and that is the real money, aka gold. And true to its anti-fragile nature, gold was peaking while equity and debt markets were doomed. Gold had gone up by more than 35% in the first six months of 2020. Such opportunities, when not understood properly, can lead to irrational decisions in panic situations.

Irrational decisions do happen and have been happening for some time with sovereign gold bonds in India. As a result, many investors were rampantly buying sovereign gold bonds—making a mockery of the basic principles of wealth creation strategies.

If you wish to disagree with me by giving the logic that you made handsome money with sovereign gold bonds, then an even bigger problem exists—a problem that sets a wrong precedent and an incorrect belief. This belief is going to drive us to many more mistakes in the future, probably risking much larger chunks of our money.

Let this be the awakening from your pre-set beliefs in gold bonds. Let this be your Foops moment which can prevent you from future disasters in gold investments.

We are going to talk about three asset classes in this Foops chapter—one, of course, is gold bonds. But since the Foops moment is not only restricted to gold bonds, we will also talk about close-ended mutual funds and ELSS funds. But lets get started with the biggest Foops moment of all—sovereign gold bonds.

1. What Are SGBs?

Sovereign gold bonds (SGBs) are government securities denominated in grams of gold. They are substitutes for holding physical gold. Investors have to pay the issue price in cash, and the bonds will be redeemed in cash on maturity. The bond is issued by the Reserve Bank of India on behalf of the Government of India.

Not only is the investment secure, but the investors are to be compensated at a fixed interest rate of 2.5% per annum payable semi-annually on the nominal value. Additionally, over and above the 2.5%, when the investor exits after the eight-year tenure, they get the market price of gold at the time of exit.

The Challenge with SGBs

All this sounds good—in fact, too good. And when something sounds too good, an investor ought to be alarmed.

So, what's so alarming about this investment? On the face of it, everything is wonderful. It is government-backed. So, you get a safe investment that follows the international price of gold and will pay us 2.5% per annum additional interest—over and above the gold price.

But here is the biggest challenge that most seekers fail to recognise, where your Foops moment could be.

Such an investment would have worked fantastically for any debt-based investment, like in most other government bonds that existed at that time. However, seekers tend to forget that gold is not a debt-based investment, though the returns seem to be at par with a debt-based investment. It is neither equity-based, but just like equity, it is a volatile investment. The volatility of gold may not be as pronounced as many equity-based investments like stocks or equity mutual funds.

But we are entering a volatile investment like gold in a lump sum format and locking ourselves for eight years. This ensures that we have lost the plot unless we are fortunate enough to have timed the gold market to perfection.

Any volatile investment, whether stocks, mutual funds or gold, is difficult to time. Therefore, wealth-investing basics guide us that the most advisable route for any volatile investment is a planned, systematic entry via SIPs and an equally well-planned systematic exit via SWPs.

Unfortunately, a gold bond does not provide an option to either enter or exit slowly and systematically. If we are not entering and exiting a volatile investment systematically, we are taking a considerable risk and an unwanted one at that.

Let me try and explain what happens when we get stuck with gold bonds or any such locked-in investment of gold or any other volatile asset class over a long period.

Sovereign gold bonds (SGB) started in 2015. It is a locked-in investment typically for eight years. Let us try and analyse what would have happened had we invested in gold via SGBs eight years back. So, let us look back in time and assume that gold bonds (something similar to SGB) were available to you, and you lock in your gold investments in 2012.

The average gold price in 2012, as shown in Figure 14 later, was ₹31,050. So, let's assume that we went ahead and purchased an X amount of gold at this rate of ₹31,050, and locked ourselves into the bonded hands of SGB for the next eight years.

Come 2020, and gold is trading at a lifetime high price of about ₹53,000. While this may feel like handsome returns, it comes out to a compounded annual growth rate (CAGR) of just 6.91% (as seen in the table below). This return is just below the fixed deposit rate today (remember that a fixed deposit is highly liquid, less risky and more predictable in growth). This return is also significantly below any equally safe debt mutual fund with a lock-in of only one year. A typical gilt fund today is returning around 11-12%.

Now, let us even top these gold bond returns with the additional 2.5% interest that you have been getting as an earning from the bonds. That makes the gold bond returns 9.41%—still below the debt fund returns with just a one-year lock-in.

Note that the above SGB returns of 9.41% are from 2020, when the gold was at its all-time high. If our SGB matured prior to 2020 or after it, then the situation would have been even worse.

Imagine buying SGB in 2011 at ₹26,400 and selling after eight years, in 2019, at ₹35,220. Can you guess the annual returns of this SGB? It's a pathetic 3.67%—not even half of the running inflation in 2019.

Where did we lose out? We lost out when we forgot that gold is not a linear investing tool. It is volatile, and if we invest our money as a lump sum in a volatile investment, we carry a high risk.

So, what is the way out? The way out is simple: SIPs. If the investment is volatile, you should enter systematically and exit the same way.

Let us re-evaluate what would have happened had we invested systematically in gold since 2012 by buying gold ETFs[17] at regular intervals.

The last column in Figure 14 on the next page shows the systematic investment every year in gold ETFs (not gold bonds) from 2012 until 2019 (eight years) and then the exit in 2020. The IRR (internal rate of return) method shows that the annual returns from such a systematic method of investing would have been 12.77%. This is almost 85% better returns than what SGB would have given in the same period (6.91%) and almost 33% higher returns than the 9.41% maximum returns you would have gotten with gold bonds after factoring 2.5% interest (Figure 14).

You might feel that many investors are already aware of systematic entry and exit in volatile investments since this is an oft-repeated point in personal finance. Then why would they go on and make the same mistake in case of gold?

I can see three possible reasons here.

Year	Avg Yearly Gold Price*	Gold Bond Investment	Systematic Gold ETF Investment
2007	10,800		
2008	12,500		
2009	14,500		
2010	18,500		
2011	26,400		
2012	31,050	Cost Price	31,050
2013	29,600		29,600
2014	28,006		28,006
2015	26,343		26,343
2016	28,623		28,623
2017	29,667		29,667
2018	31,438		31,438
2019	35,220		35,220
2020	53,000	Selling Price	4,24,000
CAGR Returns		6.91%	12.77%

Figure 14

One, yes, investors are aware; but they still do not follow these principles strictly enough. In my interaction with thousands of freedom seekers as a part of the ELITE program, around half of them were prone to making irrational entry and exit decisions despite all the knowledge. The primary reason is the noise around them, which is loud—in fact, deafening. Noise puts pressure on the investor. They assume the opportunity would get lost, never to come back. Insulating themselves from outside noise does not come easy to humans. They are driven and biased by what people around them feel and speak.

Secondly, SIP methodology somehows seems to be more associated only with mutual funds. I have rarely seen people talking about SIPs for gold, silver, debt funds, stocks, etc. That's probably because SIP has been sold ferociously by mutual fund houses.

However, the fact remains that SIP is as applicable for gold as it is for debt mutual funds or cryoptocurrencies or stocks or any other investment which is volatile and non-linear.

The third point is a little more subtle. Look at the way this investment is positioned in the market. It is a 'bond', giving the impression that it is a debt-based investment that rises linearly at a given interest rate (coupon rate). Being termed a bond, and that too a 'gold' bond, adds more sanctity to its safety. It has the other assurance of 2.5% interest over and above what the market gives us. And to top it all, the capital gains are tax-free on the maturity of the bonds. This makes us feel that the government has suddenly become our well-wisher and is ready to shell out something extra for us. It would have been a different game had it been named a gold fund or gold stock. But it is cleverly positioned as a gold bond. On top of all this, these 'bonds' are issued by the federal bank. So, double safety. By the way, no gold fund has ever failed in the market because gold has never failed.

This misconception about returns is just one part of the Foops moment associated with SGB. The lack of liquidity is the other one.

The illiquidity with bonds ties our hands to move our own funds around when the market demands so or when we have an emergency. The lack of liquidity does not sound like a big issue to most investors. That's a mistake—a big mistake. That's a Foops moment—a big one.

Does Entry Point in Gold Matter?

We all understand by now that we must go systematically with gold investments. If an investment opportunity does not allow systematic investment in a volatile asset like gold, we better let it go.

But what about the entry point? Does the entry point matter?

Should we try and start this systematic investment in gold when the prices are low?

It could very well be your Foops moment when I tell you that your entry point does not matter in a volatile long-term investment. Your money is supposed to spending time in the market. That is the only way it can grow. So, the more time your money spends, the more wealth it creates.

Some of you may argue that if the entry point is immaterial in a long term volatile investment, then what is the point of doing value analysis for stocks and buying only if the current price is significantly less than the intrinsic value of the company, as clearly stated in the book *The Autobiography of a Stock*?

The question is definitely valid. And to answer it, we must understand a key difference between investing in gold and investing in stocks. Though both of them are volatile long-term investments, there is a critical difference between the two.

A stock's market price may be running quite far from its current intrinsic value since the market price of a stock is usually illogical and driven by the collective perception of all investors rather than any concrete data. Therefore, a value analysis can give us a distinct advantage if we catch a good stock at a price significantly lower than its intrinsic value.

On the other hand, this scenario of catching gold below its intrinsic value is theoretically and practically not feasible. In the case of gold (or any other commodity for that matter), the scenario is quite different. The market price of gold is not driven by perceptions. It is driven by the actual international price of gold (or its current intrinsic value). And the international prices are not driven by perceptions. They are driven by actual demand and actual supply. So, there is never a gap between the market price and the current intrinsic value of gold.

Once you know that a commodity's market price is always mapped to its intrinsic value and you decide to make a systematic long-term investment, the entry point becomes immaterial.

2. Close-Ended Mutual Funds

Locking investments in a volatile asset class is not only restricted to gold as an asset class. It happens in equity as well. Yes, you probably guessed it right—close-ended mutual funds[6].

Close-ended mutual funds work on the same principle as gold bonds. They have a fixed start date, by which you can invest a lump sum amount and a fixed end date, at which you will get the value as on that date.

No one can redeem or enter during the entire tenure of a close-ended mutual fund, as is the case with a sovereign gold bond.

The risk is much higher in an equity market than in a gold bond because of the difference in volatility of the two asset classes. Equity markets are obviously more volatile than gold. Therefore, close-ended mutual funds tend to be risky, even riskier than gold bonds.

Look at the state of some of the close-ended mutual funds as of writing this chapter. IDFC mutual fund has extended the maturity date of IDFC Equity Opportunity Fund Series 4, a close-ended multi-cap scheme launched on December 29th, 2017. Initially set to mature on January 4th, 2021, IDFC extended it by two years. They are not the only ones. Nippon India Mutual Fund wants to roll over the maturity of its three-year close-ended equity scheme Nippon India Capital Builder Fund IV Series B by 730 days to January 2023.

HDFC Mutual Fund has gone one step further. It has lost faith in the concept of a close-ended scheme. As a result, it is converting its Housing Opportunities Fund Series 1 into an open-ended scheme a month before maturity.

And the list is endless.

The common thread binding all these close-ended schemes is their anemic performance, to say the least. As of 2021, of the 85 such close-ended schemes that exist , as many as 55 were underperforming their benchmarks, some even with negative returns. And this is the state when the markets were at an all-time high, and the bull run was not ceasing.

The flaw is in the structure itself—the same flaw as with gold bonds. A fixed lump sum entry, instead of a systematic investing—and a fixed withdrawal—instead of a systematic withdrawal, is an absolutely flawed structure in any volatile asset class, whether equity or gold. It becomes more pronounced in equity because the volatility of equity asset class is higher.

Lock-ins, as in gold bonds or close-ended mutual funds, are supposed to aid the fund manager with greater leeway and comfort in executing the fund mandate since the fund manager is protected from lumpy inflows or sudden redemptions. It also aids the investor and protects them against their worst impulses.

However, the problem with this structure is that the entire investor experience in this format hangs on market conditions prevailing at the time of entry and exit. In rare cases, the wind may turn in favour of the investor, and they may make a hefty profit. But that's relying on chance rather than on sound investing principles, like with a lottery ticket.

3. What about ELSS?

You may argue that ELSS (equity-linked savings schemes) are also mutual fund schemes with a lock-in of three years. But remember that though they have a three-year lock-in, they allow for systematic entry and exit any time after three years. This effectively eliminates any additional risk. On the other hand, the three-year lock-in allows the fund manager to achieve the relative long-term benefits of an equity fund, which may not be feasible without lock-in.

So, if you are one of those who has been through a Foops moment of investing a lump sum amount in a volatile investment and that too with a long lock-in like with SGBs, you may not be able to do much with your existing investment other than keeping your fingers crossed. However, you should be very careful before your next investment.

Foops # 12: Locking Investments in a Volatile Asset Class	
Awakening	Action
• Volatility doesn't exist only in equity stocks or mutual funds. They are a feature of other asset classes like gold and real estate too. • Sound investing principles call for entering or exiting any volatile investment systematically. • A lump sum entry or exit in a volatile investment is a big risk.	• Don't go for sovereign gold bonds. Gold is a volatile asset class and calls for systematic entry and exit. Rather, go for gold ETFs. • Don't go for close-ended mutual funds. They do not allow for systemtic entry or exit. Rather, go for open-ended mutual funds. • ELSS, while it has a lock-in, does allow for systematic entry and exit, thus making it a sound instrument.

FOOPS 13

NOT BEING A RESPONSIVE INVESTOR

> **LIFE IS 10% WHAT HAPPENS TO US, AND 90% HOW WE RESPOND TO IT.**
>
> – CHARLES R. SWINDOLL

Warren Buffet, the legendary American investor, after 70-plus years of investing experience, says,

> "The real fortunes have been made by people who have been right about the investments, and not right about timing of the stock market."

Bernard Mannes Baruch, an American financier and stock investor who devoted a significant time advising US Presidents Woodrow Wilson and Franklin D. Roosevelt on economic matters, says,

> "Only liars manage to be out during bad times and in during good times."

Benjamin Graham, the dean of Wall Street and Warren Buffet's mentor, says,

> "In financial markets, foresight is legally blind. Thus, for most investors, market timing is a practical and emotional impossibility."

Peter Lynch, a renowned author and a legendary American investor, says,

> "Far more money has been lost by investors preparing for corrections, or trying to anticipate corrections, than has been lost in the corrections themselves."

Daniel Kahneman, an Israeli psychologist and economist, a 2002 Nobel Memorial Prize recipient in economic sciences, notable for his work on the psychology of judgment, decision-making and behavioural economics, goes a step ahead. He blames market timing as the biggest reason for lower returns, just the reverse of why an average investor attempts market timing in the first place. He says:

> "The average investor's return is significantly lower than market returns primarily due to attempts for market timing."

Despite all the above legends talking with their experience, every investor is tempted to time the market at least once in their lifetime.

Everyone had this feeling at some stage of life:

> "I have been crafted with a different clay, and I can do it."

And while in the short term, some investors may be able to prove the legends wrong, this principle has proven itself time and again over the long term.

If I talk specifically about my experience, so many investors have been after my life to recommend profit-booking since the market picked up after the Covid-19 dip in March 2020.

Here is how the chart looked in August 2020, with a year of history:

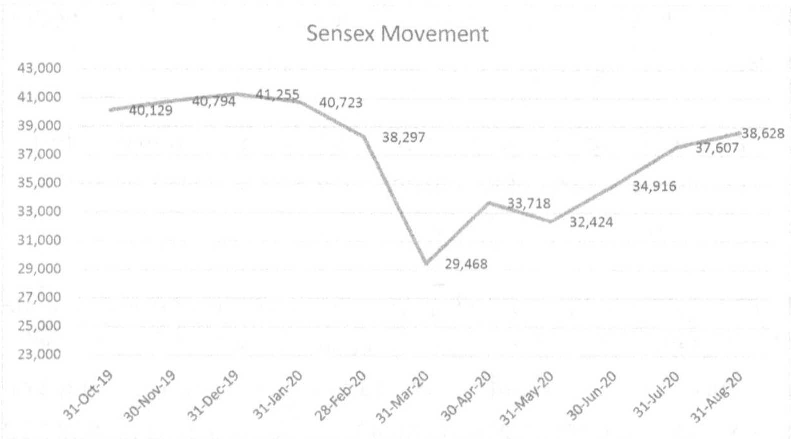

Figure 15

An inexperienced investor's mind, in March 2020, would be blaming Covid-19 for his misfortune. Half of the investors would actually exit the market at this stage, fearing a further collapse. However, those who managed to hold on through this period heaved a sigh of relief as the markets started to pick up from March 2020 through August 2020.

With every passing month post-March 2020, there was pressure to 'come out' of the market and 'get in' when it gets lower. That's precisely what trying to time the market is. It looks logical to take action, ignoring one of the most fundamental rules of equity investing that wealth is created more by 'inaction' than by 'action'.

One of the investors, in fact, went ahead in August 2020 to redeem his major equity, saying that he would come and reinvest after a 10% dip. And his logic was sound and historically correct—markets were running at an all-time high P/E, businesses were struggling after lockdown and markets were rising without businesses picking up on earnings. There was nothing wrong with this investor's reasons, but this is what has happened in the market since September 2020.

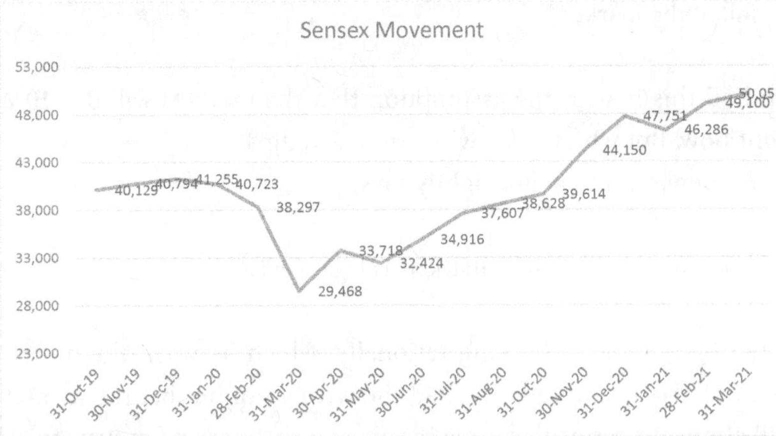

Figure 16

He was still waiting for a 10% dip while the markets had already risen from 38,628 in August 2020 to 50,051 in March 2021—a whopping 30% jump in the seven months since September 2020.

Even if this investor gets a 10% dip in the market now, he would have lost the differential as compared to those who stayed invested even during the 10% dip. Effectively, 30% returns were lost in an attempt to time the market, out of which only 10% in the actual fall, assuming that the fall happens after March 2021.

But what happened after March 2021? Markets touched 59,000 in September 2021. This is 53% higher than the August 2020 prices. The markets just kept going up. No logic justifies this meteoric rise. But who said that the market prices are driven by logic? Definitely not in the short run.

As Peter Lynch says,

> "More money is lost in trying to time the market rather than the fall of the market."

And all this is with the assumption that the markets will dip 10% right now. But who knows when they will dip?

As Benjamin Graham rightly says,

> "The future in financial markets is legally blind."

If the investor was thinking rationally, which he was, why did he lose out? He lost because he had the wrong notion that the market will always be rational and we can master the market's movements.

The fact is that no one on the planet can consistently predict the market correctly.

So, what do we do if we cannot time the market? Do we keep investing? The answer is no. We learnt earlier in Foops #7 that it is a stupid approach to keep investing.

You may belong to either of the extremes: the passive extreme, which keeps buying irrespective of the market situation, or the active extreme, which considers itself smarter than the market and tries to buy or sell as per the market situation.

Whether we are insulated from the market situation or reactive to it, both turn out to be inefficient strategies for building wealth.

There is another path, which is not only efficient but also keeps you in full control. On this path, you are neither insulated from the market nor reactive to the market. On the contrary, you are, what I term, *responsive* to the market. Let this Foops moment sink in.

Being responsive involves two key elements:

1. **You Are Not Insulated**

   One thing that becomes very clear when you are trying to be responsive to the market is that you should not remain insulated from the market. This means that you must understand and be aware of what is going on around you. You cannot just keep investing as per your investing strategy. You have to respond to market situations. But, of course, not all situations.

   The question now arises: how do you choose a situation to respond to. The answer is better addressed in the upcoming section on black swan events.

2. **You Are Not Reactive**

   You do not react to every volatility in the market. Instead, you stay insulated for the most part in the market until the volatility passes a threshold that nudges you to take massive action. But how do we define that threshold? That threshold is typically defined by the occurrence of a black swan event.

What Is a Black Swan Event?

A black swan event is an unpredictable occurrence beyond what is typically expected and has potentially severe consequences. Black swan events are characterised by their extreme rarity, their severe impact and the widespread insistence they were obvious in hindsight.

The term was popularised by Nassim Nicholas Taleb, a finance professor, writer and former Wall Street trader. Taleb wrote about the idea of a black swan event in a 2007 book before the 2008 financial crisis. Taleb argued that because black swan events are impossible to predict due to their extreme rarity yet have catastrophic consequences, it is important for people to always assume a black swan event is a possibility, whatever it may be, and plan accordingly.

Some examples of black swan events are worth mentioning here.

The dot com bubble of 2001 when America was enjoying rapid economic growth and increase in private wealth before the economy catastrophically collapsed; the financial crash of the US housing market in 2008, the effect of which was catastrophic and global; Zimbabwe having the worst case of hyperinflation in the 21st century with a peak inflation rate of more than 79.6 billion percent—an inflation level of that amount is nearly impossible to predict and can easily ruin a country financially; and the Covid-19 pandemic which brought the entire world's economy to a grinding halt as countries struggled to control the pandemic by implementing strict lockdowns.

These are four incidents in the last 20 years that reshaped the global economy. These are the black swan events that we ought to be responsive to. These are typically global events that generally occur once in five to ten years.

A responsive investor would respond to black swan events and ignore everything else.

You might argue that it is difficult to predict such events' intensity initially, and I would fully agree with you. However, we do not need to catch the events in the beginning when the markets start to fall. Instead, we need to catch them when they have shown their full impact, and the markets have already fallen. And that is not too difficult to detect.

The most recent case of a black swan event has been, of course, the pandemic, which has been marked by markets falling all across the globe. India was no exception, with markets falling as much as

30% within a few weeks of the outbreak. In India, before Covid-19 (that is, by January 2020), the markets were anyway starting to move southwards in an already crippled economy. Covid-19 only accelerated the inevitable.

Now, you do not need to be a financial expert to see the Sensex fall from 40,723 in January 2021 to 29,468 in March 2020. This is close to a 40% fall in around two months, purely because of the black swan event.

I completely understand that it is easy to look at all this in hindsight and say that we should have responded to this event around the end of March. But it is also understandable that it is difficult to know how much more the market would fall. The fact is that it does not matter how much more the market would fall. A black swan event is characterised by sharp falls and global impact. Even if we had been responsive after a 20-25% fall, we would have reaped immense benefits today.

How to Respond to a Black Swan Event

Once you have recognised a black swan event (multiple steep falls, significant shredding (like 25%-plus) within a short period, global impact, rarity of occurrence (one or two such events in a decade)), the next step is to decide how we respond to such an event.

Some seekers believed that we should stop all existing SIPs, wait for the market to reach the bottom, and then start investing again. Though it is easy to stop existing SIPs, the problem with this strategy is that it is difficult, rather impossible, to know when the market's bottom is reached. And more often than not, since we cannot clearly see the bottom unless it is gone, we miss the opportunity to reinvest.

Some other seekers grew worried and withdrew their money

from their existing equity-based investments, fearing that the bottom could be too deep and recovery could be too slow. Well, emotions like fear and greed are known wealth destroyers.

In the past, the human race has overcome many obstacles far more severe than Covid-19 or any other black swan event. It has seen pandemics, world wars and famine much worse than what we can even imagine today, and it has survived through all that.

The whole point is that if we can survive, we stand to benefit when the market bounces back.

German philosopher Friedrich Nietzsche, in the 19th century, once said,

"What doesn't kill you, makes you stronger."

Each such black swan event may seem like the doomsday, but then, we have always bounced back, survived and then thrived.

And if we are unable to survive, well, money was of no use in that case anyway.

So, how do we respond to a black swan event, assuming that we will bounce back sooner or later? My experience is that the best response to such black swan events is starting a top-up SIP[47]. Let us understand more about top-up SIPs.

Top-Up SIP

As the name suggests, a top-up SIP is a SIP over and above your existing SIPs. This means that we do not touch our existing SIPs and let them benefit from cost averaging. On top of that, we use our portfolio liquidity to start a top-up SIP with amounts much bigger and tenures much shorter.

In response to Covid-19, we suggested a three-month top-up SIP to all our ELITE subscribers in mid-March 2020. We recommended that all seekers invest as much amount as they comfortably can by splitting that amount over three months—as a top-up SIP to their existing SIPs. Many did. Some did not.

Those who did were proud of their actions after three months.

This top-up strategy thus proved a very effective response to this black swan event. I am eagerly awaiting the next black swan event to help seekers generate their next big chunk of wealth, while their existing SIPs continue to weave magic slowly, but surely.

Foops #13: Not Being a Responsive Investor	
Awakening	Action
• Market is the king. Timing the market is futile. • Neither be insulated or reactive to the market movements. Instead, be responsive. • Black swan events are an opportunity to make massive wealth. Learn to identify them.	• Never try to time the market based on short-term movements. • Don't be completely insulated from the market's movements. Keep looking out for black swan events like Covid-19. • Start top-up SIPs to invest during black swan events to generate massive wealth.

FOOPS 14

AUTO-RENEWING OUR FIXED DEPOSITS

> **A SMALL LEAK WILL SINK A GREAT SHIP.**
>
> – BENJAMIN FRANKLIN

We live in a world of automation, robotics, machine learning and artificial intelligence (AI). The one thing that the human race is short of is *time*. This also gives us a unique opportunity to innovate and create smart products that also save us time—the most precious commodity for all of us.

In many cases, it works pretty well. The advent of the internet, mobile phones, net banking, scheduled transfers, etc., has made our daily transactions smarter and faster. And the future looks even more automated. Advanced technologies will take automation to a whole new level.

But we have to be very careful with what we are automating. It is never harmful to learn what is being automated in what way and how it impacts us.

Automation in Banking

When it comes to banking, auto payment of bills and auto-renewal of fixed deposits are widespread now. It has become so common that if we are not a party to these things, we may be at the risk of being tagged as 'outdated' or 'old-gen'.

However, what we get tagged as is not the point here. The point is that we must be open to technology and go for anything that saves time for us. But at the same time, we must understand what is being automated and its consequences for an investor. If any automation leads to a loss of returns, we must do a careful analysis of the trade-off between time saved and returns accrued.

Auto-renewal of bank fixed deposits is one such investment where we must be extra cautious, because, as with me, it will turn out to be a big Foops moment for so many investors.

Auto-Renewal of Bank Fixed Deposits

Gone are the days when we had to visit the bank branch, apply for a fixed deposit on a paper form, submit the form along with a cheque, and then visit the bank after a few days to collect our fixed deposit certificate. And there are no points for guessing the amount of work needed if you ever wished to cancel or renew your deposit. Same stuff—visit the bank branch, fill up an application form and wait for a few days. That too, with the assumption that you filled up everything correctly, else you would come to know about the issues in your form only during your next bank visit. Then, you correct the anomaly, submit the revised form and wait for a few more days.

Today, the internet and net banking revolution have enabled us to do everything online—just with a few clicks—whether booking, cancelling or renewing the fixed deposits.

One of the features that the online net banking facility provides us is the *auto-renewal* of fixed deposits. We need to be extra careful with this feature. Auto-renewal of fixed deposits may not make sense in many cases—in fact, in several cases.

Auto-renewal of fixed deposits make a lot of sense if the deposits have to be manually renewed by visiting the bank branch. However, in an era where everything is online, a deposit renewal might take less than a minute every year when done on a computer.

Now, you might argue, why not automate this process of spending even a minute as well. Of course, we can. But we must understand what we are trading off this minute with.

If I tell you that this small luxury (of saving a minute) might cost you thousands or lakhs of rupees over the next few years, you might start to wonder whether your one minute is truly that valuable.

And this could be your Foops moment. This is a mistake I kept making for many years before I realised what was happening and how banks were behaving smartly.

Before I tell you how this is a costly luxury to avail, let us look at the typical slabs of fixed deposits along with their tenures.

Below is a snapshot from the HDFC Bank website, as of August 14th, 2020:

Tenure	Regular FD Rates	Sr. Citizen FD Rates
7 days to 14 days	2.75%	3.25%
15 days to 29 days	3.00%	3.50%
30 days to 45 days	3.25%	3.75%
46 days to 90 days	4.00%	4.50%
91 days to 6 months	4.10%	4.60%
6 months 1 day to 9 months	4.50%	5.00%
9 months 1 day to 364 days	4.75%	5.25%
1 year	5.25%	5.75%
1 year 1 day to 2 years	5.25%	5.75%
2 years 1 day to 3 years	5.35%	5.85%
3 years 1 day to 5 years	5.50%	6.00%
5 years 1 day to 10 years	5.50%	6.00%

Figure 17

Now, let us look at the regular deposit rates across various tenures. There are a few interesting observations you can make. But the most crucial observation is the difference in deposit rates when we switch from one tenure to another.

For example, let us consider that you already had a two-year running deposit with HDFC bank, and you have put it in auto-renewal mode. Let us assume that your deposit matures today. So, as soon as your deposit matures, it will be auto-renewed for another two years, at the current rate of 5.25%.

But what if this fixed deposit was not on auto-renew mode?

The Opportunity for Manual Renewal

If it was not in an auto-renew mode, the money, both the principal and the interest, would have come to your savings account, and you would be required to book the deposit yourself online.

This is an opportunity which we ought to grab with both hands. If I was to book the FD myself today, I would not book it for two years. I would rather book it for two years and one day. And I am sure you know the reason. It is no rocket science. The interest on a two-year-one-day FD is 0.1% higher than the interest on a two-year FD. So, just by keeping my money for one extra day with the bank, I would earn an additional 0.1% on the entire deposit amount and for the whole tenure.

Isn't this exciting as well as ridiculous? To put things in perspective, a deposit of ₹40 lakhs for two years and one day would earn me an additional ₹8,000 over two years. What did I do to deserve this additional ₹8,000? I spent a minute.

So, you need to ask yourself is whether your one minute is worth more than ₹8,000? If yes, then it is wise to put the deposit in auto-renew mode. If you think that it is not, as was the case with me, then it makes no sense to get the deposit auto-renewed. Rather, let the money come into your savings account, have a look at the interest rate in each tenure, and accordingly get a new deposit done to maximise returns.

If you watch closely, the gap is even higher when you move from a three-year deposit to a three-year-one-day deposit. The difference is 0.15% due to an additional day of tenure.

What if the deposit amount was ₹80 lakhs instead of ₹40 lakhs? The value created by your minute would be ₹16,000 in that case. Sounds interesting, doesn't it? Does that cause an awakening? Does that push you to act? Is this your Foops moment?

If you wonder why we cannot put the FD for two-years-one-day in an auto-renew mode, then I must tell you that these tenures keep changing over time. The logic behind the incentivisation of tenures is driven by the banks' need for money. The tenure structure is different for different banks. Moreover, the tenure structure for the same bank also keeps changing over time.

So, it pays you handsomely to let the deposit mature and then renew your deposit manually, online. Most investors have access to the net banking facility. Therefore, spending a minute renewing your deposits sitting at home is not a big deal.

Are additional returns the only incentive that motivates us to never put our deposits in an auto-renew mode? Of course not.

There are many more reasons why a freedom seeker should renew the deposits manually.

Let me list down a few of those.

Generates Positive Vibes

When I was chasing my own financial freedom, I truly used this concept to keep myself motivated. The idea of seeing money flow into your bank account with accumulated interest generates tremendous positive vibrations. It reaffirms your belief that you are generating passive income and you will get to your goal sooner rather than later.

Staying positive in a long and volatile journey is crucial. And this is one of the sure-shot positive vibes you can capture during the journey that makes it enjoyable and worthwhile.

Increases Portfolio Liquidity

One of the critical factors, which is often undervalued, is the liquidity of your invested money. When your money keeps flowing regularly (as in the case of a manual renewal of a deposit), it improves the liquidity of your portfolio.

And liquidity is a vital aspect in determining the health of your portfolio. A portfolio with high liquidity is definitely more preferred over a portfolio with a relatively lower liquidity. A liquid portfolio allows you to deploy the money more efficiently based on the market conditions. Such a portfolio is also an amazing fall-back option in case of emergency needs.

Depending upon an individual's financial needs, a portfolio with lower returns, but higher liquidity may be better suited than vice versa.

Allows You to Include 'Small' Add-On Amounts

Another critical factor, which is also often not valued enough, is the small add-on amounts that keep lying here and there in your savings account. Fixed deposits getting matured and credited to your savings account allow you to use these add-ons and inflate the size of your deposit before the next renewal.

Now, if you happen to think that things like add-ons are too small a factor in your wealth creation, then let me share that nothing is too small in finance to influence your wealth massively. If you have understood the concept of compounding well enough, you would definitely understand and appreciate that every rupee is an opportunity for the next million.

With these distinct advantages associated with the manual (but online) renewal of deposits, you get to harness immense advantages that you would have missed had you opted for auto-renewal. Auto-renewal may have saved you a few minutes per year but would also have deprived you of the magic of compounding, portfolio liquidity, better interest rates, and above all, the positivity to excel in the beautiful journey of wealth creation.

If you have not been doing it so far, then this just might be the Foops moment for you. And every Foops moment is an opportunity to become better, take charge and set the path right for ourselves and our coming generations.

Foops #14: Auto-Renewing Our Fixed Deposits	
Awakening	**Action**
• Generally, we put our bank deposits in auto-renewal mode. • Auto-renewal leads to missing out on great additional returns from deposits • Not only returns, you miss out on positive vibes, liquidity, compounding and piling up add-ons if you continue keeping your deposits in auto-renewal mode.	• Check all your deposits which are kept in auto-renewal mode. • Change the mode of such deposits so that money flows to your bank account on maturity of the deposit. • Renew your deposit online after looking at the optimal tenure and adding on whatever little you can from your side.

FOOPS 15

LOOKING FOR 'RISK-FREE' INVESTMENTS

LIFE IS FULL OF RISKS ANYWAY. WHY NOT TAKE THEM?

– LINDSAY LOHAN

"I want to invest only in risk-free investing options."

"At least in FDs, there is no risk. Am I right?"

"I only want to invest in government bonds. They are backed by the government and therefore risk-free."

"Gold is absolutely risk-free. Please increase my gold allocation."

"I will hold on to the cash in my savings account. I do not want to take any risks."

"I am not sure where to invest now as debt funds also carry risks."

These are some of the pleading statements I get from my freedom seekers, and I get to read such emails quite often. Every investor wants to take minimum risk and maximise their returns. Of course, that should always be the intent. But is there anything like a risk-free investment? How about simply holding cash in a bank savings account?

September 16th, 2019

Andrew Lobo, 71, was brought home from a hospital in Mumbai after undergoing treatment for a lung infection. Andrew had no reason to be relieved, however. He had come home to the devastating news that Punjab and Maharashtra Co-operative Bank (PMC), where he had a savings account, had been placed under 'directions' of the Reserve Bank of India (RBI) for six months after irregularities were found in lending. This meant that the RBI was practically taking over the bank's operations. Crucially, it meant that customers like Andrew could withdraw only up to ₹1,000 of the total balance in any account they had in the bank.

The infection had already weakened Andrew's lungs; he needed oxygen machines to breathe. While his family had managed to pay for his treatment, they had been relying on four of his fixed deposits in PMC Bank to fund the oxygen machines needed to pull him through. Each of the machines cost ₹49,000. With no access to the fixed deposits, Andrew could not recuperate.

As per his relatives, Andrew was a strong and independent person. But the family had no other money to pay for the oxygen machines because not just Andrew's uncle but even his father and all of his close friends had accounts in the same bank.

The family said stress had caused Andrew's health to deteriorate further. He couldn't believe that he had no access to his own money. He refused to eat. Andrew's family could only helplessly watch as he began waning away in front of their eyes. On October 31st, all of a sudden, he started breathing heavily. Within five minutes, he succumbed. He had suffered a cardiac arrest, becoming the seventh account holder of PMC Bank to lose his life.

Andrew was among the hundreds of depositors with PMC Bank who suddenly found themselves financially crippled for no fault of theirs. Ironically, the same bank that customers had trusted to safeguard their money had become responsible for their misery.

And bear in mind that PMC is not a small bank. PMC is a

multi-state scheduled urban cooperative bank with operations in Maharashtra, Delhi, Karnataka, Goa, Gujarat, Andhra Pradesh and Madhya Pradesh. Started in 1984, the bank boasts of as many as 137 branches pan-India.

What was the reason for such a crisis? Could the customers have known it beforehand and taken action? I do not think there was any way a retail customer would ever have seen this coming. The bank had been hiding bad loans for a long time.

The suspended managing director of PMC Bank, Joy Thomas, admitted that ₹2,500 crores of exposure to the Housing Development and Infrastructure Limited (HDIL) group had been left unnoticed in the annual audit of RBI. Thomas was arrested days after the press conference.

You may argue that this was a cooperative bank and not a nationalised bank. Sure, valid point. So, let us move a few months forward.

March 5th, 2020

The Reserve Bank of India (RBI) imposed a 30-day moratorium on Yes Bank and superseded the private-sector lender's board. Yes Bank was the seventh-largest bank in India when it went under the moratorium.

Under the terms of the moratorium, deposit withdrawals were capped at ₹50,000 per person. In addition, the central bank proposed a reconstruction scheme under which SBI might take a maximum of 49% stake in the restructured capital of the bank. Analysts believed the new management of Yes Bank, headed by former Deutsche Bank India head Ravneet Gill, who joined the bank in early 2019, could turn around the ship. Gill, however, has struggled to do so thus far.

Yes Bank was neither a cooperative bank nor a small one by any means. What went wrong?

Where do you keep your money if it is not safe in the savings account of some of the country's largest banks? At home?

No. Because cash at home carries an even bigger risk—of theft and dacoity. There is enough evidence of cash owners losing their lives just because they had money at their homes.

Where else do you put it? In debt-based mutual funds?

Let us move forward by another month.

April 23rd, 2020

On the morning of April 23rd, 2020, several investors woke up to nightmarish news. Franklin Templeton wound up six debt schemes in an overnight decision. Investors who put their hard-earned money in supposedly safe debt funds do not know what will happen to their investments. When can they expect their money back? And these crippled funds were not small by any means. The total corpus of the six exposed Franklin funds stood at ₹47,658 crores—and that's massive.

Even after eight months of this fiasco, the fund house had not given any clear indication about the possible timeline within which it will liquidate all its investments and return investors' money.

So, where do the investors go now?

Equity-based mutual funds? Stock markets? Real estate? All these were already considered too risky for the average investor.

Well, if your argument is PPF, EPF or bonds, then we should understand that they all lack liquidity. This essentially means that you do not have access to your money in times of need. While they are good tools for very long-term wealth creation, they cannot occupy more than a defined percentage of anyone's portfolio.

Then what?

Investment = Gains + Losses (Risk)

The bottom line is that investment means risk. When you are going out to invest, you are taking a risk. In fact, you are being compensated in proportion to the risk you are taking. If you still cannot believe this Foops moment, just read on.

Life goes the same way.

When you are going out of your house, you are risking your life. You may meet with an accident or just trip down the stairs. Interestingly, sitting inside the house is also a risk—of a different kind. You may be a victim of a sudden earthquake, or an airplane might just crash into your neighbour's house while you are enjoying your favourite TV show, as it happened with Hendra.

Hendra, a resident in the air force housing complex in eastern Jakarta, ran out of his house after hearing several loud explosions and saw flames engulfing neighbours' homes.

"I could hardly believe my eyes... there was a military plane that crashed and hit the houses!" he said.

"At once, the situation turned into chaos. All the residents fled in panic. Women and children were screaming hysterically."

Six people in Hendra's neighbourhood died in the crash. Did they take a risk? Not to the best of their knowledge.

And these are not one-off incidents.

Brandon Lee, 28-year-old film actor, martial artist and son of Bruce Lee, was accidentally shot to death by co-star Michael Massee while filming a scene for *The Crow* due to an improperly loaded prop gun.

An entire football team of 11 in Eastern Kasai, Democratic Republic of the Congo, was fatally struck by lightning while playing. The other team left the scene unharmed.

And such things are not isolated to underdeveloped countries.

Hitoshi Nikaidoh, a doctor in Houston, Texas, was decapitated after his head got trapped between elevator doors at his workplace.

Heval Yildirim, 13, of Turkey, was killed when a sacrificial goat bought for Eid al-Adha jumped off the roof over a protective fence and fell onto him. His father had placed it on the roof of the building where he lived because he could not find another suitable place to keep it.

Lottie Michelle Belk, 55, was fatally stabbed in the chest by a beach umbrella blown by a strong wind.

Michael Kosanovich, 21, was crushed to death by a 2002 Lexus IS300s after its owner started it by remote control. It rolled forward, and he was pinned between two vehicles

And there are ample more examples to prove that the risk never ceases to exist—in life or investments.

Here is the takeaway.

You are always taking a risk with your investments—whether you keep them in your savings account or invest in deposits or in your own house. You can only manage or mitigate risk. But risk will always exist.

One of the Foops moment for many investors come when I tell them that no investment is risk-free. They have to be ready to take risks. How much risk one should take will depend on the individual's risk profile, of course.

At the same time, there is always a trade-off between risk and reward. The more risk you take, the more rewards you are likely to reap. Many seekers consider this statement as a license to take more risks.

And suddenly, everyone is of the view that they are ready to take risks and want rewards. What they sometimes miss is the fact that when you accept risk, risk will likely occur someday. And when it occurs, the investor should be ready to bear losses that day because they also enjoyed rewards on the other days.

Do not get into the mould of entering risk-free investments. Nothing of that kind exists in our world. This is a Foops moment for all those investors who are looking for risk-free investments, or for those who want to take risks but not suffer losses midway.

We have to take risks. The amount of risk that we can take depends on our risk profile and many other financial and non-financial factors. Based on all those factors, we should decide on an appropriate investment for ourselves.

Foops #15: Looking for 'Risk-Free' Investments

Awakening	Action
• Risk exists everywhere you invest, or even if you do not invest. • We are compensated in proportion to the risk we take.	• Get yourself assessed for your risk profile to understand the extent of risk that you can take. • Create an investing strategy based on your risk profile.

FOOPS 16

CREATING SEPARATE POOLS TO FUND LIFE EVENTS

> **IT'S YOUR REACTION TO ADVERSITY, NOT ADVERSITY ITSELF THAT DETERMINES HOW YOUR LIFE'S STORY WILL DEVELOP.**
>
> – DIETER F. UCHTDORF

Every challenge in life comes packaged with opportunities. There is an intriguing chapter in my last-published book, *A Father's Diary*. This chapter has conversations with my daughters on converting negative energy around us into positive energy—just with the aid of our dreams. It is such a critical aspect of our lives that I do not get tired of overstating this fact. There is so much negativity around us, and if we can get a *converter*, we can all transform that energy in our favour, and to aid the achievement of our goals and dreams.

There are more than enough examples around the world where a handicap was converted into a massive opportunity.

Even in the ELITE program that we run for financial freedom seekers, we make it a point that all feedback received from the subscribers is acknowledged, read, analysed, responded and then acted upon without fail. Because feedback and criticism are a massive opportunity to look at our flaws, which we cannot see for ourselves.

There are times when investors do get nervous. One such time is when big-ticket life events are staring at them. Their Foops moment would be to convert this big-ticket expense into an opportunity. Let us see how.

Vandana was a committed investor and wealth creator. And as with all investors, she had certain big-ticket events planned for her life. We call them 'life special events'. These are one-time, big-ticket expenses that are properly budgeted in any financial freedom plan. Typical examples are higher education for your child, their marriage, opening up a new venture, buying a new house, etc.

Each such event poses a unique challenge to the seeker—on all fronts including, of course, the financial front. I have seen many investors getting worried about their finances as the big-ticket expenses approached. On the other hand, the Foops moment is in realising that each challenge provides a massive financial opportunity if we can set the right perspective.

However, Vandana was not one of those to grow worried. On the contrary, she had a very pleasant outlook towards life. She wanted to enjoy every special event and make them memorable for herself and her family. And I fully support her on this vision towards life.

But as her daughter's marriage event approached closer, she actually started to get a bit rattled about the finances. The reality seemed to strike her harder than she thought it would. But then, the strong lady she was, she recouped and started to accumulate some money in the *virtual box* of funds she had earmarked for this event. Her daughter's marriage expenses were marked to be funded by one of the mutual funds she had been investing in for almost ten years now. She already had significant money in her designated mutual fund. We term such designated assets as 'boxes'. Additionally, she was adding more to the box and getting ready for the life event[29].

There are many like Vandana who feel that dipping into our existing designated boxes is far better than dipping into our other investments. Her strategy was to liquidate the designated mutual fund as and when she needed the money to spend on her daughter's marriage and other related ceremonies. Many financial advisors would recommend moving the funds to liquid debt funds sometime before the actual event rather than continuing to keep the funds in the designated box. Well, yes; debt funds might make sense. But then it adds to its own complexity in terms of choice of funds, calculation of gains and applicable income tax, management, etc.

Regardless of which asset you keep your funds in, almost everyone around you will tell you that you should keep one dedicated asset for each future event in life—like one box for one event.

But this idea of keeping a pool of funds dedicated for every event does not hold much logic. In fact, this is a Foops moment when you realise that the reverse is actually far more advantageous, which means that dipping into your box is worse than dipping into other possible assets. Yes, I am asking you to dip into your other existing investments and fund the special event rather than dipping into your box that you have been so strategically planning and investing in for years.

And it is not because of just one reason. There are many. Let us go through some of them.

1. Awesome Opportunities On the Way

Be it the Covid-19 crisis or the banking and financial fiasco, opportunities keep coming all along our financial journey. A smart and well-balanced portfolio should never create 'blocks' of wealth meant only for specific goals. Such acts create rigidity in the portfolio. Rather, the portfolio should just do the reverse. It should create more harmony and more liquidity within itself so that it is easier for your funds to be moved around in case of emergencies or opportunities like the black swan events we talked about. Our portfolio should be liquid enough to grab as many such opportunities as feasible.

If we can dip only into our designated blocks, we lose opportunities big-time. Remember the Covid top-up SIP (we talked about it in one of the earlier Foops moments) that was crafted just to make use of the opportunities arising out of a black swan event. There were many freedom seekers who had a highly liquid portfolio and could move around funds quick enough to make use of black swan events. They could respond well to the unexpected situation and set up their top-up SIPs only because of the freedom they had to move the money around. Those who had created goal-specific blocks of money within their portfolio could not move the money around as easily. They stood as the biggest losers in terms of wealth that was created post the black swan event. And Covid is surely not the last of the black swan events. There will be many more opportunities coming along in the future as well.

2. Churn the Non-Performers

Whatever analysis we do prior to investing our hard earned money, there will always be times when some of our investments will go bad. As we read earlier, nothing is actually risk-free—neither in life and definitely not in personal finance.

What do we do with investments which have gone bad, which had to go bad? The answer is simple. We convert this setback into an opportunity by churning these non-performing investments at the time of such important life events. I am not advocating that we have to really wait for any event to occur before churning non-performers. The churning of non-performers should be a scheduled activity in every portfolio. This is precisely what we do in our ELITE Program, reviewing the performance of each asset and sub-asset every six months.

Having said that, you are likely to have a situation where the box of funds that you have created for a specific event does not have non-performers, but the other box of funds (probably meant for some other event) has serious non-performers. What do you do in that case? Sticking to your event boxes in such situations can do no good to your portfolio. In fact, the fewer the boxes are, the better. During or around the event, if we have non-performers, which we will most likely have, we should make this event count as an opportunity to further increase the efficiency of our portfolio by churning them out, irrespective of the box in which they hide.

3. Rebalance the Portfolio

As we read in Foops #7, we have to keep balancing our portfolio as per our customised investing strategy since a balanced portfolio gives us the most optimum returns for our needs. Based on the market situation and our own financial situation in life, portfolios do get imbalanced by themselves. Life events provide us with a great opportunity to rebalance our portfolio as per our investing strategy. Liquidating the right assets at this stage to fund the upcoming life events will allow us to rebalance our portfolio for optimal returns.

Imagine a portfolio where an investing strategy recommends 40% equity and 60% debt. Let us say that the equity portion in this portfolio has already swelled to 50% instead of the recommended 40%. On the other hand, the event block that was created for an upcoming event has funds lying in the PPF account, which was the designated box for the event. If we just liquidate the funds for the event from the designated PPF block, we are going to do more harm than good to our portfolio balance. This is because the equity percent will shoot up further as soon as we withdraw a significant debt portion from the PPF. Rather, in an *open* portfolio, we would have actually sold some equity ('sell high'). Doing so would have also brought the portfolio back to the desired balance as per our investing strategy.

And the above portfolio imbalance is not a rare occurrence. This happens in most portfolios almost all the time since the equity percentage of a portfolio at any given point of time is as unpredictable as the markets are. Despite our best efforts, portfolios will keep going out of balance. And blocks in a portfolio just don't help us convert this situation into an opportunity.

4. Churn and Save Taxes

As we read in Foops #9, we have the potential to save significant taxes if we learn to churn even the good performers. So, the time of the event provides us with an opportunity to do our annual churning and save taxes. A boxed portfolio restricts making use of the churning possibilities that our portfolio may present during our life events.

Let's carefully consider all the above points. We may start to wonder whether a life event is a time to get stressed about our finances or an opportunity to set things right in our portfolio and make it much more efficient than it has ever been. I feel that the occurrence of an event has far more positive outcomes for us, provided we have allowed our portfolio to have the suppleness it needs to take advantage of each of the so-called adverse situations instead of boxing our events. Therefore, boxing funds for an event is definitely not the right solution. Doing so only boxes the growth of our wealth. It doesn't allow our portfolio to blossom the way it is capable of.

So, should we do nothing at all to plan for our life events? This is not at all what I am advocating. We do need some planning for such high-ticket outflows from our portfolio, but boxing is not the solution. So, what is?

Based on my experience, the best way to deal with significant expenses on account of upcoming life events is to have a matrix of assets, goals and events and do a smart mapping of events to multiple assets across equity and debt (rather than one single asset) in a way that our portfolio balance is not disturbed after executing the event. We give it a lot of value in our ELITE Program. There is a designated step just to do the right mapping of assets to events, where one or more assets are mapped to a single event in a way that's most efficient for our portfolio. The life event execution should ultimately lead to a better-balanced portfolio and more optimised returns.

Next time, when we have a life event staring at us, we should be all excited about making our portfolio more supple, efficient and high-performing. Let the excitement of an event be the Foops moment leading to much greater wealth creation than you originally envisaged.

Foops #16: Creating Separate Pools to Fund Life Events

Awakening	Action
• Life events need to be properly integrated into your financial planning. • The age-old idea of keeping one dedicated pool of funds for every life event puts you at a serious disadvantage.	• Every life event should be considered an opportunity to increase the suppleness and efficiency of your portfolio. • Create an asset-life event map and keep monitoring it to maximise efficiency.

BELIEVING THAT EVERYONE NEEDS LIFE INSURANCE

THE CHIEF BENEFICIARY OF LIFE INSURANCE POLICIES FOR YOUNG, SINGLE, OR NON-EARNING PEOPLE IS THE LIFE INSURANCE AGENT.

– WES SMITH

There is an interesting and funny clip from a Jerry Seinfeld comedy show that is indirectly related to life insurance.

Here is what he says in the show.

"Sky diving was definitely the scariest things that I have ever done. Let me ask this question from all those who do sky diving. Why do sky divers wear helmet? So, I mean, if you dive from the plane and the parachute does not open, how exactly does the helmet help?"

Life insurance is your helmet, but a helmet for what? For you? For your wealth? For your income? Most of us actually do not even see life insurance as security, forget about grasping what it is a security against. Instead, we prefer to see it as an investment. I think these questions are enough to trigger your next Foops moment.

I wish to emphasise in this Foops moment that we ought to be clear why we need the helmet. Only when we know the reason for wearing the helmet can the helmet be expected to do what it is supposed to. Only by understanding the "why" of a helmet can the investment in the helmet be made worthwhile. Similarly, only if we are clear of the helmet's purpose can we take it off when we think it is not serving the desired purpose.

So, before giving you any clue whether you need life insurance or not, I will spend some time trying to explain the true need for a life insurance product. I am aware that many of you might feel that this explanation may be too naïve for you or may not be needed at all, but that is precisely where the problem actually starts.

Purpose of Life Insurance

I have spent a major part of my life in Delhi—the national capital of India. And it is not uncommon to see young 20-something teenagers riding bikes with a helmet tucked under their arms rather than placed on their heads. Why? My judgement is that it is probably some *style quotient*. But if they do not want to wear the helmet on their heads, why carry it along for the ride? Well, that may be needed to avoid being penalised by the traffic police.

The greater point here is that if you wear the helmet for style, the arms are the right place to wear it. However, if you wear it for safety, then the head is the right place for it. The helmet is the same, but everything changes once you are clear about why you are wearing it.

The same goes for life insurance. Therefore, it is important to understand why we are taking any life insurance policy.

Now, you may argue, "Obviously, we all understand the purpose of life insurance." However, my experience says that most do not. If we knew the purpose of a life insurance product, we would never go for a child plan or an insurance cover for a homemaker or even term plans in many cases.

Let me try and explain this in a little more detail.

It is common to see a security guard at the door of every bank or a jeweller's shop. What do you think is the purpose of paying a salary to the security guard? The answer is pretty straightforward. The bank and the jeweller's shop pay a monthly salary to the security guard with only one purpose—so that their assets (which could be in the form of liquid cash in the case of a bank or gold ornaments in case of a jeweller's shop) are protected.

But what is the protection against? Of course, the protection is against any unwarranted occurrences like theft or dacoity.

The bank or the jewellery shop owners feel that it is worth spending a monthly salary outgo to protect themselves against the risk of any theft. The risk impact is high since the stakes involved are high. Therefore the security guard acts as a risk-mitigation[42] strategy to deal with any eventuality arising out of the occurrence of the risk.

So, here is the first lesson in managing risks.

Whenever the risks involved are high in life, we need a risk-mitigation strategy to deal with the situation, just in case the risk becomes a reality.

There is another crucial lesson to be learnt here.

Is theft or dacoity the only risk for the bank? Are there other risks involved in running the bank operations? How about the risk of fire? Can the security guard protect the bank or the jeweller's shop against the risk of fire? Quite unlikely. The security guard mitigates only the risk of theft or robbery and no other risk. Mitigating the risk of fire requires a dedicated investment in a fire extinguishing system, training the staff on how to use that system and carrying out multiple fire drills from time to time.

How about the risk of internal theft by the bank's or the jeweller's own staff? Can the security guard or the fire extinguishing system handle this risk? Quite unlikely. A different strategy is needed to mitigate this risk, such as investing in CCTV cameras, keeping the employees motivated, etc.

So, here goes the second lesson in managing risks.

There are different kinds of possible risks on your stakes. Every risk could require a different risk-mitigation strategy.

Risks on Personal Wealth

While theft, fire and dacoity are some of the potential risks for a bank or a jewellery shop—each demanding a separate risk-mitigation strategy—the risks involved in managing your personal finance are different.

As far as your personal wealth is concerned, two key risks must be clearly understood and protected against.

1. Ability to Earn

The first risk to our personal wealth is our ability to earn money—active money, that is. This is the biggest thing of value. Nothing is bigger than this.

It is difficult to start generating passive money without first earning active money or enough of it. I am not saying that everyone who generates active money will be able to generate passive money. No, that may or may not hold true depending on the guidance, mindset and skill set of the person involved. But the flipped side is absolutely true. That is, without leveraging active money, it is tough, really tough to generate passive money.

We develop some niche skills over time. In a job or a business setup, we can convert these skills to earn money for ourselves and our families. We use this money to fund our life by incurring expenses, which keep increasing every day with inflation. Over and above these regular expenses, there are some future special events which must also be catered to through our income. This could include our children's marriage, their higher education, etc.

All these need a regular flow of money. So, we have to keep earning until we reach a tipping point, called *financial freedom*, where our passive money is enough to take care of everything.

Until that tipping point is reached, we have got to carry on earning money. To do this in a competitive world, we need to keep honing our ability to earn money. If our ability to earn money diminishes, our life can get caught in a serious financial challenge. The ability to earn, therefore, is a vital element. The loss of such ability is a massive risk to our survival, and we need to mitigate this risk.

But, as they say, risk comes from the unknown. What happens if we meet with a fatal accident or suffer a cardiac arrest? Probable? Of course, it is probable. While there is no way that our loss can be compensated to our family, there are ways we can reduce their financial suffering in such situations.

This happens to be, precisely, the purpose of life insurance—it is supposed to protect our ability to earn *active income*. If we are unable to earn for such unforeseen but possible reasons, our life insurance policy should take care of our family's financial needs for the rest of their lives.

Therefore, a life insurance policy is a risk-mitigation strategy for our ability to earn money. The risk impact is very high in case the risk actually occurs. Therefore, it becomes important for an earning family member to hold a valid life insurance policy. This is the purpose of a life insurance policy, and this purpose should always be kept in mind when you decide which policy we want and whether we need it at all.

2. Managing Accumulated Wealth

We may have protected our ability to continue earning money by taking a life insurance policy. And we may be earning well. But is that the only risk to our wealth? Of course, not.

The second important risk to our personal wealth is the risk to the already accumulated wealth, which is lying with us in the form of various investments (or a portfolio). This accumulated wealth serves many purposes. For example, it takes care of our unforeseen expenses, post-retirement life, family's health and education needs, etc. This accumulated wealth also helps us become financially free if we can hit a certain threshold and invest our wealth in the right places to get optimal returns.

There can be unplanned and unforeseen situations in our lives, which can lead to our accumulated wealth waning off—whether we are still earning active money or are financially free.

Let me share a few examples.

What if our house catches fire, and it is not protected? We may have to shell out a big kitty out of our accumulated wealth to rebuild the house. What if our house is hit by an earthquake? What if an airplane crashes into our house? What if our brand-new car is stolen? What if there is a burglary?

All the above are feasible events. The probability of their occurrence may be less, but they do occur. And they can occur in our lives as well. And since their impact is very high, they can be deep wealth stealers. They can play havoc on our accumulated wealth. These incidents, therefore, pose a risk to leading a comfortable life in future.

And therefore, they need to be protected against—each with a proper risk-mitigation strategy. The resultant risk-mitigation strategies can vary depending upon how we try to mitigate this risk.

The risk of a house fire or an earthquake can be mitigated via home insurance. The risk to your new vehicle can be mitigated by buying proper vehicle insurance. The risk while travelling can be mitigated with travel insurance, and so on. They key is to understand the risk involved, and adopt an appropriate risk-mitigation strategy.

Both our ability to earn money and our accumulated wealth need protection. Neither is more or less important than the other.

Many seekers, in my experience, feel that the accumulated wealth is far more important and needs protection than the ability to earn. Fortunately, or unfortunately, this is not the case. I say this because of two reasons.

First, to be able to accumulate wealth, you need to have the ability to earn. Only when you earn, save and invest will you have some accumulated wealth. So, your ability to earn is a prerequisite to accumulated wealth—and therefore equally important, if not more.

Second, even if you lose all your accumulated wealth, you can accumulate it again as long as your first skill, the ability to earn, is intact.

Having understood that we need to have life insurance as a risk-mitigation strategy to protect our ability to earn, and other forms of insurance (like vehicle insurance, home insurance, travel insurance, etc.) to protect our accumulated wealth against other known risks, it is also important to understand some key aspects related to insurance, and life insurance specifically.

How Long Do We Need Life Insurance? Who Needs It?

Now we know that life insurance helps us mitigate the risk to our ability to earn active money. It serves this essential purpose, just like the security guard is essential outside the jeweller's shop.

Similarly, we understood earlier that a security guard can only mitigate the risk of robbery and nothing else. Again, life insurance can only mitigate the risk to our ability to earn money and absolutely nothing else.

Knowing, understanding and appreciating this fact goes a long way in making wise decisions related to life insurance. To enable you to make the right decisions, let me help you get started with some very straightforward questions.

- Do we need life insurance after we retire from a job at the age of 60?
- Do we need life insurance after achieving financial freedom, probably at the age of 40?
- Do our children need life insurance?
- Does our spouse need life insurance?

The key to answering all these questions is to go back to the purpose of life insurance that we just understood, that is, to mitigate the risk to our active income.

So, here are the answers to the above questions, along with my reasoning.

- Do we need life insurance after we retire from a job at the age of 60?

  No, since it is unlikely that we will have any active income. If we don't have any active income, why do we need protection against its loss?
- Do we need life insurance after achieving financial freedom, probably at the age of 40?

  No, since either we will not have any active income or our family will not be dependent on our active income.
- Do our children need life insurance?

  You should try this one. It is easy. Do they earn active income? The answer is a most likely no. If they don't earn active income, then what protection are we talking about?

- Does our spouse need life insurance?
  Yes, if the spouse is earning active income and the family is dependent on it. And no, if she is not actively earning, or even if she is earning and the family is not dependent on it.

When you know why a particular product exists, the answers are pretty straightforward, aren't they?

But none of us, and that definitely includes me, are immune to ignorance.

I got a life insurance policy from LIC for my first child when she was not even two years old. My thought process was that this policy is going to assure financial security for my daughter. Just a couple of years back, she turned 18, and the first payment of that 'money back' policy was due to me from LIC. I had been paying premiums and waiting for 18 long years—waiting for this day when I would be paid back. I was super excited. I checked the policy papers to find out the exact amount we were likely to get so that I could plan to pay her college fees accordingly. After the initial hassles of getting our bank account linked to the policy, LIC finally paid us.

LIC paid us ₹20,000 on her 18th anniversary—an amount which is approximately 1/5th of our monthly expense today. This is an amount with which we cannot even pay as token money for her college admission. The next amount due from LIC is after two years, when she turns 20. The amount remains the same. Over the next two years, the value of ₹20,000 would have degraded further.

Insurance products that have 'child' or 'children' in their name have been around since eternity. Most parents feel that these products have some unique advantages for their children over other insurance products. However, the fact remains that there is nothing distinctive about them. They are just what they are—

insurance products—sold in your child's name. Since we are usually very emotional and protective of our children, we get swayed into buying such policies without understanding whether such policies are mitigating any risk or not.

Child insurance policies are thus just a sales gimmick. Let this be your Foops moment. Let this drive you to action.

Most Do Not Need Any Life Insurance

If you are financially free, retired, not earning (child, spouse, parent), or even earning but your family is not dependent on your earnings—you absolutely do not need any life insurance cover.

You can still take one, but it serves no real purpose.

I have seen so many seekers having a life insurance cover for their family members who are not even earning. How much money they waste on such a cover over a 30-40-year period is for you to guess. Wait—there is also a compounding impact here since the holding period is quite long. And as we know by now, it will be tough for the human mind to understand compounding's power even after going through a series of examples. So, let me help you with a simple case.

Consider a simple life insurance product where you pay a premium of ₹25,000 per year for the next ten years. No more premiums are required to be paid after the tenth year. The policy runs for 30 years, and you are insured for a risk cover of ₹5 lakhs during this period. On maturity, the insurance company pays you back the ₹2.5 lakhs you paid them through annual premiums. Additionally, they pay you a near-guaranteed bonus of around ₹2.5 lakhs. Sounds fascinating? I always got lured by such policies. What about you? It just sounds too good to be true. It feels like we are getting insurance for free. Not only that, we are getting double the amount of money back. What a great deal! But this emotion only lasts until we understand that the power of compounding is being utilised as an instrument to fool us. So, let me help you.

₹2.5 lakhs invested at 7% per annum compounded over 30 years fetches you approx ₹19 lakhs. Even if you discount the ₹5 lakhs you got back from the insurance company (including the bonus), you are still at a loss of ₹14 lakhs after 30 years of locking your money. A loss of ₹14 lakhs on a base of ₹2.5 lakhs of total investment. So, you now know why an insurance agent is always running after your life. They do make a lot of money.

So, get set, plan your insurance cover based on the risk it mitigates, not because your parents also got it for you or because your insurance agent is pushing you to get one. Always remember that a life insurance policy is an extremely long-term commitment. Therefore, you need to be extra careful before you opt for one. Long-term commitments also happen to lead to a lack of liquidity in your portfolio—another wealth stealer.

Having said that, I must also warn you that even if you may not need a life insurance cover, you and each of your family member would still need to address the remaining risks to their health, home, car, etc.

What Kind of Life Insurance Do We Need, If at All?

Vineet was about to give the cash down payment for a brand-new car. He and his family were pretty excited. This would be their first-ever SUV. Rajvansh, Vineet's son, was excited to quickly take the car out of the showroom and get to McDonald's for a family outing.

The dealer was getting all the paperwork ready—one of which was the car insurance papers.

Vineet was very particular about the vehicle insurance he wanted to choose. He had thought through this much in advance. Before the dealing salesperson could take his signature on the default insurance company, Vineet insisted that he would like to choose the insurance company rather than going with the default option.

The salesman had no issues considering the big sale he was about to complete.

"Sure, tell me, sir. There are five options. We recommend the first one to all our clients since we consider this the most value for money. But if you have a specific preference, we do not mind at all."

"Yes, I do have a preference."

"Sure, sir. Tell me. We will get this changed."

"But you need to help me choose a company that helps get the maximum mileage out of my car."

The salesman was as confused as you are right now. Yes, obviously, the mileage of the car has nothing to do with insuring the car.

While Vineet's request seems absurd to us, we keep playing with the same mistake almost throughout our lives. Let this be another Foops moment for you.

The mileage of the car can depend on car engine efficiency, running conditions, quality of fuel, or the skills of the driver, but definitely not on the insurance cover—precisely the same way the returns of your portfolio can depend on your future goals, market performance, current investment and your financial and behavioural skills, but definitely not on your life insurance cover.

So, if your life insurance cover has nothing to do with the returns that your wealth generates, why do we keep looking for returns from an insurance policy? This is tantamount to looking for good mileage from your vehicle insurance.

Apart from a select few individuals I know up-close or have been mentoring one-to-one, most either do not care enough to have any life insurance policy (a big mistake) or have a policy where they seek high returns (another big mistake).

And I do not blame them even a bit. Life insurance is sold like an asset that will fetch us decent returns. Quite ironically, the returns from a life insurance policy seems like the main product and the life insurance cover itself seems like a by-product.

If you don't trust me, open up any life insurance company's brochure and start reading it. The terms will often have nothing to do with risk cover or life insurance. Instead, they use terms like returns, taxes, savings, guaranteed, bonus, etc. Ironically, no one talks about the life insurance cover, claim settlement ratio, how long the insured is covered, or anything linked to life insurance.

By the way, a lookout for returns is not the only goof up we do when buying insurance. We buy insurance to save taxes as well. Again, it is not the customer to be blamed. It's how this sells quite well.

When you google the 'best endowment plans', the top result is policybazaar.com—the largest aggregator of online policies in India. When you click on the associated link of Policy Bazaar, these are the first seven sentences you read (in this order):

- 100% guaranteed returns
- Best investment plans
- Save up to ₹46,800 in taxes under Section 80C
- Inbuilt life cover
- Tax-free returns, unlike FD
- Invest ₹5,000 per month and get 100% guaranteed returns
- You pay (X amount), you get (Y amount), which is 2.4 times the original amount

Out of the top seven sales pitches, only one (the fourth bullet from the top) relates to the purpose of life insurance. Everything else is not even remotely connected to the purpose of life insurance. And please reread the last bullet point—2.4 times the return on your investment. Who will not get lured? But what annualised returns does this 2.4 times actually translate into? We just saw an example, but who has the time to calculate that? And that's where we all get it wrong.

And look at the third bullet. All those workaholics who slogged the entire year serving their companies are now left with three days to invest and save taxes. They become easy prey to the insurance companies. It has been made so simple by technology. Go online. Buy a life insurance policy and save taxes for that year. We forget that we are committing something for 10-50 years, or maybe even more.

Term Insurance

So, if there is any policy giving you anything in return, please understand that the policy can never be an efficient life insurance policy. Therefore, you have to look for a life insurance cover, a pure cover with absolutely no returns. A security guard outside the jewellery shop can only provide you risk cover but cannot give you anything in return. If he opens his small shop in front of your shop and starts paying you a percentage of income from that shop, then understand that your risk cover is compromised and that he cannot be an efficient security guard in that case.

Such a policy that gives you only the risk cover is called a *term plan*.

Nowadays, the sales teams of most insurance companies have become even smarter. They are starting to realise that people are beginning to understand the earlier trick and are looking for term plans. So, they are rebranding their existing plans to a 'term plan with returns' or similar sounding names.

Do not get fooled with anything other than a term plan, and that too, if needed. In quite a lot of cases, life insurance is not required at all.

Foops #17: Believing That Everyone Needs Life Insurance	
Awakening	Action
• Life insurance protects us against the risk to our ability to earn, and nothing else. • For other risks, we ought to be looking for health insurance, vehicle insurance, travel insurance, etc. • Pure term cover is the only life cover that makes sense.	• Avoid any kind of child insurance plans. • Go for pure term cover and nothing else. • We do not need any life insurance cover if we are not earning active income or have no financial dependants on our active income.

BEING LURED INTO AN INVESTMENT

WHAT APPEARS TO BE, ISN'T ALWAYS THE TRUTH AND WHAT IS TRUE ISN'T ALWAYS CLEARLY VISIBLE.

– ANONYMOUS

Would you ever rent a house without knowing the rent you will have to shell out at the end of the month?

Would you ever book a flight for a vacation without knowing whether a return flight is available or not?

Would you ever start solving a mathematical problem without knowing what needs to be calculated as a part of the solution?

How about starting to play a game without understanding all the rules of the game?

Would you ever join a course without understanding the expected outcome of the course?

And how about booking a fixed deposit without understanding the expected interest rate that will be paid to you at the tenure's end?

Would you ever dive in a swimming pool if you did not know how to swim and come out of the pool?

The most likely answer to all of the above questions is a clear no. In fact, the questions themselves may sound stupid to most readers.

Why in the world would we enter anything without knowing how to exit?

But we do. Yes, we do so happily. Don't believe me? Then, this has to be one of your Foops moments. Let me share prime examples that demonstrate how we get blinded by certain factors and enter arenas whose exit is unclear.

And it is not only the investors who get blinded. This *chakravyuh* has been documented in our mythology as well.

The *chakravyuh* in Mahabharata was a military formation, so made that a person entering the *vyuh* began to anticipate that he was gradually coming out from it when actually he was being driven deeper inside while passing the layers of soldiers as he fought them. After moving in the first three rounds of the *vyuh*, it felt as if one has come out of the *vyuh* when all of a sudden, in the fourth turn, one leapt inside the formation again.

It's the same thing with investors.

To start with, why would we ever enter a long-term agreement with a life insurance provider without clearly understanding our takeaway at the time of exit or en-route?

Of all the freedom seekers that I have interacted with until today, not more than 5% are aware of the amount they will get at the maturity of a life insurance policy which they have been holding for years or even decades. To ask them to calculate the returns generated by such policies is expecting far too much.

Almost all of them have never ever gone through the policy document, even once. Forget that; a good majority do not know where their policy documents are lying in the house. Quite a few of them do not know that they have an insurance agent who is getting a commission from every premium they are paying to the insurance company.

And as if this was not enough, many sign 'some' papers, not even knowing that they are buying a life insurance product. They have been depositing money in the form of premiums all these years, assuming that they are putting their money into 'some unique' saving plan. When they are told that the asset they are holding is actually a life insurance policy, they stammer in disbelief. Believe me, this happens with many, most of whom are actually quite well educated.

Of course, misselling by the insurance company or the insurance agent is one cause for this misery, but can we really blame everything on the seller? Is it not the buyer's responsibility to understand some rudiments of the agreement they are entering into, like returns, risk cover, lock-in, safety, etc.? We are so explicitly clear about all these things when booking a one-year fixed deposit but so hopelessly casual when entering a 40-year contract with an insurance company. This is just inexplicable. We cannot blame a swimming pool or the swimming instructor because we dove into the pool without knowing how to swim.

If we feel that the insurance agent has falsely sold the policy to us, then this may not be an entirely true statement. Let me share another example that should clear some more air around this misconception.

National Pension Scheme (NPS)[35], the biggest and only public pension scheme in India, attracts millions of subscribers every year. The most recent data from the Pension Fund Regulatory and Development Authority (PFRDA) shows us that there were 3.83 crores (38.3 million) NPS Subscribers as of the end of October 2020. Not only that, NPS added 7 million subscribers in the last year—no mean achievement.

All this looks hunky-dory and gives a feeling that it is a 'go-to' product. But you might be surprised to know that a majority of the subscribers, who enter this product with many expectations, do not even know what will happen at the time of exiting this account. Again, the same mistake—people enter a long-term agreement without understanding the consequences at the time of exit.

At the time of writing this book, there are big consequences at the time of exiting an NPS account. Things can change in the future, new laws can be passed in the coming years, but you should definitely be aware of what's going to happen to your money upon exit. First, you cannot access more than 60% of your corpus at the time of exit—whatever be the emergency in your life. This essentially means that 40% of your corpus will always be illiquid—not at all a healthy sign for a portfolio. We talked about the importance of liquidity and suppleness in our portfolio in one of the earlier Foops moments. And trust me, 40% is not a small amount. To put it in the right perspective, it's close to half of your NPS corpus. Note that its not 40% of what you invested. It's 40% of your corpus at the time of exit. That's big, really big—especially if you were banking on NPS to meet your future expenses.

Worse is to understand what happens to your illiquid 40% money. Does it continue to get interest like EPF? The answer is no. Your money is automatically moved to a government-backed annuity scheme—the returns of which are likely to be much worse than fixed deposits. And to top it all, the returns that you finally get from this "forced annuity package" are all 100% taxable. If you compare all this with EPF, NPS would stand nowhere and would be defeated hands down. Logical, right?

But the logic stops right here, as NPS continues to add millions of new subscribers every year. Why?

Just like in the case of buying a life insurance policy, the investors have been blinded into buying an NPS subscription. But blinded by what?

What Blinds Us?

There was a pretty popular advertisement once run by Maruti Suzuki for its cars. The commercial showed the salesman selling a ship to a prospective owner and talking about the ship's features. After listening to all the jazzy features, the prospective buyer asks, "Kitna deti hai?" which essentially meant, "What is the fuel economy of this ship?"

The buyer was focused on a popular talking point when buying cars—the fuel economy of a car, however irrelevant it may be from the perspective of the vehicle he was buying. Maruti Suzuki went on to publicise that they manufacture some of the most fuel-efficient cars in India.

For an economy car, it may make perfect sense to talk about fuel economy as a deal maker or breaker. But if we are buying a ship, the point is meaningless.

The same thing happens when investors try to get into investment vehicles like a life insurance policy or National Pension Scheme. Just like fuel economy, here it is the tax saving that pulls the investor towards greed. Without looking at the consequences of locking their money for decades and a very poor exit, the investor only looks at the tax benefit in that particular year.

We often get so *blinded by tax-saving* that we fail to understand what we are doing with our money. An insurance policy will block our money for 10, 20 or even 30 years and deliver us a meagre 5-6% annualised returns in the end, at best—albeit via a string of fancy and lucrative terms like guaranteed bonus, return of principal and what not. These names sound like the insurance provider gives us something over and above what they are expected to give.

Even if the returns of our insurance policy are tax-free, such returns are shabby, to say the least, because you have to lock in your money for many decades.

Any subscriber of NPS can claim tax benefit under Section 80CCD (1) within the overall ceiling of ₹1.5 lakhs under Section 80CCE. NPS adds to the same bucket of ₹1.5 lakhs, just like other tax-saving instruments like life insurance, EPF, PPF, tuition fees for your children, etc. However, where it attracts entry is somewhere else—an additional deduction for investment up to ₹50,000 in NPS (Tier I account) is available exclusively to NPS subscribers under subsection 80CCD (1B). This is over and above the deduction of ₹1.5 lakhs available under section 80C of the Income Tax Act.

This additional investment of ₹50,000 can be made tax-free if you are investing in an NPS Tier 1 account. This is what lures the salaried class to it. But look at this from the right perspective. To save taxes on ₹50,000 for one year—which would turn out to be anywhere between ₹5,000 to ₹15,000 annually (depending on the tax slab), we lock in lakhs of rupees in a futile annuity plan with 100% taxable payments. The tax that we saved initially is all lost later at the time of exit, notwithstanding the huge lock-in and meagre returns.

In the lure of saving taxes, we tend to enter investments without looking at how we will exit them after decades of investing. Tax saving should never be the intent of any investment. Returns, liquidity and safety are the biggest pillars of any investment. Tax saving is a byproduct or an add-on to help you distinguish between two equally good or equally bad investments.

If you have been investing to save taxes, then wake up and realise your Foops moment.

Foops #18: Being Lured into an Investment	
Awakening	Action
• Do not look for short-term benefits when entering into a long-term commitment in any asset. • Investors often get blinded by the lure of tax saving and they end up committing too much money that is blocked for a very long duration in investments with meagre returns.	• If you are planning to take an insurance policy or an NPS to save taxes, then please avoid. • Tax saving should never be the criteria to invest and block your hard earned money. • Talk to your financial advisor on your need for NPS and life insurance before committing.

INVESTING IN INDEX FUNDS

> **I AM MUCH MORE INCLINED TO BUY A STOCK THAT HAS BEEN KICKED OUT OF AN INDEX BECAUSE THEN IT MAY HAVE VALUE CHARACTERISTICS.**
>
> – SETH KLARMAN

If you have come this far in the book, I am sure that by now you have a fair idea of the 'buy low, sell high' strategy of equity investing. I am confident that you will be able to easily answer the question that appears after the scenario that I am just going to describe.

I have a stock that is worth buying at ₹100 today. So I go ahead and buy it. This stock happens to be a part of an index, say Nifty 50. This stock will stay in this index as long as it continues to be in the top league. Else it will be replaced with a similar one that beats it. So the selected stock continues to rise and reaches, let us say, ₹200 over the next 12 months. Of course, needless to say, this stock deservingly stays in the top league of the Nifty 50 index.

But now, it seems overpriced and too hot to stay at this level for a very long time. It may fall any day. The stock price has been driven this high by public perception, which does not match the company's actual earnings performance.

What would any rational investor do?

- Option A: Sell this stock since it is overpriced, make some neat profit and invest the proceeds in another similar stock that is currently underpriced.

  OR

- Option B: Buy more of this stock at an already high price of ₹200.

What would you do?

If you chose option A, then you are in the league of rational investors who understand the basic wealth management principles.

But here is your Foops moment. The index fund[22] will, however, choose only and only option B. And there is absolutely no choice or two ways about it. It has to choose option B by design. Now, get ready for an even bigger Foops moment.

Not only will the index fund[22] continue to invest in an overpriced stock as per option B, but it will also increase the weight of its investment in the stock since this stock is performing exceptionally well, and there is no active manager to make any intervention. If the index fund was earlier investing 20% of its allotted money in this stock, it would now invest 30% or even more of the total allotted money in this stock. Yes, let that sink in. Index Funds are designed against the rudiments of investing.

With this background, let's dig deeper into index funds.

Today, as I write this topic, markets are at an all-time high post-Covid-19 lockdown. Index funds have been posting decent returns. And they deserve all the applause. They also happen to get a lot of media attention. There are at least 130 books on index funds—way too many for a fund as passive as this.

But before we get to the positives or negatives, we must understand what an index fund is and then handle the perceptions surrounding it. And even before we learn about index funds, let us understand what an index is.

What Is an Index

With thousands of companies listed on a stock exchange, it is hard to track every single stock, and therefore, evaluate the market performance at any given point in time. So, then, how do you judge the performance of a market?

Here is the solution.

A smaller sample is chosen from these thousands of stocks, which represents the entire market. It is just like what you do in surveys. You survey a well-distributed sample and then extend the findings to the whole population base or community.

Along similar lines, the sample of stocks is chosen so that it is a close representation of the entire market. This small, carefully picked sample, is called an index, and it helps measure the value of a section of the stock market. The index is computed from the prices of selected stocks.

For example, Sensex, also called BSE 30, is the market index comprising 30 well-established and financially sound companies listed on the Bombay Stock Exchange (BSE). And Nifty, also called Nifty 50, is the market index that consists of 50 well-established and financially sound companies listed on the National Stock Exchange of India (NSE).

What Are Index Funds

As the name suggests, index funds are the funds or the schemes that invest in a particular index. These funds purchase all the stocks in the same proportion as the index it is benchmarked to. This means the scheme will perform in tandem with the index it is tracking. For example, if an index fund is benchmarked to Nifty 50, it will buy all the 50 stocks in the Nifty index in exactly the same proportion as the Nifty 50 index.

Let's take an example.

SBI Nifty Index Fund is an index fund (where SBI is the fund house) and tracks the Nifty index. On a similar line, you have the UTI Nifty Index Fund, or ICICI Prudential Nifty Index Fund, and many others.

Big institutions such as the Employees Provident Fund Organisation (EPFO) also invest a defined sum in the market via index funds.

It is, therefore, not tough to understand that Index funds are process-driven rather than person-driven. And the reason is obvious. These funds invest in an index, and the manager doesn't have to really choose the stocks to invest in. Instead, up or down, their performance just follows the performance of the index. This is termed as 'tracking the index'. The index funds are, therefore, also known as passive funds.

What Are Actively Managed Funds

Actively managed or active funds, sometimes simply referred to as mutual funds, are just the reverse of passive funds.

In an active fund, the fund managers choose the bouquet of stocks to invest, based on that fund's goal, performance or liquidity. Here, the manager tries to beat the market by choosing better-performing stocks or using volatile opportunities in the market—irrespective of whether these stocks are a part of any index or not. Since these funds have more freedom and flexibility on investments, they are expected to outperform the passively managed index funds.

Nevertheless, the problem with active funds is that the return on these funds depends on the goal and efficiency of a specific person (the fund manager). Moreover, even if you can find a good fund with a sharp manager, there is still some uncertainty if the fund manager quits and moves to another company.

In most cases, you would not even know about any such movement. Tracking a good fund manager along with the fund becomes a headache for many investors.

There are hundreds and thousands of actively managed funds to choose from. Some of the examples are ICICI Prudential Value Discovery Fund, Nippon Small Cap Fund, etc.

Well, if an actively managed fund can outperform the index fund, then why would anyone invest in an index fund? And why is there even a comparison being drawn between index funds and actively managed funds?

To understand that, one must first understand the origin of index funds.

History of Index Investing

In the 1950s, American investor John C. Bogle conducted a study for his undergraduate thesis. He found that most mutual funds in the US failed to beat their benchmark index. Moreover, the funds that did beat the benchmarks couldn't pass on the benefits to the investors as the fund-running charges (covered in various expense ratios) were higher than the margin of outperformance. Therefore, Bogle concluded that retail investors were better off investing directly in the index.

In 1976, Bogle launched the first passively managed fund, also known as an index fund, based on the S&P 500. The fund was called Vanguard 500 Index fund. This index constituted the 500 largest companies in the US market. Because it was passively managed, Bogle charged a meagre fee. Later, Bogle launched more funds, but the Vanguard 500 Index fund remains the most popular fund to date in the history of index funds.

From there on, index investing became popular in most countries. And for some, it happened to be the preferred vehicle of investment.

Why Index Funds Are Preferred

The media noise and hundreds of books on index funds primarily point to the following two advantages of getting into index funds:

1) Low Total Expense Ratio (TER)

These funds incur significantly lower expenses than actively managed funds. For example, UTI Nifty Index Fund has an expense ratio of 0.20%. In contrast, actively managed funds may charge around 1% on direct plans and about 2% on regular plans.

Can lower index fund charges cause a significant difference in your portfolio returns? Of course. We saw in Foops #6 that it is humanly impossible to comprehend the power of compounding, especially if done for a long tenure, like 20 or 30 years.

So, this is definitely a plus with the index funds compared to actively managed funds, but whether this positive makes the index funds worthy contenders over actively managed funds? That is something we will deal with very soon.

2) No Dependence on a Fund Manager

In the index funds, the stocks are not picked by the fund managers. Instead, these funds are merely copying or—as we say technically—tracking the index. That's why even if the fund manager of an index fund quits, it won't create any havoc (unlike in actively managed funds). In fact, there is no fund manager in index funds in the true sense, other than managing operational work related to managing the financials.

The absence of a fund manager, the associated tools, analytics, reports and the team in index funds leads to lower charges. This leads to better returns for the investor, which is already covered in the first point.

Index Fund's Positives Turn Out to Be Its Biggest Handicap

The absence of a fund manager can both be a positive or a negative, depending on how skilled or unskilled the fund manager is, respectively.

The fund's movement in index funds is directly related to the movement of the index it is tracking, which is directly related to the market. The market itself is directly related to the sentiments of the people involved in buying the underlying securities.

So, effectively, an index fund is driven by the collective perception of all investors of the underlying securities across the globe.

At least to me, all this does not exude much confidence in the performance of the fund. Unfortunately, everything is left so much to perception, luck, and sentiments. As an investor, I would be actually worried if the public, in general, would decide the future of my investments. So, I see this passive tracking more as a negative than a positive.

You have to insulate yourself from the noise around the index funds and make your own judgment. If you sit down with an open mind and try to judge this for yourself, it will most likely turn into another Foops moment for you. For now, let me further trigger your brain cells and get them thinking.

Are Index Funds an 'Investment' at All?

Effectively, the only benefit of an index fund over an actively managed fund is the lower charge. However, before we see the worth of this delta, let us come to a very fundamental question.

Are index funds an investment at all?

Now, please do not get shocked by the question. Get set for your Foops moment. You have to have the patience of an investor and read through. This is the same scared look that crosses many people when I ask them whether insurance is an investment at all. Let us read through.

Now that we understand what index funds are and that the flow of money invested by index funds is not controlled by anyone other than the public, I would rather say that they are a measure of the public feeling rather than an informed investment. You do not need any skill to measure public perception about a particular index and, therefore, about the index fund. All you need is a process or a tool. The money you have invested in index funds, strangely enough, actually gets invested into a *measuring device* rather than an *investing device.* In other words, index funds are actually a measuring tool rather than an investing tool—just like a thermometer in your home.

When you are sick, your body temperature rises. A thermometer is a handy device in such a case. It can track your body temperature, measure it and display it. But it cannot do anything to proactively control the temperature. You have to take some other parallel action to control the body temperature—be it via medicines or any other therapy.

If your body continues to be sick or becomes even sicker, the thermometer cannot do anything. It will just keep tracking your temperature—high or low. What you want at this stage is not a thermometer, but a doctor, who can look at the temperature, look at various other symptoms you are exhibiting, apply his skill and experience and then take some action on your behalf. You can, of course, decide to stay passive and not go to the doctor and take a chance with your health. Of course, not going to the doctor is a cheaper option, but is this option is really worth the money saved? To me, it would absolutely not be worth the money saved in most cases. Of course, you must make sure that you go to the right doctor with the right experience and skills. Researching for the right doctor may take some time, but it is definitely worth it.

Index funds are nothing but a thermometer of the market. They are tracking an index, which is not proactively controlled by anyone, but the public. Index funds are not investing devices; they are measuring devices.

On the other hand, the fund manager of an actively managed fund is your doctor. He can look at the situation, apply his skills and experience and then proactively switch your investments where the valuation is more worthy. Yes, he is going to charge his fees, just like a medical doctor. But you have to decide whether it is worth it or not. To me, it is always going to be worth it if you do a bit of research and pick a good mutual fund with a good fund manager, just like you make the effort in shortlisting a good specialised doctor

Concentration Risk of Index Funds

Nifty 50 is considered a diversified index with 50 stocks spanning all major sectors and industries. Theoretically, everything sounds so good. You get diversification. You get the best of the blue chips from across the spectrum. You get low costs.

But theory is what it is—just theory. Reality, on the other hand, can trigger your Foops moment. As they say, the devil is in the details.

Here are some details to ponder about the reality of Nifty 50 index fund

- The top three stocks of the Nifty 50 index have 32-33% weight, while the top five accounts for 44-45%. So much for stock diversification, but half of the 50-company index is occupied by just five companies rather than the theoretically expected 25 companies. It's not diversification. Rather, it is concentration.
- The combined weights of few sectors such as financial services, oil and gas, information technology and consumer goods are more than three-quarters of the Nifty 50. Yes, 75% of the index is spread across three to four sectors, and that's about it. So much for the sector diversification. This is nothing but sector concentration—just the reverse of sector diversification.
- SEBI has guidelines for actively managed mutual funds that restrict them from owning more than 10% in a single stock. So, unlike index (or index funds), there are some rules to protect common investors from the concentration risk of over-exposure to a few stocks, groups or sectors in the indices. Nothing of this sort can exist in index funds by design.

The above points clearly point to the often-ignored concentration risk for these indices. And since index funds (or ETFs) mimic these indices, the concentration risk is also replicated in index fund portfolios.

And it does not take rocket science to conclude that this isn't correct from a risk management perspective. On the other hand, active funds have a much lower concentration risk. Their managers can take discretionary calls to reduce exposure to stocks/sectors when they become too large from an allocation perspective. This makes good fund managers (and therefore good, actively managed funds) worthy of the fees we pay.

Where Do Index Funds Find Value?

Now that you understand that index funds are not actually an investing device, can you completely ignore what John Bogle did in the US markets? No, actually not. Index funds do find value in some exceptional cases. Let us delve into those as well.

Going back to the doctor-patient example, let me share some special scenarios.

1. Naïve Investor

What if the sick person does not happen to be literate enough, and for likely kidney disease, lands up with a neurologist? Is it better for a neurologist to attend to such a patient and recommend medicines, which may do more harm than good? Or is it better for the patient to take general advice from the people around him and start his own treatment?

This is a special case where the investor is too financially illiterate to find a good fund manager and a good fund. In such cases, the investor is better off investing with an index fund where the results are driven by the public. This can happen if someone is new to investing, has no clue about investing or has no support from a financial coach.

So, index funds are a welcome addition for newbie investors who wish to get into the market with no financial support system.

That's not the only special case. There is one more.

2. Mature Markets

What if the sick patient is located in a remote area, hours or days away from a doctor? Will it make sense for the patient to travel for days to go to the right doctor, or rather take neighbourhood advice and try their own treatment? Of course, the latter solution holds much more promise.

This is a special case where the investor is in a country, system or process which is still not mature or robust enough. And it takes time for the system and processes to mature. New York Stock Exchange, which has a market cap of $25 trillion, opened in 1817 for its first-ever transaction. That was when India was not even thinking of independence from British rule, and Mahatma Gandhi was not yet born.

John Bogle launched its first index fund in 1976. This is after 159 years of process and market maturity has already gone in, starting in 1817. India got its independence in 1947, though the Bombay Stock Exchange was established much earlier under British control. National Stock Exchange was established as late as 1992. So, as of date, it is a maximum of 73 years of market maturity since independence. Compare 73 years of the Indian stock market with 159 years of US market, and you would start to understand that our markets are still not mature enough to benefit from index funds.

For example, if you just compare the size of the mutual fund industry in India with the total market capitalisation, it is insignificant. The size of the mutual fund industry is around 16% of the total market cap. As opposed to this, asset under management (AUM) for mutual funds account for over 85% of the total US market cap.

Having said that, we can obviously not have a comparison between India and the US. Things change at a faster pace nowadays. And there are many indicators that the markets in India are maturing at a rapid pace.

For example, just a few years back, SEBI has laid down a strict mandate for schemes after recategorisation. This is resulting in less disparity in the return given by most schemes within a category. Earlier, we used to compare oranges to apples. For example, 80% of assets of all the large-cap schemes will now be chasing the top 100 companies. There is obviously not much room for experiment. When the fund house's universe is strictly defined, they will more or less be betting on the index. Still, the fund manager can pick better stocks and beat the benchmark, but the quantum of outperformance is likely to be lesser than what it used to be. But this restriction of the universe is primarily constrained for large-cap funds. Big money is, however, made in the mid- and small-cap segments. And there is still enough room to experiment here.

Another move by SEBI was to make the outperformance of schemes more transparent by introducing the total return index (TRI). The regulators believed that the performance claimed by the mutual fund schemes (actively managed ones) was not fair because the returns shown by the schemes had dividends from their stock-holdings. In contrast, the benchmarks were based only on price. This bought the percentage of outperformance down by 1.5% annually.

Such moves by the regulating authorities are a step towards market maturity. They have created an environment where a shift towards index funds looks inevitable in India in the long run. And that is why you see index funds beat the poorly managed active funds—at least in mature categories like large-cap funds, though they still cannot beat well-managed active funds in any category yet.

However, it is difficult to predict when index funds would become a default choice. It will definitely take some more time—probably 20 years, as I see it. We, as a market, are still not mature enough to welcome index fund investing all out.

The Data Is in favour of Actively Managed Funds

We understood that our markets are not yet mature enough for large-scale index fund investing. Therefore, my view is that it still makes a lot of sense to stay with the actively managed funds, at least for the next 10-20 years, in a country like India.

I will now show some data points to support my point.

1) Actively Managed Funds Do Better

Look at even slightly longer-term returns, and you will find actively managed funds, on average, doing better than the indices, with better-managed funds (above-average funds) doing significantly better.

On a three-year rolling return basis, apart from the large-cap category, all other categories beat their indices over 70% of the time in the last eight years.

The large-cap category still managed to beat its index 53% of the time. This itself should be a good enough reason to avoid index funds.

2) Margins of Outperformance Are Pretty Big

The average margin of outperformance by actively managed funds may be getting smaller for the large-cap category but is much more for multi-cap and ELSS funds and much bigger for mid-cap and small-cap funds.

Multi-cap and small-cap funds have almost always beaten their indices on a five-year rolling return basis over the last six years.

ELSS and mid-cap funds have managed to beat the indices around 90% of the time—and these facts are nothing short of massive.

3) Long-Term Outperformance Is Unbeatable

Investing in any of the ten largest actively managed equity funds in India would have given you 1.5 times the return of the Nifty index over the last five or ten years. The longer the term, the more significant the outperformance.

Why So Much Noise Around Index Investing?

Having just talked about the data, you might be wondering why there is so much talk about index fund investing nowadays. And that is where you will find your Foops moment.

There are three reasons you will continue to hear about index investing:

1) Indian equity space is expanding like never before. There are too many new investors entering the market. And a naïve investor, as we just understood, has the best chance of making money via index funds. Index funds will make more money than poorly managed active funds. For a naïve investor working without guidance from any financial advisor, index funds are a wonderful starting point.
2) There are enough people with a bias towards index funds, and they tend to look at short-term returns for periods less than three years. Unfortunately, short-term performances are always unreliable in the long term.
3) The new kid on the block is always the talk of the town—be it in index investing or cryptocurrency. Instead of understanding the issue at hand, we have a tendency to get our hands on something new, which we feel is going to solve

all our problems. This is like getting into a new stock or a mutual fund since your existing ones are not doing that well.

We are approaching a hybrid market where the differences will get blurred. It is crucial that you get the basics right. Know how much equity percentage you need—and what should be the split of large-cap, mid-cap and small-cap that suits your needs. These proportions are continuously changing in an evolving market like India. Once you know how much of which category you are looking for, take the help of your financial advisor to pick the best actively managed funds from those categories. You will always beat the index funds in the long run.

Foops #19: Investing in Index Funds	
Awakening	Action
• Index funds are a measuring device, not an investing device. • In the long run, good actively managed funds will always beat their index fund counterparts. • Index funds may be suitable only for naïve investors, or in a highly mature market.	• If you already have index funds, stop investing more in them. • Consult your financial advisor to create a strategy for you to define your allocation to large-, mid- and small-cap segment. • Go for good performers in actively managed funds for each category. Avoid index funds, atleast for the next two decades.

FOOPS 20

THINKING THAT AN INVESTING STRATEGY IS OPTIONAL

WITHOUT A STRATEGY, INVESTING IS LIKE DRIVING A CAR WITHOUT KNOWING THE DESTINATION, TIMELINE OR ROUTE.

– MANOJ ARORA

In many of our earlier Foops moments, we spoke plenty about having the right investing strategy in place. Unfortunately, the word 'strategy' has been used so often that it has become immensely underrated.

But let me try and give you a fresh perspective of the need for the right strategy—suited for you and just for you. To get the right perspective, let me try to take you back in time, sometime in 2003.

2003

She started from home in her car at around 11 AM and was not expected to be back before 5 PM after seeing her sister. Her sister had just moved to a new home, and she was an obvious invitee to the house warming lunch organised at the new abode.

Unexpectedly, she was back after 60 minutes—disturbed and agitated. On enquiry, she disclosed that she lost her way after driving for about 30 minutes, and everyone she asked gave inconsistent and unsure directions. And she found it safer to return back.

2020

Before starting the car, she opened the Google Maps app on the car dashboard and started to type the address where she wanted to reach in the next 15 minutes. Even before she could type the fourth character of the address, the name of the destination apartment and the address, sector and other details popped up on the screen with a few other related options. She clicked on the one which was her intended destination.

Google Maps recommended the shortest path she should be taking and the time she is likely to take with the current traffic conditions. She clicked on 'start', and a soothing female voice started to guide her towards her destination as she listened to her favourite song on the way.

She was there, dot on time.

The lady in both the incidents above is the same. She also happens to be my spouse.

Google Maps has changed her world for sure. She has all the freedom to go anywhere, anytime—without the need to seek directions from anyone on the way. She starts in the nick of time after finding out the current traffic conditions on the mobile app.

If it were not for this app, she would have struggled with the directions, speed and it is quite likely that she would have come back unsuccessful many times.

Why am I telling you all this?

I am sharing these incidents with you because I want you to understand and appreciate that an investing strategy is as important for your financial goals as Google Maps for my spouse's driving freedom.

Investing strategy, just like Google Maps, will show you the direction at every moment, will tell you how much time you are going to take to achieve a particular goal, whether you are currently headed in the right direction, and what do you need to do to get there—one step at a time.

Of course, you must put in some work, just like the car has to be driven and the directions have to be correctly followed. But if there is someone to guide you, that is a lot of help indeed.

With no maps, you may feel that you are going at a high speed but probably in the wrong direction. You are very unsure about everything. And course correction can be extremely painful, if not done in time. The same applies to your financial journey.

Factors Influencing an Investing Strategy

If an investing strategy is that important, then you may be wondering where is yours. I can bet you with a 99% success rate that you do not have a meaningful investing strategy as of now. You are most likely running without a strategy. Let this be your Foops moment.

If you are thinking that investing in high returns assets is an investing strategy, then think again. This is like driving your car at high speed. But how high is high? Are you really driving at high speed, or is it just your notion of high? Is the speed going to be the same in every phase of your journey? What should be the speed, and in which phase? Are you going in the right direction? Can you control the car at high speed? Will this speed take you to the goals at the right time?

There are hundreds of questions that will pop up as you get deeper into it.

Most freedom seekers that I have interacted with in my lifetime did not know how much money is enough for them for this life span. When we do not know where we want to reach, any direction can be right or wrong.

Still more seekers have taken a financial portfolio service to invest money on their behalf with just one aim—high returns, as high as possible, higher than high. There is hardly any element of consideration for stability, liquidity, balance, profiling, future needs, etc., before investing. Most of us are just running after good returns. Like so many other races, this is a mad race with no upper limit, fierce competition, painful experiences for most and tragedies for many.

Are investments done just for good returns? Or does investing have other purposes also?

If you have hired the services of a financial advisor and your advisor is investing money on your behalf—just for returns—and without understanding every single financial and non-financial factor that impacts your life like your specific needs for cash flow stability, liquidity, balance, risk profiling, future needs, etc., then let me assure you that you will have to do course correction at some stage of your journey. The more the delay in your course correction, the more painful it is going to be.

I am not saying that your financial advisor is not skilled, but they usually do not have all the inputs needed to frame the right investing strategy for you.

You may find it useful to understand what inputs frame an investing strategy so that you can seek your financial advisor's suggestions accordingly.

Many factors frame up a meaningful investing strategy. I am not sure if you have ever seen an investing strategy, but let me discuss some aspects that must be considered before creating one.

1. Age

Age impacts your risk-taking capacity as well as tolerance. As your net worth changes with age, you can potentially take more risks. But the amount of risk is also constrained by your mindset towards risk, which is also impacted by age.

2. Risk Capacity

This is your financial capacity to take high risks and seek higher returns. It depends on your current net worth, age, financial dependents, planned future life events and many other factors. Your risk capacity[41] is calculated by using a series of financial questions and arriving at a score. If your risk capacity is high, you can potentially take more risks.

3. Risk Tolerance

This is your mental tolerance for big risks. Will you be able to tolerate extreme volatility? Will you be able to display patience and consistency even if the markets are doomed? Or are you a safe player? Your risk tolerance is calculated by using a series of non-financial questions and arriving at a score. If your risk tolerance is high, you can potentially take more risks.

4. Target Returns and Target Year

When you seek directions from Google Maps, the first thing it will ask you is your destination. Unless you share the destination, Google Maps won't be able to show anything. This is a big factor and somehow missed by most. How much money do you need in life? How much time do you need to get there? How much returns per annum will take you there? When do you reach your freedom? If you have not yet found the answers to these questions, then your investing strategy will always lack focus. It will always just try to seek returns instead of satisfaction. The purpose of sound investing is not to generate high returns but to help you lead a good life.

5. Liquidity

Unless you tell Google Maps that you wish to stop at a petrol pump en route to your destination, it will most likely skip the petrol pump and take you via the shortest possible route. The only problem with missing the petrol pump is that you might not reach the destination on account of a lack of fuel, rendering the entire journey worthless. Precisely the same way, your financial plan has to consider the liquidity needs that will arise on the way—be it for your children's education, world travel, children's marriages, opening up a new venture, or anything else that you may have in mind.

Now, these are the bare minimum needs to come up with a customised investing strategy for you. Any investments done without an investing strategy is like starting to drive a car without knowing which route to take and where to reach. If your investments are being made without considering these factors, then you need to realise that you may be headed nowhere and will need to rework at some point in time.

An investment strategy is not something that expert financial guys make for themselves. It is not something that you can think about later in your financial journey. It is, in fact, the starting point for the execution of your financial freedom plan. It is the foundation upon which all your dreams and goals will be erected and stay erected. You need it right now and need it badly. Stop all your investments and focus on building your investing strategy first if you do not have one. The dire need for an investing strategy was a Foops moment for me. Was it for you as well?

Foops #20: Thinking That an Investing Strategy Is Optional	
Awakening	Action
• Having a clear and customised investing strategy is a must, before you start investing your hard earned money. • Without a clear investing strategy, you will keep chasing returns, and keep losing satisfaction.	• If you don't have an investing strategy, stop investing any further until you have a clear strategy in hand. • Ask your financial advisor to help create a customised strategy for you, and then start investing as per the strategy.

FOOPS 21

BELIEVING HIGH RISK TOLERANCE IS ENOUGH TO TAKE RISKS

RISK CAPACITY AND RISK TOLERANCE ARE TWO SIDES OF THE SAME COIN.

– MANOJ ARORA

Who does not want to be the next Sachin Tendulkar? But how many are actually willing to consistently slog the way he did without any surety that they would ever make it big.

Who does not want to be the next Jeff Bezos or Elon Musk? But how many are ready to face adversity, burn the midnight oil, face rejections, keep persisting and cut through all the negativity without being impacted.

We all want results, but most of us are not ready to pay the *price* for the result. The fact is that there are no free lunches. Every big success comes after innumerable defeats, countless sacrifices, discipline, commitment, rejections and frustrations. You have to be ready to pay the price for success. At the end of the day, the price you pay for your dreams is usually far less compared to the value you get out of living those dreams.

Zig Ziglar, a renowned motivational speaker, once said,

"There is a price you pay for your dreams. But there is a bigger price you pay for not pursuing those dreams."

Even to become financially free, you have to pay a price—discipline, commitment, consistency, frugality—and those who are willing to do it will get there quite easily in the end, and then reap the value of the price they paid.

Among the critical factors determining anyone's speed towards financial freedom is their capacity and tolerance for risk-taking.

Before I explain what risk is, it might be interesting to set the context with this short story.

There are two wrestlers in the ring, playing for everything they have.

The first wrestler is physically weak compared to his opponent. He knows that. His opponent also knows that. But while he is physically weak, he is prepared to be aggressive in his moves. He wants to attack the stronger wrestler during the match.

The first wrestler's coach is a level-headed person. He tells his man not to use physical power to defeat the opponent because that is just not his forte. Instead, he should play intelligently. However, the wrestler is mentally prepared to get aggressive as soon as the match starts. He feels that physical strength will follow as long as one is mentally prepared to take the risk.

Now, if this is the only information available, let me ask you whether the first wrestler's thought process is prudent.

Different people may have varying answers, but the more rational explanation is that you need physical strength as well as mental toughness to win a game. Even if one of them is absent, like the absence of physical prowess in the case of the first wrestler, there are high chances of defeat.

The above bout resulted in the first wrestler being thoroughly defeated. Foops moment? This is no heroic or exceptional story. This is the *most likely* outcome of the story. We have been so used to hearing and reading about heroic stories in the media that we forget that heroic stories, though true, are one in a million. The majority end up with the expected results.

The first wrestler took the risk because he thought he was mentally prepared to take it, but his mental strength was not backed by physical strength. He forgot that one needs a mix of both mental and physical strength to win. We cannot choose one over the other.

And this is not only related to risk in sports. This is equally applicable to personal finance.

When we talk of risk in personal finance, we are essentially talking about two dimensions—risk capacity and risk tolerance. We have encountered these two dimensions earlier in this book.

Risk capacity is your actual ability to take a risk. This comes from your current net worth, age and other factors and is equivalent to the physical strength of the wrestler.

Risk tolerance is your mental attitude towards risk—your ability to tolerate losses. This comes from your response to volatility and is equivalent to the mental strength of the wrestler.

Just like the wrestler, if we have to win the battle of money, we need to possess a good combination of capacity and tolerance. But that is not how many seekers think, and that's precisely where the Foops moment lies.

Varun is one of our esteemed freedom seekers from Hyderabad. He wants to take big risks and is already investing 80% of his savings in equity, but has a negative net worth, a poor risk capacity and many life events earmarked in the next five years. He definitely has a high-risk tolerance but poor risk capacity—just like the first wrestler of our story.

He feels that taking a risk would result in higher rewards. Well, risk can potentially lead to higher rewards, but much before the reward, the risk explicitly means that you have a decent enough chance of making losses as well. Investors like Varun want to take high risks only knowing that it will lead to rewards. However, such investors will be unable to bear the losses since they are already running low on risk capacity. Varun is like that physically weak but mentally strong wrestler. With all the mental strength, the wrestler can take the risk and attack the opponent. But once counter-attacked, this wrestler may not have enough physical strength to hold the game. In the heroism of taking risks, the chances are high that he may bear irreparable physical harm, making him unfit for any future games.

If equity goes down for Varun for a sustained period of time, then there is no way Varun will be able to settle his liabilities (being in negative net worth), feed his family and take care of important future events of life. This is because he has not yet developed enough physical capacity, that is, risk capacity. To develop that risk capacity, he has to build up his net worth and have some emergency funds, life and health insurance before taking risks. Just because someone is mentally ready to take risks does not mean that they should go ahead and take risks.

Both risk capacity and risk tolerance should be high to be able to take risks. Of course, both the dimensions being high does not guarantee rewards in the market but enables the person to handle the situation if the market is down for an extended period.

If you are one of those daring, raring and risk-taking personalities, please avoid the temptation to start investing in high-risk instruments unless you have gauged your risk capacity. Only when the combination of risk capacity and risk tolerance is good enough should you be moving to high-risk investments.

Let this Foops moment sink in because this is becoming increasingly vital in today's world where everyone wants to get everything done quickly.

Foops #21: Believing High Risk Tolerance Is Enough to Take Risks

Awakening

- Just because you feel you are ready to take the risk or are naturally a risk-taking person doesn't qualify you to take risks in personal finance.
- Both risk capacity and risk tolerance are essential for financial risk taking.

Action

- Assess your risk capacity as well as risk tolerance levels.
- Only if you have a balance of both these dimensions, should you attempt to take risks.

FOOPS 22

SETTLING OUR HOME LOAN

THERE IS HARDLY ANYTHING 'EQUATED' ABOUT 'EQUATED MONTHLY INSTALMENTS'.

– MANOJ ARORA

One of my old-time friends from Larsen & Toubro, Mumbai, Vinod Unniyal, once mentioned that one of his mentors, a famous author on financial topics in the US, had told him to follow the first ground rule in personal finance. When I asked him about the ground rule, he mentioned that the first rule is to settle all your liabilities. Only once their liabilities are settled should one go on to build assets. Sounds logical, right? But this could just turn out to be the next Foops moment of your life.

My belief has always been to not define any rigid rules, and have a critical look at the existing rules even if they were defined by you sometime back. I also believe that different countries, regions and, more importantly, individuals have very different needs. To top it all, situations, circumstances and life generally evolve with time, and the rules must follow suit.

Therefore, having a *one-rule-fits-all* strategy rarely works in personal finance. It's 'personal' finance, after all. It's unique for each person you are building an investing strategy for. And that is one of the foremost reasons we take in a very limited number of selected seekers in our ELITE program. We ought to pay personal attention to each participant since the needs and situations of every person are very different, and that puts a constraint on the number of participants.

Each person is different, the same person is also changing with time and situations in life. The same person with a very high-risk profile at 30 may have a diagonally opposite risk profile at 50. And trust me, this is not only driven by age. This is primarily driven by experiences in life and future needs. So, there is no way that general rules can truly fit into personal finance.

To me, personal finance must be driven by common sense. If we understand tenth-standard mathematics and have fairly decent common sense, then we have all the qualifications needed to become one of the most successful wealth creators and accumulators in the world. Unfortunately, common sense is not a widespread commodity on this planet. We tend to blindly follow rules propagated by 'big' investors, undermining the fact that what works for someone else may never work for you. I am, in no way, undermining the investing stalwarts or their skills. Who am I to do that? I respect them from the bottom of my heart. But I also realise that I am different from them. My situations, life, needs and experiences are all different. These times are different. Therefore, I always encourage you to read and listen to anyone who is your hero. But please avoid following them blindly. Rather, try and judge for yourself if those rules make sense to you, your situations, your needs, your geography and your life. Adopt what makes sense and drop what does not.

One of the situations where you should never go by any rules is the liability portion of your portfolio. Irrespective of who says what, apply your own common sense and logic. Of course, emotions are also involved in personal finance, and we would also make emotional decisions in life. But the lesser the emotions and more the logic, the better it is for your wealth. Emotions create biases, and biases are never wealth enablers.

More important than *what* you do is *why* you are doing it. If you have enough money, and you or your family members are getting stressed or disturbed over your existing liabilities, then no logic is justified. In such cases, no technical financial calculations are ever going to be worthy enough. You should simply go ahead and settle your liabilities. But if you are willing to handle the liability without you or your family getting stressed about it, you may be in for a great opportunity to save a significant sum.

Assuming there are no emotional needs to settle, I will give you five strong reasons to continue with your liability, especially if it is a home loan. Yes, I don't want you to settle your home loan. Foops moment? Let it be. Understand these reasons and take your own call.

1. Most Interest Is Already Paid

Bankers always knew that after taking a loan and paying EMIs[13] for a few years, the borrower would not only realise that the loan term is too long but would also be more capable of paying back the loan—assuming career progressions, salary increases, etc.

So, the banks created the concept of equated monthly instalments (EMIs). But though the total monthly outflow from our bank is 'equated', 'equal' or 'same' every month, there is a big catch in the break-up of that 'equated' amount.

The principal and interest components in that breakup are anything but equal. So much so that your first EMI may have as much as a 95% interest component and just 5% principal, without you even noticing.

With that trick, most interest on the entire loan is paid in the first four to five years of the tenure. So, by the time the borrower reaches the potential to pre-pay the home loan, bankers are safe. In fact, the bank would welcome a pre-payment. Having gotten a majority of the interest for, say, 20 years, the bank could never have asked for anything better if we paid back the entire remaining principal after five years. For banks, this is a gold mine. Give the money on loan for 20 years, take the interest for 20 years, and get the principal back in five years.

Until just a few years back, bankers were so smart that they charged the borrowers with pre-payment charges if they ever decided to pre-pay their pending loan amount. Sounds absolutely ridiculous, but that's how it was. Instead of giving incentives, they penalised the borrowers for paying back the principal early. Anyways, today, there may be no pre-payment charges, but there are no incentives either.

To take this idea further, nowadays, even the total monthly instalment may not remain the same since they are linked to market interest rate fluctuations.

Let me give you an oversimplified example to show how it all works.

If you have taken a home loan for ₹100 from any bank and are supposed to pay ₹140 as the interest over the next 20 years, the most logical EMI distribution would be as follows:

a) Principal to be paid back every year = ₹100 / 20 = ₹5
b) Interest to be paid back every year = ₹140 / 20 = ₹7
c) Total EMI to be paid every year = ₹5 + ₹7 = ₹12

But this is not how the loan is actually amortised.

The actual EMI break-up changes every year—in fact, every month—though the borrower does not feel the impact since the total EMI remains the same.

For example, in the first year, a typical EMI goes something like this:

a) Principal to be paid back in the first year = ₹0.5

b) Interest to be paid back in the first year = ₹11.5
c) Total EMI to be paid in the first year = ₹1 + ₹11 = ₹12

And something like this in the next year:

a) Principal to be paid back in the second year = ₹1
b) Interest to be paid back in the second year = ₹11
c) Total EMI to be paid in the second year = ₹1 + ₹11 = ₹12

So, what has happened in just two years of a 20-year loan tenure? The borrower, who should have ideally paid approximately 10% of the interest (two-year interest of a 20-year loan), has paid ₹22.5—which is 16% of the total ₹140 interest. By the time you come to the end of the fifth year, the borrower would have paid almost 50% interest instead of the expected 25%. Interestingly, he would have paid back approximately only 5% of the principal amount (₹5 out of ₹100), instead of the expected 25%. Now, if the borrower decides to pre-pay the principal amount at this stage, he faces a situation where he has paid 5% principal and 50% interest. He will have to pay back 95% principal now.

So, in many cases, it actually does not make any financial sense to pay back the home loan after approximately a quarter of the original loan period has passed, simply because you have already paid too much interest to the bank. You are trapped. The simplicity of EMIs has taken you by surprise. Let this be your Foops moment and drive you to take action.

2. You Stop Getting the Tax Benefits

It's not only the extra interest that you paid to the bank already that pinches you during pre-payment of home loan. You lose many tax benefits as well.

There are multiple income tax benefits that the loan borrowers get in India. The benefits are both on the principal amount as well as on the interest paid each year.

Depending on our tax bracket, we may lose a significant benefit if we prepay our home loan.

3. You Lose the Opportunity to Earn Double the Money

If you are a reasonably well-informed investor, it is not tough to beat the home loan interest rates and earn much more money rather than paying the money back to the bank. In effect, you have the bank's money lying with you, usually at a much lower rate.

For example, in India, home loans are currently available in the range of 6-7%. On the other hand, a typical well-managed debt fund like a dynamic bond fund or a gilt fund will easily give you 9% returns in the long run. And if we can balance it with good equity-based mutual funds, we are up at 11-12% returns from that money.

So, here we are. We borrowed money from the bank, paid 6% interest on that money and earned 12% returns by investing it in the right places—making double the amount of money than the interest we are paying to the bank. You decide how you want to use the bank's money.

If you wish to precisely calculate whether it actually makes sense for you to settle the home loan early or not, you may log on to our official website and look for the 'Calculators' section under 'Wealth Management Tools'.

In general, while bank loans may sound like added pressure on you, they can create wonderful wealth creation opportunities provided you learn to manage your money with discipline and common sense.

Foops #22: Settling Our Home Loan

Awakening	Action
• There is hardly anything which is 'equated' in the equated monthly instalments (EMIs). • You pay a significant portion of your total interest in the first few years of your home loan. • It makes no financial sense to pre-pay your home loan after the initial few years.	• If you or your family are stressed about carrying a home loan liability and you have the financial capacity to pay it back, then there is no need to think twice. Just go ahead and pre-pay your home loan. • If you have paid EMIs for even a quarter of the loan tenure, then it may never be a financially wise decision to pre-pay.

FOOPS 23

INVESTING IN REAL ESTATE

EVERY TIME YOU ARE TEMPTED TO ACT IN THE SAME OLD WAY, ASK IF YOU WISH TO BE A PRISONER OF THE PAST, OR A PIONEER OF THE FUTURE.

– DEEPAK CHOPRA

Real estate is 'real' estate. So true. But every truth has an expiry date. And trust me, this truth expired at least a decade back, if not more. Get set for your next Foops moment.

We live in a virtual world today. Physical things continue to carry lesser importance as time passes. Of course, you need a home to live in. It could be rented, or it could be purchased. That more people prefer not to buy a house for their own living, but to take it on rent is an entirely different topic for discussion. But this topic does emphasise the fact that buying a house as an investment is definitely not the 'in thing'.

Let us briefly talk about the history of real estate as an investment vehicle.

In the period between the 1950s to the 1990s, real estate was the investment vehicle of choice. And that was understandable. Mutual funds and demat accounts did not exist back then. Buying stocks involved massive paperwork—just for applying and then preserving the share certificate papers. I clearly remember when I had to get the dematerialisation of physical shares of Tata Steel which my father purchased in his heyday. It was a three-month-long procedure with several follow-ups, signature mismatch issues, affidavits and everything else.

There was no internet in those times—so nothing could be done online—no net banking, mobile, SIP, online fund transfer, Paytm, nothing. Even creating a fixed deposit took many days. I remember seeing my father going and enquiring the rate of interest from multiple banks, applying for the deposit in the bank which gave the most interest, going and getting the deposit certificate. And then following the same process to redeem or renew the fixed deposit.

So, in such times, where does an investor go with all these constraints? Real estate, of course!

To a certain extent, real estate became a handy investment in the late 1990s and 2000s. Banks started giving easy loans, and the governments started to encourage home buying by giving significant tax exemptions for taking home loans. I also happened to buy one. Many in my network bought more than one house. They were the ones who were able to leverage the bank's money to capitalise on the real estate boom.

Yes, that was the time when you could leverage a bank's money and make money out of it for free.

Let me try and explain how it worked.

Take a loan of ₹50 lakhs, put some ₹10 lakhs as downpayment, and get a property worth ₹60 lakhs. Since real estate was booming at that time, expect the property to zoom by an average of 15% per year (on the most pessimistic side). On the other hand, banks will ask only 7-8% interest on the ₹50 lakhs you borrowed from them.

Therefore, you leverage the bank's ₹50 lakhs to earn 15% appreciation by paying only 8% interest. That's a neat profit of 7% of ₹50 lakhs out of thin air. The principal money of ₹50 lakhs was not even ours in the first place, but we managed to earn significant net interest out of it. Not only that, we enjoyed tax savings for paying the EMIs—on both the principal and the interest amount. If this deal was not lucrative enough, we also received rental income if we bought a ready-to-move-in apartment. In fact, in many cases, the rental more or less covered the EMI, and we started to own a home for almost nothing.

Today, 20-25 years down the line, the fact is that real estate is fast becoming an outdated asset class to invest our money in.

There may be exceptions, but let me give you eight strong reasons in support of my belief:

1) Illiquid Investment

Technology has changed everything. Liquidity is more and more vital in today's uncertain world. Unfortunately, when we get into real estate investment and need our own invested money for any life emergency, there is no way to get it back—not even a fraction of it. We need to wait for 6-12 months from the time we decide to liquidate this investment.

Such illiquid investments that cannot serve in times of need should be kept to a bare minimum, especially if we have a choice. And today, we have no dearth of options.

2) Infeasible to Invest or Withdraw Systematically

Real estate is a volatile asset class like equity. And we understood in one of the earlier Foops moments that locked volatility is a flawed strategy. In real estate, there is no option for systematic investment or withdrawal since the cost of the real estate is locked at the time of signing the agreement.

An investor is, therefore, relying too much on luck when buying or selling real estate. This is a massive risk since it is possible that the lump sum amount is being invested at a high point and being taken out at a low point of the real estate curve.

3) Tax Inefficient

Everything is relative in this world. So, while the tax structure on real estate investments has not changed significantly for many decades, new asset classes have mushroomed in the past two decades, whether online stock trading, mutual funds, etc., which pose a serious competition to real estate on tax efficiency.

For example, for short-term capital gains on real estate, you pay taxes as per your tax bracket, which can go as high as 30%. On the other hand, the short-term capital gains on equities—be it stocks or mutual funds—are just 15%, half of the real estate tax.

The long-term capital gains scenario is even worse. You have to pay a flat 20% tax on long-term capital gains (though it is with indexation of costs). On the other hand, if you act smartly and make use of techniques like investment churning, you may not have to pay any taxes at all for equity.

You end up paying too much tax on your capital gains in real estate or, in an attempt to avoid paying those taxes, end up investing your gains in some dud bonds.

4) Transaction Process Is Tedious

No one will go through the painful process of selling real estate just a few years after buying it. In most cases, the process is not worth it. Typically, our investment gets locked in for many decades before we actually redeem it. It takes many months to shortlist and buy and almost the same amount of time and effort to sell. You are always on your toes. Your heart is in your month until the deal is successfully completed and you get the original papers or the money in your bank account.

If you are thinking that this tediousness and chaos is because of the size of a real estate investment, then you have a potential bias towards real estate. Look at the competition. Whatever the size of your investment, an equivalent investment like a mutual fund can be accomplished within minutes—both at the time of buying and selling. Moreover, it can be done sitting from the comfort of your home. There is no need to go to the broker, bank or registrar's office.

Without an iota of doubt, the entire process of getting in and out of a real estate investment is chaotic and tedious.

5) Money Leakage

Too much money is lost at the time of buying and selling real estate. First, there are the typical leakages when buying real estate like 6% registration and stamp duty, 2% brokerage fees. Then, add another 2% for all the running around, paperwork, CA fees for ITR filing, money equivalent of all the effort you put in, etc. This pegs the total leakage at about 10% of the cost of our investment.

Now, 10% is a real big leak. Why do I say that? That's because the equivalent leakage that happens in any direct mutual fund investment is around 1% of your transaction. Even if you go with a regular mutual fund via your financial advisor or broker, at most, your leakage would be around 2%. If you invest in equity via ETFs, the leakage costs could be as low as 0.2%.

Now, this difference is massive—five to ten times the leakage that you would incur when you invest in real estate. When you compound this difference over a long period, you may be able to get a grip of what you are losing.

6) Illegal Money Involvement

Despite the government's efforts to curb illegal money, the fact remains that real estate transactions are still prone to the exchange of illegal money. Properties registration is still done at the minimum allowed published rate (also called *circle rate*). This is usually much lower than the actual amount of the sale.

The differential in the rate of registration and the actual sale causes illegal money to seep in—the money on which no taxes are paid and is unaccounted.

As we move towards a more digital and transparent technology-driven world, let me assure you that it will not be easy to handle this money.

On the other hand, mutual funds, e-gold or any other modern-day asset class transact in 100% legal money.

7) Running Expenses Are too High

There are a lot of hidden expenses that are usually not considered in our real estate gain calculations, be it society maintenance, house maintenance, missed rental months, property tax, home insurance, etc.

So, despite the rentals, the true yield from real estate will rarely be able to beat inflation.

8) Unregulated Industry

I know a few of my IBM friends who had booked an under-construction property with the hope of getting possession in two to three years. Even after seven years, they lived in a rented home that they should have vacated long back and were also paying the EMIs—a double whammy. The builders have expressed their inability to continue, citing fund shortage, and raised their hands in the court. The cases are still under trial, and only God knows when justice will be done.

Such cases are not one-off. Go and ask your friend circle, and you are most likely going to find a few such cases for sure.

The reason for such cases coming to light is that the real estate industry, despite all the hue and cry, is still largely unregulated. This is quite unlike the mutual fund or stock investments which are regulated and monitored strictly by SEBI (Securities and Exchange Board of India). SEBI regularly places checks and balances to ensure that the investors' interests are protected and they are never taken for a ride.

So, whether you like it or not, real estate is an old-fashioned, outdated and inefficient asset class. If this is your Foops moment, then it is better to set our perspectives right and take massive action to get rid of your real estate at an appropriate time. Break all shackles to get into new and more reliable investments. And trust me, there are plenty nowadays.

Foops #23: Investing in Real estate	
Awakening	Action
• Real estate was the 'real' investment just one generation ago. • Then came the era of internet, online investing and redemptions that changed everything. • This was a technological disruption. • Today, real estate is an outdated asset class compared to the new possibilities.	• Unless your real estate is giving exceptional returns of the tune of 15%-plus per annum, get rid of them as soon as you can. • You have more efficient investment options that can work silently and offer amazing results.

ASSUMING THAT VOLATILITY IS BAD

> **THE PARADOX OF SIMPLICITY IS THAT MAKING THINGS SIMPLE IS REAL HARD WORK.**
>
> – BILL JENSEN

"But this is for your long-term good," I was arguing with my daughter.

"It hurts, it pains. How can it be good for me, Dad? I am not going to go for it," remarked the younger fairy, Harshita.

Sitting at the doctor's clinic, Harshita and I were arguing over the usefulness of her vaccination shot. This was, of course, when she was quite young. No child likes to be vaccinated, and for a good reason. It is painful to be injected with a needle. But then, in the case of vaccinations, all of us understand that it is for the child's long-term good.

Here is my point.

Things that look dangerous, risky or hurtful today may actually be designed to deliver benefits in the long term.

The reverse is also true.

Things that look good to us today may actually be harmful in the long term. Whether we are aware of it or not is a separate issue.

Harshita and I continued our discussion.

"I know it hurts, baby. But this Hepatitis B vaccine is going to prevent you from various viral attacks in future."

"I mean, how can that be? How will today's vaccine do that after 20 years?"

"Well, that's because, with the vaccine, an inactive version of the Hepatitis B virus is injected into your body. These viruses stimulate our immune system to create antibodies against the virus over time. So, as our body creates antibodies to a specific virus, we become immune to that virus in future."

"What are you saying?" she was shocked. "We are injected with the disease! Really?"

"Yeah, that's true. That's a paradox."

"Paradox. What's that?"

"The virus that can hurt you is the one that saves you. This is the dual nature of life."

"Oh, interesting."

"And vaccination is not the only area where life shows duality. The oxygen that you breathe gives you life and is also responsible for the deterioration of your health in the long run."

"What? Is oxygen a killer? What are you saying, Dad?"

"Yes, the oxygen that you breathe gives you life, and the same oxygen oxidises your body parts, leading to ageing. You cannot survive without oxygen, but ultimately, oxygen itself will age you and cause you to die. That's the dual nature of life."

As we continued this discussion on the way back home after the vaccination, I wondered if this duality of life exists in the personal finance space as well. I realised it does.

Volatility

Volatility in the market is an apt example of a personal finance paradox.

Many financial analysts consider volatility a bad thing. Several investors fear volatility. There is so much fear that there are matrices that track a particular product's volatility. The ones with higher volatility are tagged as 'bad' or 'not so good' products.

Volatility is the primary reason that people shy away from equity markets or even commodities.

The entire system is built in such a way that volatility is considered bad. Let me start with a very common metric to measure the suitability of a mutual fund for investors.

Beta

Let's take an example of one of the indicators of risk while investing in mutual funds, that is, Beta. Let me explain Beta with an example,

Rohan scored 45 marks, and Vinay scored 80. Both scores were out of the benchmark score of 100. Though Vinay's performance is undoubtedly better than Rohan's in this particular case, can we really conclude that this outstanding performance makes Vinay a better performer in the long run?

What if this was a one-time fluke by Vinay? What if Vinay's scores have been utterly unpredictable—that he has scored less than Rohan many times.

So, consistency or stability (or, for that matter, volatility) is a vital factor that the market wants you to account for. Beta registers and quantifies a fund's response to market volatility, that is, the degree of conformity of a fund's prices in response to any change in the benchmark index.

The baseline for Beta in mutual funds is one. The value one suggests that a specific fund responds to market volatility equivalently. That the shift in its price is equivalent to the benchmark movements.

A beta value of more than one for a specific fund indicates that the fund demonstrates a more significant price shift than the benchmark's movement. This indicates more volatility.

A value below one represents the opposite, that is, more stability.

In general, a high Beta score means high volatility and high risk. The higher the risk, the less the probability that an investor would be attracted to it.

That's the irony with volatility. It is considered to be something that brings risk to an investment. Not that it does not, but the problem is that our understanding of volatility stops there. It's like limiting our knowledge to the fact that the hepatitis virus kills us. We ignore that the same virus, when inactivated and injected into our body, also saves us. It's like stopping at the fact that oxygen is a killer and ignoring the paradox that oxygen is also a life-giver.

And this one-sided view of volatility (that it adds risk) creates a perception that keeps the investors at bay from the market.

What is the other side? Yes, we are going to talk about it, because that is precisely where your Foops moment lies.

If you re-think this perception around volatility, this might just turn out to be one of your biggest Foops moment.

IIFL Securities recently published a study that sets the context for what we are discussing.

One of the study's findings states that only 1.5% of the Indian population invests in equity markets. Compare it with that of the US, where this statistic is over 50%. It's not that Indians do not invest; they just don't invest in equity. They invest in deposits, PPF, post office schemes and even insurance policies—but not in equity.

This is even though equity has outperformed all other asset classes in the last 40 years, with the BSE Sensex giving a compounded annual growth rate of 13.71%, much higher than gold, silver, public provident fund (PPF) and fixed deposits (FD). Equity has given more than double the returns compare to assets like FDs over the last 40-plus years.

So, why do investors still keep away from equity? No marks for guessing this.

The one big factor that keeps the investor away from equity is the perception of volatility in the equity market. Annualised growth of 13.71% over 40 years has not been 13.71% growth every year. It may have been 30% growth in some years and a 20% decline in others as well. That's precisely where the challenge starts for a common investor who has been so used to growth from a debt-based asset.

Volatility is considered tantamount to risk, fear, loss and panic. Most investors cannot bear the sight of erosion in their invested amount. It feels like they have been cheated.

The facts are, however, diagonally opposite. So, let me phrase your Foops moment here.

Volatility is a trait that allows for stellar returns from the market.

Yes, volatility, a seemingly disturbing characteristic of the market, is paradoxical in nature—just like oxygen and vaccines. Volatility is the big reason you would earn double the returns from the equity market compared to any other asset class. If it was not for volatility, the returns from the market would have been muted, at best.

Don't believe me? You need not because that is how Foops moments are—unbelievable in the beginning and awesome in the end.

As they say, knowledge removes fear. So, let me help you with a simple example that should help us understand the positive side of volatility to a good extent.

Let us consider two different investments: investment A, which gives 10% per annum linear returns with zero volatility, and investment B, which offers 10% average returns but is volatile.

In the end, both are expected to offer 10% annualised returns. So, which investment would you choose if you were to invest your hard-earned money? Most of you would choose investment A. That's natural because, even though it offers no additional returns than investment B, it is, at least, stable. And this stability creates the false impression of 'goodness' about such an investment.

We forget that volatility is paradoxical and can potentially allow you to push the returns from investment B to go way beyond 10%. Yes, the average return will stay 10% in both cases if we invest and forget the two investments.

But if we are smart, if we can handle our emotions, if we understand the nature of volatility, if we look at volatility as a good trait rather than a bad one, if we can insulate ourselves from the noise all around us and if we can be patient, then we can get ourselves returns way beyond 10% from investment B. In that case, my vote is all for investment B, and I am all for volatility.

Even if you invest every month or every day in a linear investment like investment A, you will still get 10% returns at the end of the year.

However, in a volatile investment like investment B, there would be phases of crests and troughs. If you invest during a dip, your average purchase cost will decrease, and your year-end returns would be far higher than 10%.

No one talks about this is the side of volatility. This volatility makes equity a star performer. This volatility will help you get inflation-beating returns. Yes, volatility involves non-linear growth, but that is its nature—just like oxygen oxidises and ultimately kills.

Of course, volatility will test your conviction, and not everyone can withstand it. But those who can will emerge wealthy.

All those who cannot exhibit the resilience, patience and adaptability to withstand volatility need not be disappointed. There is a way to take advantage of the volatile nature of the market—a way that actually thrives on volatility and can definitely be called anti-fragile.

Anti-Fragile

In his book by the same name, one of the foremost philosophers of our time, Nassim Nicholas Taleb, talks about the concept, 'anti-fragile'. Anti-fragile is one step beyond robust, as it benefits from adversity, uncertainty and stressors, just as our muscles get stronger when subjected to physical stress and pressure.

Taleb turns uncertainty on its head, making it desirable, and proposing that things be built in an anti-fragile manner. Anti-fragile points out the value of systems that gain from disorder, chaos or volatility.

And here we are—staring at volatility—and thinking how could we develop a system in personal finance that could not only prevent us from volatility but goes a step ahead and takes advantage of this volatility.

And finally, this system was developed. It exists today, and you probably also use it. Yes, you do. It is called a systematic investment plan (SIP). SIPs do not only protect you from volatility by averaging your buying costs but takes it one step further. The higher the volatility, the higher the returns from the SIP. SIPs actually gain from volatility and are an exemplary anti-fragile mechanism to handle volatility.

Don't believe me? See for yourself

Let us say that you start with a SIP of ₹100 for 12 months. The below figure shows three different cases—one, two, and three. In each case, the SIP amount remains the same.

The only way these three cases differ is in their extent of volatility. Case one is an investment with low volatility. Case two has medium volatility and case three has high volatility.

You can see the difference in volatility by the NAV variation in the three cases. Note that in all the three cases, the NAV starts at 100 and ends at 110 after 12 months. It's just that the volatility between months 1 and 12 varies depending on the case. Case one's NAV varies from the extremes of 90 and 110—the least variation of all the three cases. On the other hand, case three's NAV varies from 58 to 134, while case two lies somewhere in between these two extremes.

So, over 12 months, if you invested ₹100 in month one and forgot about your investment, all three investments would end up with ₹110 after month 12, thus giving you 10% returns. But then, we are not using the invest and forget philosophy here. We are going to use SIP as an anti-fragile strategy to handle and benefit from volatility. So, let's look at the returns in all three cases if we continue the SIP of ₹100 for 12 months.

SIP Amount 100

Month	Case 1 Low Volatility		Case 2 Medium Volatility		Case 3 High Volatility	
	NAV	Units via SIP	NAV	Units via SIP	NAV	Units via SIP
1	**100**	**1.00**	**100**	**1.00**	**100**	**1.00**
2	104	0.96	109	0.92	115	0.87
3	103	0.97	107	0.93	112	0.89
4	100	1.00	100	1.00	100	1.00
5	97	1.03	90	1.11	83	1.20
6	95	1.05	86	1.16	76	1.32
7	90	1.11	76	1.32	58	1.72
8	94	1.06	83	1.20	71	1.41
9	98	1.02	95	1.05	85	1.18
10	103	0.97	110	0.91	120	0.83
11	105	0.95	120	0.83	134	0.75
12	**110**	**0.91**	**110**	**0.91**	**110**	**0.91**
Total Units		**12.04**		**12.35**		**13.08**
% Difference in returns		NA		2.55% (wrt Case 1)		5.91% (wrt Case 2) 8.61% (wrt Case 1)

Figure 18

As you can see from the above figure, in case one, we end up with a total of 12.04 units after month 12. However, a similar SIP of ₹100 for case two reveals that we end up with a total of 12.35 units.

Case two's investment was more volatile than case one but yields more units, therefore, more gains at the end of month 12. If we compare the returns of case two (12.35 units) versus case one (12.04), you would realise that case two yielded 2.55% more units (and therefore more returns) compared to case one. And if you keep getting 2.55% higher returns in any investment year on year, then compounding comes into play and unleashes its own magic.

Now, let us look at case three. Case three is the most volatile. While your advisor may consider this a risky investment (which actually it is if your risk tolerance levels are low or if you do not trust volatility), volatility being paradoxical also allows SIPs to take advantage of it. Our ₹100 SIPs in the third case yields 13.08 units at the end of 12 months. This is 5.91% better than case two and a whopping 8.61% better than case one.

In an investment that is expected to give us 10% returns, if we get 18.61% returns (8.61% higher), then what else needs to be said about the power and anti-fragility of the SIP method? More volatility, more gains. That's the anti-fragile nature of SIPs. SIPs love volatility.

Of course, we can get even smarter by opting for VIPs (variable investment plans) rather than SIPs, but that's for some other day. For now, we have a very simple SIP methodology at hand, and we should be excited when the NAVs of our mutual funds fluctuate—because the more the fluctuation, the more we will benefit. Do you love volatility now? If yes, go ahead and cherish this Foops moment for the rest of your life.

Foops #24: Assuming That Volatility Is Bad	
Awakening	Action
• There are many paradoxical things in life—volatility is one of them. • Higher volatility signifies higher risk, but if managed well, leads to higher returns. • SIPs are an effective anti-fragile strategy which takes advantage of volatility to provide higher returns.	• Volatility is good for you, provided you belive in it. • Never invest lump sum in any volatile investment. Go for SIPs. • SIP provides an effective mechanism to take advantage of the volatility of an investment. • The higher the volatility, more are the returns from the SIP.

FOOPS 25

CATEGORISING ASSET CLASSES AS GOOD AND BAD

> **THERE ARE NO BAD INVESTMENTS, ONLY BAD INVESTORS.**
>
> – ROBERT KIYOSAKI

Here is an interesting conversation between two of my friends while we were sitting in Café Di Milano—a joint owned by one of my other friends, Sandeep, at Dwarka, New Delhi.

"I think this is some allergy on my skin."

"Yeah, looks like it," said Mukesh as he checked Sushil's right hand. Both of Sushil's hands were showing blisters and were turning purple.

Both Mukesh and Sushil were good friends since the IBM days, and we were having a mini get-together at Sandeep's café—a place where we regularly meet.

"I think that I must show this to a good doctor." Sushil sounded a bit concerned.

"Yes, you shouldn't delay, Sushil," Mukesh reverted.

I was equally concerned for Sushil, but I also found this a great opportunity to intervene and pass on a lesson to Sushil, which I have been trying to awaken him to for a very long time.

"Sushil, let me share Dr. Bhatia's number with you. He is a good friend of mine and one of the best dental surgeons around."

"Ok. Thanks... But what did you say? He is a what?"

"The best dental surgeon," I responded.

"Are you kidding with me, Manoj? Why should I go to a dentist for a skin problem?"

"Well, because he is the best doctor around."

"Brother, he may be the best, but he is not the best fit for me in my current situation."

"Hold on to this thought, Sushil. There is a big learning in here. He is the best but may not be the best for you."

"What is so special about this thought? I mean, I just do not get it, Manoj," he remarked puzzledly.

'Best' vs. 'Best for Me'

And if you are also puzzled by the aim of the above conversation, just be a little more patient. Foops moments do demand patience and in-depth understanding. But as you know, these moments are capable of changing your whole perspective.

The possibility of the best not being the best for you has far-reaching consequences.

Day in and day out, there are hundreds of seekers asking for the best investment in the market where they can put their hard-earned money and see it multiply at the best possible rate.

This is a question that has no answer simply because the answer depends on understanding the problem. When we understand that Sushil's problem is related to skin disease or allergy, then pointing him even to the best dental surgeon is of no use.

Just like the best doctor does not make any standalone sense, the best investment does not either. Because the question itself is flawed. What is the best investment in the market? Is X a good investment? Is Y a bad investment? These questions are all flawed, just like: Is Dr. Bhatia the best doctor?"

Then what is the right question?

The right question is what Sushil asked later—who is the best doctor for me?

'Best doctor' and 'best doctor for me' carry two vastly different connotations. Those last two words—'for me'—make a world of difference in how you look at various investing options. It did make a big difference for me and was one of my most transformational Foops moments.

To suggest the best doctor, I need to know your disease—its symptoms, severity, impacted body areas, etc.

Similarly, to suggest the best investment, I need to know your financial disease. I need to know what you want from your money. What is your current financial state? What is the current health of your financial portfolio? What is your age? What is your current risk profile? What are your future liquidity needs? What returns are you already getting, and what are you targeting?

Based on all these data points, I can guide you in the right direction. Each investment vehicle exists to serve a specific purpose for a particular set of investors. If they do not serve enough investors or there is a superior product available in that segment, such a vehicle will automatically cease to exist with time.

Does that mean that fixed deposits earning 5-6% returns are also good investments? Of course, they are—if you ask the right question. And the right question is, "Are fixed deposits a good investment for Mr. X?" The answer would be a resounding yes for a significant number of people, even with their miserly tax-inefficient returns.

For example, fixed deposits make a lot of sense if you are just a teenager trying to understand the concept of compound interest, a senior citizen trying to avoid risks, looking for a regular monthly cash flow, you can stay invested for a very limited time frame, or you have a poor risk-taking ability.

Similarly, stocks are a good investment for certain people. Stocks, specifically long-term investments, are useful for an investor who is ready to take entrepreneurial decisions, has high risk-taking ability, understands and appreciates volatility, is ready to stay invested for at least seven to ten years, is willing to learn and spend time in the market.

Mutual funds are the best investments for someone who has a moderate risk-taking ability, cannot spend enough time in the market but is still ready to invest in a volatile market for at least five to seven years.

And so on. Each investment vehicle has a purpose and a target audience.

But dealing with financial freedom seekers is always very interesting. For example, one of our freedom seekers from Dubai understood this concept very well that there are no bad investments. So, after a lot of thoughtful consideration, he concluded that mutual funds are the best investment vehicle for him.

I was happy that he understood the concept and was clear that the mutual funds are good for him. But my happiness was short-lived.

"Ok, seems that I am fit for mutual funds. Tell me the best mutual funds in the market today."

Bad habits die hard. I smiled and asked him to re-frame his question. But in the end, I had to reframe the question for him.

"'What are some good mutual funds?' may not be the right question, buddy."

"Then what is it?" he asked.

"'What are some good mutual funds for me?'"

"Does it really matter that much?"

"It matters the world to you. Those two words make the biggest difference. For example, someone with a high-risk profile may find thematic funds a good fit, while someone looking at stable income might find debt funds the best for him. It's different for everyone."

"Oh yes, I get that."

"So, depending on numerous financial and non-financial factors, we take a call on whether we should go for debt funds, equity funds, hybrid funds, etc. Even within equity funds, depending on various factors, we need to decide the type of equity funds like small-cap, mid-cap, large-cap, etc. Or if it is a debt fund, understanding the risk factors of the underlying securities, fund durations, etc."

"Wow! Never knew that all this required such in-depth study. And where do investments like PPF and EPF fit?"

"These investment tools are designed for those who are not disciplined enough—those who want someone to push them into the habit of saving and leverage the power of compounding; they are looking for virtually risk-free investments."

"ELSS also?"

"ELSS lies somewhere in the middle. It allows you to invest in equity, still saves taxes for you and has a lock-in to ensure that you do not make irrational decisions before the lock-in period is over."

"Quite interesting. And gold, bonds, etc.?"

"Gold provides a hedge for your market risk. Bonds may provide you slightly better post-tax returns. Each has an investor base. And, of course, a portfolio contains not just one type of investment. Every portfolio is like a bouquet, having different types of investments to balance out the class of investors who are somewhere in between these extreme traits. Nothing is absolute—black or white—in this world, and it is the same with humans."

"Same with humans, how?"

"Is there anyone who is 100% honest, 100% corrupt, 100% free from anger or 100% angry? We are all a mix of different shades of grey. And so is your portfolio. It is a mix of different investments, the weightage of each investment depending on various financial and non-financial factors we already discussed."

"Hmm... I get it. For the first time, I think I have started to appreciate the power of each investment tool. Today, I understand that there is nothing like a bad investment or a good investment. The only question is whether a particular investment is good for me or not."

He finally got the point, at least for the moment.

No investment is a bad investment, and similarly, no investment is a good investment. Asking such questions from your financial advisors or from anyone else is redundant. Each asset serves a particular class of investors. We need to identify the class that we belong to, depending on our situation, portfolio and investment needs. Then, we must pick up our investment from the beautiful bouquet of available options accordingly.

Most investors are majorly looking for 'good' investments because of their narrow focus on returns. There is a feeling that the investment which provides the maximum returns is the best. Nothing can be farther than the truth.

Today, cryptocurrency is yielding around 300%-plus returns per annum. Does that make it the best investment for all of us? Or does an EPF returning tax-free 8%-plus returns with government security become the best investment? An investor may actually need both and many more to complete one's portfolio.

Return on investments (ROI) can never be the sole deciding factor for picking an asset. There are so many other factors that decide the right option for you. It could be liquidity needs, the safety of principal amount, risk factors, etc. That is why we take so much time on each step when building your financial freedom plan as a part of our prestigious ELITE program. We truly want to understand you, your existing portfolio, future needs, risk-taking capacity, attitude to risk, current portfolio liquidity, etc., before we conclude what is the 'best' investment 'for you'.

Foops #25: Categorising Asset Classes as Good and Bad	
Awakening	Action
• Investors often confuse a 'good investment' and 'a good investment for them'. • Every investing option has a target audience, and is therefore not bad. • Returns should not be the only criteria to judge an investment.	• Instead of looking for 'good' investments, look for 'good for me' investments. • You need to choose a bouquet of investments for your portfolio that meets your personalised needs for the present and the future.

BELIEVING THAT WE ARE NOT BIASED

EVER SINCE I CAME TO KNOW ABOUT CONFIRMATION BIAS, I HAVE STARTED SEEING IT EVERYWHERE.

– JON RONSON

"Confirmation bias is the mother of all misconceptions," says Rolf Dobelli in his best-selling book, *The Art of Thinking Clearly*.

Confirmation bias happens to be a silent wealth killer as well. All the while, you may be assuming that you are taking good and informed decisions based on concrete data points, and you would not even know how confirmation bias is influencing your mind to look at a biased set of data points in the first place.

Confirmation bias is probably the biggest Foops moment for all those investing in the equity market. Undertanding this bias helps us realise this Foops moment and take massive permanent action.

What Is Confirmation Bias?

Confirmation bias is a natural human tendency to interpret new information to become compatible with our existing theories. It is so natural that it is tough to know whether we are thinking and acting under the influence of this bias.

Buffet has seen investors lose big money in the equity market simply because they ignored facts that contradicted their pet theories.

You might wonder why an investor would ignore contrary facts. I used to wonder the same. But when you scrutinise this mindset, you realise that no one does it intentionally. It happens. It is a human trait, and we need conscious, persistent efforts to overcome this bias.

Bettina J. Casad, Assistant Professor at Department of Psychological Sciences, University of Missouri at St. Louis, says that this biased approach to decision-making is largely unintentional. People are especially likely to process information to support their beliefs when they are highly important or self-relevant.

Why Do Humans Display Confirmation Bias?

There are various theories on this topic. In fact, this is one of the most talked-about topics in human psychology.

One explanation why a human being is susceptible to confirmation bias is because it is an extremely efficient way to process information. Humans are bombarded with information and cannot possibly take the time to carefully process each piece of information to form an unbiased conclusion. Decision-making and information-processing are often automated in the brain, based on shortcuts that the brain creates based on prior experiences and feelings. It is adaptive to rely on instinctive, automatic reflexes that keep humans out of harm's way. The brain, therefore, gets wired to seek out information that conforms to our existing beliefs. This automated response often results in biased decision-making.

Another reason people show confirmation bias is to protect their self-esteem. People like to feel good about themselves, and discovering that a belief that they highly value is incorrect makes people feel bad about themselves. Therefore, people will seek information that supports their existing beliefs. Have you ever experienced people coming up with supporting evidence in political or religious debates on social media? I have experienced it many times. Neither side is wrong. Both act under the influence of their confirmation bias, which pushes them to only look at the evidence which confirms their thought process and ignore any contradicting evidence.

Another motive for a human being to display confirmation bias is the desire for accuracy. People want to feel intelligent, and information indicating that one holds an inaccurate belief or has made a poor decision suggests they lack intelligence. No one wants to be in this category of low intelligence.

Impact of Confirmation Bias

Confirmation bias, by the way, has implications not only in personal finance but in most other fields as well. Research has shown that doctors are just as likely to have confirmation biases as everyone else. Doctors often have a preliminary hunch regarding the diagnosis of a medical condition early in the treatment. This hunch can interfere with information that may indicate an alternative diagnosis is more likely.

We judge people, opportunities, government policies, political parties, and of course, the markets. When we analyse our world with our own biases, we put our observations through several filters manufactured by our experiences. This is not simply for stock screeners. We're talking about the bias-inducing filters we put our decisions through. Individuals may or may not necessarily rationalise that their decisions are being made based on biases they have developed.

Broadly, investing biases fall into two main categories: cognitive and emotional. Both are usually the result of prejudice towards one thing over the other.

We've all seen movies where a thief wears a police uniform to pass through a security checkpoint. The real police officers assume that since the person is wearing a uniform like theirs, he must be a real police officer. That's an example of a cognitive bias.

Emotional biases typically occur spontaneously based on the personal feelings of an individual at the time a decision is made. They may also be deeply rooted in personal experiences that also influence decision-making. Such biases are usually ingrained in the psychology of investors and are more challenging to overcome than cognitive biases. Emotional biases are not necessarily always errors. In some cases, an investor's emotional bias may help them to make a more protective and suitable decision for themselves.

There are more than one examples where we see such confirmation biases in investing world. Investors who continue to hold on to low-yielding real estate display typical traits of emotional confirmation biases. They expect to recover the cost someday. They do not want to be proven unintelligent by selling their investment at a loss. And as we studied in Foops #1, they are clear victims of the cost of lost opportunities.

Real estate is just one example. Almost every investor holding on to dud stocks in the hope of recovering their capital is biased. They keep buying dud stocks just because a renowned brand has been hitting all-time lows, and they think it just cannot go lower than this.

It's not only about dud stocks or real estate. The bias is everywhere. Even when we are going ahead with the selection of new stocks, we develop biases based on our previous success and failures with stock selections. We may be biased to go with stocks of the same industry where we have seen tremendous success earlier. We may get biased and avoid companies whose CEOs image does not fit into the image that our mind has created. And the list goes on.

Confirmation bias is so deeply rooted, so natural to humans, that most of us may never realise our bias for an entire life time. Overcoming confirmation bias is extremely vital for massive wealth creation. It requires a very conscious effort to change the way we think, to reprogram our mind to avoid short cuts and automated responses, to challenge our thinking as soon as we encounter a contrarian view.

Lets get deeper into it.

Overcoming Confirmation Bias

For most people, it is impossible to be unbiased in investment decision-making. However, just as in the case of managing risks, investors can mitigate biases by understanding and identifying them, then creating trading and investing rules that mitigate them when necessary.

I will share a few strategies that I personally use to overcome confirmation biases.

1. Exit-Entry Strategy

As the name suggests, you first exit and then decide if you wish to enter.

In his best-selling book *Deep Work*, Cal Newport gives a beautiful example of how this 'exit-entry strategy' works.

When Ryan Nicodemus decided to simplify his life, he first targeted his possessions. At the time, Ryan lived alone in a spacious three-bedroom condo. For years, driven by a consumerist impulse, he had been trying his best to fill this ample space. Now it was time to reclaim his life from his stuff. The strategy he deployed was simple at first glance but radical upon closer examination.

He spent an afternoon packing everything he owned into cardboard boxes as if he was about to move. To transform what he described as a 'difficult undertaking' into something less onerous, he called it a 'packing party', explaining that "Everything's more exciting when it's a party, right?"

Once the packing was done, Nicodemus then spent the next week going through his normal routine. If he needed something packed, he would unpack it and put it back where it used to go. At the end of the month, he noticed that most of his stuff remained untouched in their respective boxes. So, he got rid of them.

Stuff accumulates in people's lives partly because people worry, "What if I need this one day?" when faced with a specific act of elimination. They then use this concern as an excuse to retain the item. Nicodemus's packing party provided him with definitive evidence that most of his stuff was not something he needed, therefore supporting his quest to simplify his life.

Ryan's, I am pretty sure, is not a solitary example. We have the same issue in every house, in varying extremes. Using this strategy, I can confidently say that I have reduced the unwanted stuff in my house by at least half. Still, there are things I haven't gotten rid of yet. I am working on myself. It is not easy, but I am on it.

Of course, in the case of stocks, you cannot sell all of them and then start thinking about which one to buy instead. This does not make a lot of sense to a lot of people. But we can always *imagine* that we sold everything today, and are now starting from a clean slate. The vital question at this stage is, *how many* of *which* stock will we buy today. We have to be honest with ourselves.

As enlisted in the book *The Autobiography of a Stock*, we must perform a proper value analysis. After value analysis, or for that matter, any other criteria that we may have for stock selection, if our answer is in the affirmative, then we should continue to keep that stock. Else, we should sell it.

We need to drop our ego for this. We might just have proven ourselves unintelligent. Accept it. We all make mistakes. It is not the mistakes themselves that are embarrassing but the failure to admit mistakes and take corrective action that contradicts the human spirit and intellect.

This exit-entry strategy can be very effectively used for most financial assets.

2. Separation of Duties

In most IT companies that I have worked for, we followed a process called 'separation of duties', or SOD.

The process is simple. If the duties are not separated, emotions and biases are likely to play a significant role in our decisions. In that case, we are likely to make irrational decisions.

For example, any software project will undergo various phases in its life cycle—typically, requirement gathering, design, development, testing and deployment. In big software projects, these phases are handled by different teams. But if the projects are small or if cost-saving is of paramount importance, the same team members can play different roles depending on their skill set.

While the same team can do development and testing, they are always kept separate considering SOD. A development team develops the software, and a test team is supposed to test and validate the software's functions. In other words, they try to destroy the software with the intent to make it as defect-free and resilient as possible.

Development and test teams are kept separate primarily to avoid any confirmation bias. It is challenging for a development team member to test and find mistakes in their own developed software code. A developer will always have a predisposition to pass it successfully. He doesn't want to be proven wrong. He doesn't want to sound unintelligent. He doesn't want to admit mistakes.

Humans are better able to process information rationally when they are emotionally distant from the issue. And therefore, a separate team testing the software makes a lot of sense. The testing team has not slogged and burnt the midnight oil to develop the software. They are, therefore, less emotionally attached to the software.

Similarly, in the equity market or, for that matter, in any asset class, if there is a team of two in a family—one responsible for buying and the other for selling, emotional biases can be mitigated to a significant extent. Of course, both the partners need to be aware of the family's financial goals, the value analysis process, etc. Just as in software projects, both the development and test teams aim to achieve the end goal of a satisfied client. Similarly, the goal of a couple in buying and selling assets is to keep value stocks and sell overvalued stocks. This might sound a bit strange to you, or you might need some adjustments in your family discussions. But that's how Foops moments are—strange but effective.

It is much easier to handle confirmation bias using SOD than having the same person fulfill both the roles of buying and selling assets.

3. Seek Disconfirming Evidence

Development and test teams in an IT project have the same end goal—a high-quality software and a delighted client. However, there are many healthy or even unhealthy clashes before the final goal is met. These clashes while testing the software are a natural part of software evolution—primarily because of the clashing roles that both teams play.

If SOD has to be implemented in a family, clashes might be natural and should be expected. Many couples often find it tough to play opposing roles in a team. If there is no synchronisation of goals, SOD may cause friction in household activities as well.

If only one person, instead of the couple, has to perform this function of SOD, then the person can potentially adopt the following technique.

They must proactively seek disconfirming evidence to take a contrarian point of view. Do specific searches to prove that you made a mistake when selecting a stock or any other asset. Search for irregularities against the company. Specifically, look for earnings dips. If possible, try to use their products from a critic's point of view. You must play the cop and seek evidence to prove your decision wrong.

Nevertheless, it is never easy to completely eliminate confirmation bias. It is ingrained in humans. But we can adopt strategies to better control it.

Foops #26: Believing That We Are Not Biased	
Awakening	Action
• Confirmation bias is naturally ingrained in humans. • It occurs to us whether we realise it or not. • Such a bias leads to irrational buy and sell decisions.	• Adopt strategies like exit-entry, separation of duties or seeking disconforming evidence in order to minimise the impact of confirmation bias. • The lesser the confirmation bias, the more rational are your investing decisions.

THINKING THAT MASSIVE ACTION ALONE GENERATES WEALTH

> **INACTION MAY BE THE BIGGEST FORM OF ACTION.**
>
> – JERRY BROWN

"One who sees inaction in action, and action in inaction, has understanding among men, disciplined in all he performs."

– Bhagavad Gita, Chapter 4, Verse 18

The key phrase in the above beautiful line from the Bhagavad Gita is 'action in inaction'.

Inaction is not simply a lack of action. Inaction is the lack of action where you are generally *expected to take action.* And expectation causes a big difference.

You may sleep the entire day if you do not have to go to the office. That's inaction without pressure or expectation.

But if you perform the same *inaction* on a weekday when you have to report for a crucial meeting, then your inaction is accompanied by an expectation to take action.

BIG difference. The tendency to consciously not act irrespective of the general expectations happens to be our next Foops moment.

This expectation becomes pressure in no time. You may decide not to sell the equity at a market high. That's inaction.

Let's say you do not insulate yourself from the world around you, your friends, colleagues, social media, newspapers—all citing historical examples, predicting the future and imploring you to take action or face the consequences. In this case, it takes discipline, commitment and adherence to a process to withstand the pressure and stick to inaction.

Mark Armbruster is the president of Armbruster Capital Management, Inc. (ACM), a wealth management firm serving high-net-worth individuals and institutional clients in the US. As per him, *doing nothing* in the face of changing markets may seem counter-intuitive to most people. Nevertheless, when it comes to investing, inaction is often the best course of action. This is not to say that it is best to ignore portfolios entirely. Rather, the correct approach is to be highly disciplined and selective when making any and all changes to a portfolio.

In Foops #13, we talked about being a *responsive* investor. And therein lies the art—to know when to respond and to know that the response is not driven by market volatility but your portfolio situation.

Let me show you a recent real-life example of stock markets after the first Covid-19 wave in India:

Figure 19

If you look at the above chart, you would realise that every week starting April 2020, everyone had the temptation to keep selling—simply because we were hitting an all-time high almost every week. And this trend did not stop. As of writing this chapter, the markets have just hit another all-time high.

But this consistent *all-time high* can pressure many investors to take action when inaction is needed. You may feel it is easy to resist the pressure, but the fact is quite different.

Here is the key content of some of the emails I keep receiving in this context:

- I have liquidated my mutual funds and booked gains as markets are at a peak. I am planning to re-enter after the markets correct themselves. However, I would like to understand the best mutual funds for short-, mid- and long-term horizons.
- Markets are running high. We have made good returns. Let us book some profits.
- I have been hearing that all stocks are overvalued in this market. Should we exit now?
- My portfolio went out of balance because I exited the market now and made a neat ₹5 lakhs profit. How long should I wait before re-entering?

The last question triggers all kinds of emotions in me. If anyone on this planet knew this answer beforehand, that person would never have to invest any money again.

The fact remains that no one can accurately predict the market. All the above email senders (and there are thousands of them just in our circle) had been sent repeated alerts not to take any action based on the market movement and focus on their own specific investing strategy instead. But they were bested by the pressure.

This is the pressure created by everyone and everything around these investors. They are all, directly or indirectly, trying to time the market. They do not realise that no one knows if and when this 'correction' will occur, by how much the market will correct even if it does and what will happen after the correction.

The key here is inaction. And there is more than ample evidence to support this—of course, valid only in the long run.

ING Corporate Leaders Trust, based in the US, has outperformed the overall stock market over the past ten years with no investment manager and a group of stocks passed on from a portfolio set up in 1935 and not traded since. That's pure inaction.

Warren Buffett describes his investment time horizon for a stock as "somewhere between ten years and forever." That's some commitment to inaction.

A study was conducted in the US by researchers Geoffrey Friesen of the University of Nebraska at Lincoln and Travis Sapp of Iowa State University. They calculated that between 1991 and 2004, 'market timing' decisions reduced equity fund investor returns by 1.56% annually.

We have talked about not timing the market in one of the earlier Foops moments as well. But remember that inaction does not mean you should not monitor the market. Inaction simply means no unnecessary action. I would extend this statement to say that an asset is intended to be never sold, never ever.

This statement brings us to some obvious questions.

- Isn't it an investor's job to buy and sell assets to book profits?
- If we never sell an asset, then how will we fund our expenses and special events?

So, here is my take.

An investor's job is not to keep buying and selling assets. Is this another Foops moment for you?

An investor's job is to generate cash flow out of the existing assets and continue with them as long as feasible. The cash flow thus generated should be able to fund your needs from time to time.

But seriously, what if we don't sell and just die of ageing? Is that desirable? What if the asset quality deteriorates over time? What if we have a much better investment option available? Really, should we never sell? Again, the point here is that we don't want to buy and sell to prove ourselves smarter than the market. We can, however, sell in specific situations.

Never Ever Sell Your Asset Unless...

So, let me rephrase the statement.

An asset is never meant to be sold—never ever—unless, of course, any of the following five conditions are met.

1. You Need the Money for Your Life Special Events

One of the most important and probably the only purpose of an asset (or an investment) is to cater to your varying needs. Money is ultimately meant to help you lead a comfortable life and have as pleasant an experience as feasible.

So, if there are special events like a marriage in the family, children's education needs, health and life emergencies that demand liquidating low-performing assets, it makes total sense to liquidate such assets. Go on and do it happily.

As Ken Honda writes in his book *Happy Money*

"No amount of money is going to make you happy. Happiness

comes from experiences, some of which money can buy for you. So, you ought to earn more and spend more—get the money flow going. Participate in the flow."

You can barter your assets or investments for happy experiences when these special events approach. Do not miss doing so.

2. The Asset Is Not Worth Holding Anymore

You may have invested in the best assets with the best intentions. But the quality of assets can depreciate over time—and the company may not be responsible for this deterioration of asset quality.

For example, you may have invested in an excellent company. However, the company's industry itself may be undergoing a massive shift. As a result, the companies in such an industry may not have a stable future.

You may consider exiting in such cases.

Remember Kodak? Kodak was a global market leader in cameras and films until digital technology outdated it—forever.

And things will change in the future as well.

A study by Harvard Business School says that the top three future disruptors would be:

a) **Manufacturing**: The limits of what is possible with 3D printing are still being tested. But the technology is already shaking up the traditional manufacturing sector, and it's poised to make a lasting impact.

b) **Real Estate**: The iBuyer model is appealing to consumers seeking an alternative, streamlined solution to the traditional methods of buying and selling property, and it's set to continue driving innovative growth in the real estate market.

c) **Sports**: Games like football, soccer and baseball have long been at the forefront of the sports industry, but new kinds of spectator events are quickly gaining traction.

In a nutshell, assets can be sold and should be sold if you see an industry shift or a technological disruption. Inaction, as we said earlier, is not blind inaction; it's inaction with regular monitoring. But if situations like these arise, taking action is logical and sensible.

3. You Have an Extraordinarily Better Investment at Your Disposal

Almost everyone who exits investments at so-called market highs starts to ponder what to do with the liquidated money post exiting the investment. Something that they should have thought before exiting strikes them after exiting.

They cannot obviously enter the same market that they just exited. Other investment options don't seem to be lucrative enough. In the end, for most, the money ends up in some dud investment. And then they are looking out for better investment opportunities again.

The investments can change their nature over time. Therefore, their returns may also change. If you think you are absolutely clear that you have a significantly better investment available (in terms of returns, liquidity or safety), you have a genuine reason to liquidate your asset.

4. You Need to Rebalance Your Portfolio

This is something a lot of us miss out on. And we have talked at length about portfolio balancing in Foops #7.

Many investors do not know the optimal portfolio balance for them. Those who know the right mix may not know how to keep the portfolio balanced. An investment may demand movement from debt to equity or vice versa depending on whether your portfolio is getting out of balance.

And this can indeed create a need to sell your asset.

5. You Are Churning Your Investments

We studied investment churning in Foops #9. If churning is the aim, then a sell action may be justified.

But in all situations, you must do a proper analysis and study the trade-offs and see if the advantages of selling far outweigh those of not selling.

Until today, I see no other valid reason to take action and come out of an investment. So, if that means staying invested for decades, so be it. If intelligent inaction is what defines your Foops moment, so be it.

Foops #27: Thinking That Massive Action Generates Wealth	
Awakening	Action
• Action comes naturally to humans. • But its inaction that will build wealth for you. • Inaction does not mean not monitoring your assets. It means resisting the urge to act unnecessarily.	• Insulate yourself from outside noise and let inaction be the default mode of operation. • Take action only under five specific situations as enlisted. • Resist any other temptation to act.

FOOPS 28

BELIEVING THAT THE PURPOSE OF INVESTING IS PRIMARILY TO GENERATE HIGH RETURNS

INVESTING IS USELESS IF IT DOES NOT EASE YOUR LIFE.

– MANOJ ARORA

There was a time when my colleagues, friends and well-wishers convinced me that if you have to succeed in life, you have to learn corporate politics. Not only must you learn it, but you must also master it and thrive in that atmosphere. Else, you would always be a laggard and would never be successful.

Well, I don't know how you look at it or what has been your experience with corporate politics. However, I firmly believe that the above is true, only depending on one's definition of success.

Let's say someone's definition of success is to climb the corporate ladder, get a fancy designation that can be boasted off in parties and get-togethers and get a fat pay package. In that case, the prerequisite seems valid to a large extent. But if our definition of success is different, then this may not be valid for us.

My definition of success was to have the ability to decide my agenda for every single day for the remainder of my life. That's it. I never wanted to be governed. I wanted to do a lot of things. I wanted my day to include activities like planting trees, writing life-elevating books, spending a lot of time with family, seeing my fairies grow up as confident and successful adults, meditate, elevate lives around me in whatever ways I can and to keep myself happy.

Corporate politics was definitely not a prerequisite to succeed with my definition of success. So, I rejected office politics. I worked for and achieved financial freedom and quit an extremely well-paying corporate job at 42. I did that so I could pursue my definition of success. Similarly, you must define success for yourself and take a call on what you need to do to get to your success and then thrive in it.

My definition of success and my prerequisites may not match yours. Every individual is different, and that makes this life beautiful and worth living.

My wife and I have vastly different reactions to the threat of Covid-19. And neither is wrong. After all, we are both driven by our individual personal experiences and past *sanskars*.

Many investors with a relatively low risk profile are fearful of the equity market. And they are not wrong; they are just different. They are driven by certain experiences in their lives. And if someone tells them that investing in equity is a prerequisite for wealth creation, it is like telling them that corporate politics is a prerequisite for success. Such investors often panic at the thought of equity investments and, therefore, about the thought of financial freedom itself.

They don't have to abide by any such prerequisite. That's a Foops moment for several investors. Thinking about financial freedom without equity investing is almost unthinkable to many.

But, as with corporate politics, it depends on the definition of wealth and what the seeker expects from financial freedom. Your purpose for wealth creation could be to compete and beat the richest person in your locality, town, city, country or the world. And there is absolutely nothing wrong in that. In that case, it will be tough for you to 'succeed' in wealth creation unless you move a significant portion of your portfolio into equity. But if your definition of wealth is to be able to lead a peaceful and successful life, then the prerequisites may or may not include equity at all.

For anyone to take that decision, they must understand the purpose of investing in the first place.

The Purpose of Investing

The purpose of investing can be different for different people. I am giving you some of the reasons why I invest my money. I have tried to list them based on their priority.

1. To Beat Inflation and Keep Our Home Running

The primary reason we must take our money and expose ourselves to risks associated with investing is to beat the inflation monster. Inflation is like a sword hanging on our head—and if in any year, we are unable to beat it, the pressure mounts in the subsequent year. If we cannot beat inflation, our money keeps eroding at a compounded rate.

Therefore, to beat inflation and keep ourselves at par with our family's continuously rising expenses, we must continue to invest.

2. To Achieve Financial Freedom

Once we have successfully defeated inflation, the next ambitious target is to invest to achieve our personal financial freedom. Not only should we invest to achieve this milestone in our life, but we also need to continue investing so we can retain the 'financially free' title.

Financial freedom gives us immense control over every single day of our lives. It provides us with an empty canvas to craft life's direction just the way we want it.

3. To Acquire Intellectual Elevation and Satisfy Our Creative Bent of Mind

Post financial freedom, more money doesn't excite you as much.

As Bill Gates says, "I can understand wanting to have a million dollars, there is a certain meaningful freedom that comes with that. But once you get beyond that, I have to tell you, it's the same hamburger."

So, it is never only about money and freedom.

When I was in a job managing a big team of young professionals, I had seen many leave the job, some for the lure of money but a far bigger percentage in the lure of learning something new. They got bored with the technology, company, people, location, etc. Humans crave to learn new things. Expressing creativity is what gives us immense satisfaction—even more than money.

There are innumerable ways to get creative. What excites you and brings out your creative juices is very personal to you. By definition, there are no limits or constraints to creativity.

Investing is one area where we might just find our lifetime too short to learn everything. This includes learning not only technical financial skills but also developing the right attitude towards money. You will truly have to get creative to excel in this field. Such highly skilled investors are likely to see better rewards for their learning, bringing in more happiness.

This learning and creative juices flowing in our body satisfy our soul. This is what continues to drive me and so many other financially free individuals to continue to learn, invest and keep getting smarter—and to always strive to be a better version of ourselves.

4. To Lead a Worthwhile Life

The quest to keep getting better does not always mean that we are always trying to get better returns.

It could also mean getting reasonable returns and better sleep. It could also mean that we earn more and spend more to keep the flow going, enhance our and our family's quality of life, contribute more to the world around us and lead a purposeful, worthwhile life.

Let's say you are clear on the purpose of investing. You are not a part of the media-driven maddening race where people are ranked based on their net worth, where someone will always be ahead of you, and you would be trying to catch up. In that case, you would appreciate that returns are not the only thing you are looking for, at least after you become financially free. If that is clear in your mind, then, of course, equity investments could be optional for you—absolutely optional.

We have many freedom seekers in the ELITE program who have started to reduce their equity percentage based on our investing strategy. This enables them to lead a less volatile life and still earn more than decent returns, allowing them to work on their passion areas. This is what leads to a more worthwile and fulfilled life.

Equity investing is just one class of investing, with its own merits and demerits. It is absolutely optional for you to participate in this asset class, just like those who wish not to invest in the cryptocurrency asset class. Many others, including me, do not participate in the real estate asset class. That does not mean that real estate cannot give us good returns. This is a personal choice for reasons of ease and comfort.

At the end of the day, investing should be governed by the mindset to make your life easier and enjoyable. If the process of investing is making it complex for you, you may be defeating the very purpose with which you started to invest your hard earned money.

Foops #28: Believing That the Purpose of Investing Is Primarily to Generate High Returns.

Awakening	Action
• It is vital to understand your purpose before investing. • The purpose of investing could be very different for different investors. • Equity or, for that matter, any asset class is not a prerequisite to become a good investor.	• Identify what you want out of money. • Along with your financial advisor, frame an investing strategy which caters to your purpose. • Insulate yourself from the maddening race around you as everyone's purpose could be starkly different.

FOOPS 29

ASSUMING THAT FINANCIAL FREEDOM IS THE SAME AS RETIREMENT

WORK BECAUSE YOU LOVE TO, NOT BECAUSE YOU HAVE TO.

– TONY ROBBINS

People often mistake financial freedom with having money, which it is actually not.

Let me trigger your next Foops moment with this statement: "If money is even one of the side motives behind your daily actions, you are still far away from understanding what financial freedom actually is."

Let me just list down three such cases where financial freedom is misunderstood.

One of my friends, a high-profile corporate executive with a big multinational company, recently took voluntary retirement with the dream of living a relaxed life and spending time with his loved ones. However, his plans were shattered by the harsh realities that life presented to him in the form of boredom, frustration and anger. His family accepts that they were a happier lot before the head of the family decided to call it quits.

Another one of my close friends is planning to quit a job that he hates so as to work full-time on a venture he recently started. He firmly believes that he can earn much more if he diverts even a fraction of the time and energy he spends in his present job. However, he knows he is not financially secure today. The venture is too new to feed him and his family consistently until the end of his life.

I also met one of my readers who quit his job a few months back. He had been working there for a quarter of a century, but he was not enjoying it anymore. He did this knowing very well that he was just 80% through with his financial protection. Currently, this corporate executive with close to 25 years of industry experience is looking to mix his passion with a source of income that he badly needs to ensure he keeps running his monthly household expenses smoothly.

All three have had multiple discussions with me, directly or indirectly, seeking my approval on their decision to quit their jobs. They also do not believe that I am leading a happy and contented financially free life after resigning from a well-paying and highly-respected job.

I do not blame them at all. It's a misconception that many carry. They happen to miss out on understanding one of the most vital aspects of financial freedom, and therein lies their Foops moment.

They fail to realise that I am not retired, bored or venturing into any money-churning venture to replace my job. Nor am I trying to leverage my passion with the intent of earning money and feeding my family.

And why should I do any of these things? Why should I earn money when money can earn more money for me? Why should I spend even a single minute pursuing wealth when I have employed my corpus and assets to take care of it for me?

None of my three friends appreciate the true meaning of financial freedom. Therefore, they are unable to relate to the quality of life I actually enjoy. I do not do anything for my living. Whatever I do, I do for my passion and for the things I truly love in life, irrespective of their money-earning potential.

Whenever I try to explain this to anyone, they start to wonder that there must be something else that drives my finances. How can anyone just stop earning money?

For all such naysayers, I do not mind clarifying a few more things about my life.

- I have not inherited a single rupee from anyone.
- I do not possess any financial degree, nor do I intend to get one.
- No one in my family circle has anything to do with finance.
- My spouse does not work for money.
- I have absolutely no other source of active income.

In the Indian context, I understand that it is tough to explain that I have actually and truly become financially free. This is because such freedom is uncommon in our society.

But with discipline, commitment and a few sacrifices, I have accumulated a large enough corpus to fund our expenses for the rest of our life, after taking care of inflation, the current standard of living, future expenses, etc. This corpus is self-funding. It generates enough returns (or passive income) to keep growing even after meeting all our monthly expenses. This is the blissful state of financial freedom that is starkly different from the situation of all my three friends.

My first friend, who grew bored of life without any pursuit, did not realise that financial freedom was never my end goal. Financial freedom was just a means to start doing what I always wanted to do. I wanted to plant trees, spend time with my fairies, write books, understand myself and my body and mentor more people to become financially free so that they too can elevate the world around them in their own unique ways. Today, I am busier than I ever was. I am happier than I ever can be. It is vital to be clear in your mind as to *why* we are seeking financial freedom. What do we intend to do once we are financially free? Our dream, our goals should drive us towards financial freedom. If these goals are not clear in our mind, the chances are high that we might end up in a state of frustration and anger as my first friend did.

My second friend says that he wants to be financially free and quit his job. For him, financial freedom is tantamount to just quitting a job. He has seen me quit my job and wants to replicate the same. He believes that quitting a job will give him freedom. Though he realizes that he is short of the corpus to achieve financial freedom, he is hiding behind the fact that he can spend a lot more time after quitting his job on a venture that he has so fondly started. He is living his life on assumptions. It is not that entrepreneurs do not take risks and become successful. But then, he should be clear that he is moving from being an employee to being an entrepreneur. He is not going to be financially free just by this move. He must understand that he will still be in a rut to earn money because his family expenses must be met, and his daughters' school fees must be paid. We are not moving towards financial freedom when switching from one kind of active income source to another. We are still actively required to earn money—a state which is far from financial freedom.

My third friend was in a hurry to quit his job. It can happen. It almost happened to me, but good sense prevailed at the right time. I ensured that I fully become financially free before quitting my job. Now that he has already quit, declaring to the world that he has become financially free, he is looking for options to earn while doing something that he loves. If earning money is even one of the motives in any pursuit, we can never put our soul into that pursuit.

We cannot continue with the pursuit without getting impacted by the results. And if we cannot put our soul into the act, the feeling of bliss will still be far away.

But remember that these friends are still those strong-willed friends who at least had the guts to take some decision, placing them in the niche 5%. On the other hand, 95% of us will never be able to take that decision. Because taking decisions might mean going against the social norms and challenging our own boundaries.

All I can say is that life is too good and blissful to be ignored in the pursuit of earning money. There are better, wiser and more beautiful things to spend your time on—your spouse, sons and daughters, friends and relatives, neighbours, nature and this world, and YOU! Spend some time with them, and you would surely realise what I did—that financial freedom is not about finance, it's about freedom!

Financial freedom is a choice. It is liberty. It is the ability to decide your daily schedule and change it at the drop of a hat. It is to be able to pursue your passion while you are young and have all the energy with you.

This energy is the vital difference between someone who is retired and someone who is financially free.

A retired person may have the time, and in some cases, also the money. On the other hand, a financially free person will have the rare and deadly combination of time, money and energy—three ingredients to have a blissful experience on this journey called life.

Foops #29: Assuming That Financial Freedom Is the Same as Retirement	
Awakening	**Action**
• Financial freedom is not about retirement, quitting a job or getting into any money-making venture. • Financial freedom is about your daily choices and the ability to chase your passion, irrespective of its potential to earn you money.	• Think hard about what you wish to do in life after becoming financially free. • Think about what you love doing, and would keep doing, if you could never ever earn anything out of it. • Then strive towards financial freedom with the intent of chasing your passion.

FOOPS 30

NOT PRIORITISING PORTFOLIO TRACKING

ANYTHING THAT GETS MEASURED, IMPROVES.

– PETER DRUCKER

Anudeep is one of our freedom seekers who has always been quite disciplined and committed. He has a loving spouse, and they are expecting a child soon. He earns ₹80,000 per month, and his average expense is currently around ₹40,000 per month. Over the last ten years, he has accumulated an asset base of about ₹75 lakhs. This includes all his investments along with some inherited money from his parents.

He has been a good performer and likes his job as a chemical engineer with Tata Chemicals. However, he is seeking freedom because he feels that jobs are not secure. Therefore, he is unwilling to put his family's future at risk because of job situations—a perfectly valid argument. He is also interested in teaching, which he cannot pursue, considering his current job pressures.

Until he joined our ELITE program, he was not diligently tracking his portfolio like most new seekers. It is not that freedom seekers do not want to be wealthy. It is primarily because they undermine the impact of managing a portfolio. They think they do not have the time to closely track their portfolio, considering the tight job schedules and other family commitments.

He had never realised until now that it is never a question of time. Rather it is always a question of priority. And prioritisation only happens when you know the impact of not doing a particular thing. Going to work on time every day, for decades together, is a priority because we understand the impact of not doing it. Therefore, we prioritise it. If our child is sick at home, that takes higher priority than going to work on that day because we understand the impact of not tending to a sick child. Therefore, we find time for our sick child.

Before we assign a priority to any task, it is vital to understand the impact of not doing that task. Similarly, it is important to understand the implications of not actively managing your portfolio. Then, we can make a fair judgment about whether it deserves to be prioritised or not.

I had to show Anudeep the massive impact small things can have in the field of personal finance.

We did some number crunching and calculated the current approximate returns on his portfolio. We saw that he was averaging a return of around 5.8% from his portfolio, which primarily consisted of EPF, FDs, bonds, mutual funds and some gold.

It took no rocket science to calculate that his portfolio was generating about 5.8% of ₹75 lakhs, which is around ₹4.35 lakhs per annum. A better way to put it would be to say that Anudeep's portfolio is earning approximately ₹36,250 per month passively. Now, to begin with, this is no small achievement. This is almost half his current salary, with hardly any effort going towards managing the portfolio.

Now comes the vital part.

This is how our discussions panned out.

"You work on your job ten hours a day, five days a week, for an entire year, to earn a 10% increment, which comes to approximately ₹8,000 per month. Correct?"

"Yes, even this is not assured in times of Covid," remarked Anudeep.

“Very correct. But even if we assume that the increment is assured, this amounts to virtually nothing.”

“Why do you say that?” he asked, puzzled.

“Look at it like this, Anudeep. You start working on your portfolio by assuming yourself to be its CEO.”

“What does that even mean—to be a CEO of my portfolio?”

“Right, that’s a valid question. Being the CEO of your portfolio entails considering every single asset as an employee of your portfolio. In this case, you are the CEO of your portfolio. Therefore, you must start tracking every asset and monitor its performance by spending 30 minutes, two to three days a week, for a year. This way, you can increase your returns from 5.8% to a much more practical and moderate 8%.”

“Ok…”

“And this is not at all tough to achieve. In fact, 8% is the average returns that can be expected from a well-tracked portfolio.”

“Right, I agree, but how does this help me?”

“This 2.2% increase in your portfolio returns—from 5.8% to 8%—means an increment of 2.2% of ₹75 lakhs, which is an increment of ₹1.65 lakhs a year, or ₹13,750 per month.”

“Wait, wait, wait… How did you calculate this ₹13,750 per month?”

It is absolutely normal for most seekers to get shocked at this point. And the reason is simple. I am showing them how to achieve an increment of ₹13,750 per month by spending 30 minutes a day managing and tracking their portfolio against an increment of ₹8,000 per month by spending ten hours a day on their jobs. That’s roughly twice the reward for just 5% of the time investment.

I asked Anudeep to choose which option deserves a higher priority.

There was pin-drop silence, and this silence is a common sign of experiencing a Foops moment. The power of small things is immense in personal finance. Unfortunately, these small things are usually overlooked. Anudeep was dumbfounded. He did not know how to react.

"Ok, I get that. What's next for me?" he asked.

"Be the CEO of your portfolio. Your assets are your employees. They are working hard to earn you more money. They are sweating it out for you in the market, in bonds, commodities, etc. Watch their performance closely."

"Ok..."

"Have you ever been through a performance appraisal cycle in your company?"

"Yes, of course. It happens every year."

"So, what happens in that appraisal cycle if you have been one of the worst performers?"

"Well, my boss may ask me to just leave the company."

"Absolutely. It's not that your boss has any animosity towards you. It's just that your performance does not match the objectives and goals of the company, right?"

"Right."

"And what will happen if you were an exceptionally good performer?"

"I would be rewarded for my performance with a raise or promotion."

"Right. Exactly the same way, be the boss for each of your assets. Eliminate the bad performers. Invest more in high performers. That is what a CEO does, no? Just if you can track them, you can elevate their efficiency. Your money will start to work harder for you."

"But I have a query. I cannot keep increasing my portfolio returns every year. I mean, I cannot move from 8% to 10% to 12% ROI and so on. This cannot keep happening forever."

"Right. But just try and maintain it at 8% by tracking it effectively. If you can do that, your ever-increasing portfolio size will take care of the rest."

"How is that?"

"Your portfolio, which is valued at ₹75 lakhs today, will increase to around ₹85 lakhs over the next year, considering your monthly savings and the returns that your existing portfolio generates. And then, if you can maintain just this 8% returns, the next year's increment would be 2.2% of ₹85 lakhs, which is ₹1.87 lakhs per year. This translates to approximately ₹15,600 per month. This is much higher than the earlier ₹13,750 per month."

"That's very interesting."

"It is. And this increase in your portfolio will be much more than your salary increase in the times to come because it compounds and grows faster than your salary. The amount of returns multiply with the increasing size of your portfolio. Soon, you would reach an inflection point."

"Inflection point?"

"The point where you have enough assets working efficiently for you, such that your portfolio's monthly returns far exceed your job's monthly salary. Imagine that time."

Anudeep was getting a new perspective of money and of being a CEO. The inflection point or tipping point is a true perspective-changer. As Malcolm Gladwell explains in his debut bestseller *The Tipping Point*, it is that moment or critical point, which seems simple but can have a more than significant impact on the outcome.

When you become the CEO of your portfolio, the first inflection point is when your portfolio generates more passive income than your active income from a job or business. This changes your perspective towards money. You look at it not only as a service provider but also as an alternative to your full-time job.

The next inflection point is reached when you become the CEO of your time and, therefore, your life. At this point, you have the liberty to decide what you want to do with your time, when you want to do it, with whom you want to do it and how long you want to do it. This inflection point is triggered when your corpus becomes big enough to support your and your family's current and future expenses.

As the CEO of your portfolio, it is a fantastic feeling when this time comes. Your transition from working for money to having complete control over your time. This Foops moment turned my perspective of life on its head. It can change yours too.

Foops #30: Not Prioritising Portfolio Tracking

Awakening	Action
• Do not underestimate the power of small things. • A well-tracked portfolio significantly improves the efficiency of each asset in it, thus generating more passive income for you.	• Consider yourself the CEO of your portfolio. • Track every single asset. • Let the non-performers go. Reward the high performers. • Make every asset work hard for you to generate more money.

THE FOOPS HASHTAG

The 30 Foops moments described in the book are not the only ones that exist. Investors—whether novice or experienced—keep making and repeating mistakes without truly understanding their impact on their wealth.

If you have also been awakened to any such Foops moment, please share it with us on social media using #Foops.

I will be looking out for them and personally talking to the investors with the most interesting Foops moments.

MY COMMITMENT TO YOU

I am passionate about YOU. I am committed to YOU. It is my life's mission to elevate my society, in whatever way I can.

As with all my other books, this book comes with a 100% commitment to help you, guide you and mentor you on your journey. We will walk this journey together.

You have an absolute right to connect with me, and I will be more than delighted to help you elevate your life.

Feel free to connect with us at our:

Official Website	:	http://www.manoj-arora.com
ELITE Program*	:	https://bit.ly/about_elite
Blog	:	https://elevate-your-life.blogspot.com/
Email	:	help@manoj-arora.com
WhatsApp	:	+91-9871133619

*ELITE Program for Financial Freedom: On demand, we designed a unique program, which we have been running with unmatched success since 2018. Herein, we shortlist a limited set of passionate financial freedom seekers (via an interview process) thrice a year. I personally coach each selected seeker and take them to financial freedom by a defined date.

GLOSSARY OF COMMON TERMS

1. **Active Income:** An income earned by one's active involvement or participation. For example, income through a job, business venture, profession, etc.
2. **Asset:** An investment that is made with the expectation of generating positive returns. Mutual Funds, FDs, stocks and bonds are assets. Your car, furniture and TV are not assets.
3. **Asset Class:** A grouping of investments that exhibit similar characteristics and are subject to the same laws. For example, mutual funds.
4. **Black Swan Event:** An unpredictable event that is beyond what is normally expected of a situation and has potentially severe consequences. For example, the financial crash of 2008 and the Covid-19 pandemic.
5. **Bonds:** An instrument of indebtedness of the bond issuer to the holder. For example, RBI Bonds and Infrastructure bonds.
6. **Close-Ended Mutual Funds:** An equity or debt fund in which the fund house issues a fixed number of units at launch.
7. **Commodity:** Any useful material that can be bought and sold like tea, gold, beans, etc.

8. **Compounding:** Generally referred to as the eighth wonder of the world, compounding is a system of generating returns cumulated over a period of time.
9. **Coupon Rate:** The returns or yield committed/paid by a fixed income asset. For example, a fixed deposit with an 8% coupon rate or interest rate.
10. **Debt-Based Investment:** Any investment made in debt instruments like fixed deposits, bonds, PPF, etc. Usually, debt-based investments are characterised by a fixed coupon rate and tenure.
11. **ELITE Program:** A unique program to handhold you towards financial freedom by a defined date.
12. **Equity Linked Saving Scheme (ELSS):** A category of equity-based mutual funds which helps save taxes under Section 80C.
13. **Equated Monthly Instalments (EMI):** One part of the equally divided monthly charges to clear an outstanding loan within a stipulated timeframe.
14. **Employee Provident Fund (EPF):** A retirement benefits scheme in which employees of an organisation contribute a small portion of their basic pay monthly to accumulate a big corpus for retirement.
15. **Earnings Per Share (EPS):** It is a figure describing a public company's profit per outstanding share of stock, calculated quarterly or annually.
16. **Equity-Based Investment:** Any investment made in equity instruments like equity mutual funds, stocks, etc.
17. **Exchange Traded Fund (ETF):** Funds that trade on an exchange, just like a stock.
18. **Family Inflation:** A decline in the purchasing power of a particular family over time.

19. **Fixed Deposit:** An investment instrument where we can invest a certain sum of money for a fixed period at a predetermined interest rate.
20. **Financial Freedom:** A state where you have enough savings, investments and cash on hand to afford the lifestyle you want for yourself and your family—and a growing nest egg that will allow you to pursue your passion without being driven by a compulsion to earn money.
21. **Greater Fool Theory:** The greater fool theory states that you can make money even from buying overvalued securities. This is because there will usually be someone (a greater fool) who is willing to pay an even higher price.
22. **Index Funds:** A portfolio of stocks or bonds designed to mimic the composition and performance of a financial market index.
23. **Inflation:** The decline of purchasing power of a given currency over time.
24. **Investing Strategy:** A set of principles or a roadmap designed to help individual investors achieve their financial and investment goals.
25. **Initial Public Offering (IPO):** The process by which a private company can go public by the sale of its stocks to the general public.
26. **Long-Term Capital Gains (LTCG) Tax:** A tax on the profits earned from the sale of certain assets held over a long term.
27. **Liability:** Something that a person or company owes to someone else, usually a sum of money. For example, home loan.
28. **Lifestyle Inflation:** It refers to an increase in spending when an individual's income goes up. This usually leads to uplifting of an individual's lifestyle. For example, owning a bigger car when one can afford it.

29. **Life Event:** Milestone events in one's life. For example, marriage, children's birth, higher education, international trips, etc.
30. **Life Insurance:** Insurance against the risk to life.
31. **Liquidity:** This refers to the ease with which an asset, or security, can be converted into ready cash without affecting its market price.
32. **Mutual Fund:** A type of investment vehicle comprising a pool of money collected from many investors to invest in securities like stocks, bonds, money market, etc.
33. **Net Asset Value (NAV):** It is the per-unit market value of all the securities held by the mutual fund scheme.
34. **New Fund Offer (NFO):** It is the first time subscription offer for a new scheme launched by asset management companies.
35. **National Pension Scheme (NPS):** It is a social security initiative by the Central Government, open to public, private and even unorganised sector employees, except those from the armed forces.
36. **Passive Income:** It is the earnings or returns generated by one's assets. For example, rental income, FD interest, etc.
37. **Portfolio:** A collection of financial investments like stocks, bonds, commodities, cash and cash equivalents.
38. **Public Provident Fund (PPF):** A public retirement savings scheme offered by the Government of India to provide a secure post-retirement life.
39. **Promoter Shareholding:** The percentage of shares that are held by the promoters of a company.
40. **Risk:** The chance that an outcome or investment's actual gains will differ from an expected outcome or return.
41. **Risk Capacity:** The mathematical measure of how much risk you can take before it affects your financial goals.

42. **Risk Mitigation:** Action taken to reduce an investor's exposure to potential risks and reduce the likelihood of risk occurrence.
43. **Risk Tolerance:** The investor's ability to psychologically endure the potential of losing money on an investment.
44. **Sensex:** India's benchmark stock index, created in 1986. It represents 30 of the largest, well-capitalised stocks on the BSE.
45. **Systematic Investment Plan (SIP):** An investment strategy wherein an investor needs to invest the same amount of money in a particular mutual fund at stipulated intervals.
46. **Systematic Withdrawal Plan (SWP):** A strategy that allows an investor to withdraw a fixed or variable amount from their mutual fund scheme on a pre-set date every month.
47. **Top-Up SIP:** A facility wherein a SIP investor can increase the instalment amount by a fixed amount at pre-defined intervals.
48. **Value Analysis:** A method to estimate the approximate value or worth of an asset.
49. **Volatility:** The tendency of an investment to change rapidly and unpredictably, especially for the worse. For example, the volatility of equity-based investments is high, while that of debt-based investments is relatively low.

JAICO PUBLISHING HOUSE

Elevate Your Life. Transform Your World.

ESTABLISHED IN 1946, Jaico Publishing House is home to world-transforming authors such as Sri Sri Paramahansa Yogananda, Osho, The Dalai Lama, Sri Sri Ravi Shankar, Sadhguru, Robin Sharma, Deepak Chopra, Jack Canfield, Eknath Easwaran, Devdutt Pattanaik, Khushwant Singh, John Maxwell, Brian Tracy and Stephen Hawking.

Our late founder Mr. Jaman Shah first established Jaico as a book distribution company. Sensing that independence was around the corner, he aptly named his company Jaico ('Jai' means victory in Hindi). In order to service the significant demand for affordable books in a developing nation, Mr. Shah initiated Jaico's own publications. Jaico was India's first publisher of paperback books in the English language.

While self-help, religion and philosophy, mind/body/spirit, and business titles form the cornerstone of our non-fiction list, we publish an exciting range of travel, current affairs, biography, and popular science books as well. Our renewed focus on popular fiction is evident in our new titles by a host of fresh young talent from India and abroad. Jaico's recently established Translations Division translates selected English content into nine regional languages.

In addition to being a publisher and distributor of its own titles, Jaico is a major national distributor of books of leading international and Indian publishers. With its headquarters in Mumbai, Jaico has branches and sales offices in Ahmedabad, Bangalore, Bhopal, Chennai, Delhi, Hyderabad, Kolkata and Lucknow.

SINCE 1946

www.ingramcontent.com/pod-product-compliance
Lightning Source LLC
LaVergne TN
LVHW021138211026
PP19721600010B/28
* 9 7 8 9 3 9 1 0 1 9 7 1 6 *

FOOPS!